Business Essentials

Supporting HNC/HND and Foundation degrees

Business Strategy

Course Book

In this July 2010 edition:

- Full and comprehensive coverage of the key topics within the subject
- Activities, examples and quizzes
- Practical illustrations and case studies
- Index
- Fully up to date as at July 2010
- Coverage mapped to the Edexcel Guidelines for the HNC/HND in Business

First edition September 2007
Second edition July 2010

Published ISBN 9780 7517 6833 6
(previous edition 9780 7517 4479 8)
e-ISBN 9780 7517 7670 6

British Library Cataloguing-in-Publication Data
A catalogue record for this book is available from the British Library

Published by
BPP Learning Media Ltd
BPP House, Aldine Place
London W12 8AA

www.bpp.com/learningmedia

Printed in the United Kingdom

Your learning materials, published by BPP Learning Media Ltd, are printed on paper sourced from sustainable, managed forests.

We are grateful to Edexcel for permission to reproduce the Guidelines for the BTEC Higher Nationals in Business.

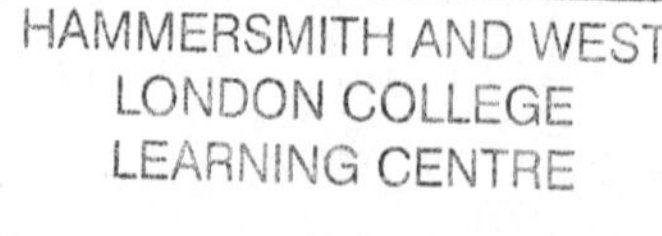

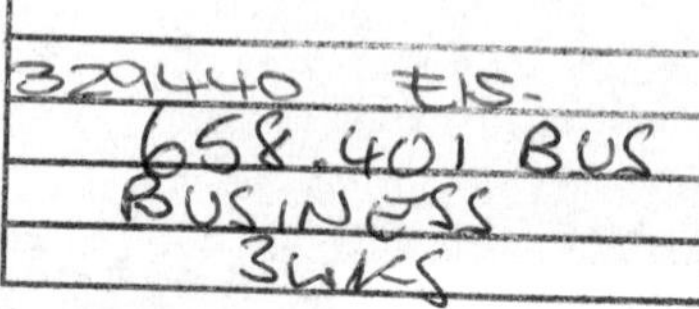

Contents

Introduction

BPP Learning Media's **Business Essentials** range is the ideal learning solution for all students studying for business-related qualifications and degrees. The range provides concise and comprehensive coverage of the key areas that are essential to the business student.

Qualifications in business are traditionally very demanding. Students therefore need learning resources which go straight to the core of the topics involved, and which build upon students' pre-existing knowledge and experience. The BPP Learning Media Business Essentials range has been designed to meet exactly that need.

Features include:

- In-depth coverage of essential topics within business-related subjects
- Plenty of activities, quizzes and topics for discussion to help retain the interest of students and ensure progress
- Up-to-date practical illustrations and case studies that really bring the material to life
- A glossary of terms and full index

In addition, the contents of the chapters are comprehensively mapped to the **Edexcel Guidelines**, providing full coverage of all topics specified in the HND/HNC qualifications in Business.

Each chapter contains:

- An introduction and a list of specific study objectives
- Summary diagrams and signposts to guide you through the chapter
- A chapter roundup, quick quiz with answers and answers to activities

Other titles in this series:

Generic titles

Economics

Accounts

Business Maths

Mandatory units for the Edexcel HND/HNC in Business qualification

Unit 1	Business Environment
Unit 2	Managing Finance
Unit 3	Organisations and Behaviour
Unit 4	Marketing Principles
Unit 5	Business Law
Unit 6	Business Decision Making
Unit 7	Business Strategy
Unit 8	Research Project

Pathways for the Edexcel HND/HNC in Business qualification

Units 9 and 10	Finance: Management Accounting and Financial Reporting
Units 11 and 12	Finance: Auditing and Financial Systems and Taxation
Units 13 and 14	Management: Leading People and Professional Development
Units 15 and 16	Management: Communications and Achieving Results
Units 17 and 18	Marketing and Promotion
Units 19 and 20	Marketing and Sales Strategy
Units 21 and 22	Human Resource Management
Units 23 and 24	Human Resource Development and Employee Relations
Units 25-28	Company and Commercial Law

For more information, or to place an order, please call 0845 0751 100 (for orders within the UK) or +44(0)20 8740 2211 (from overseas), e-mail learningmedia@bpp.com, or visit our website at www.bpp.com/learningmedia.

If you would like to send in your comments on this Course Book, please turn to the review form at the back of this book.

Study Guide

This Course Book includes features designed specifically to make learning effective and efficient.

- Each chapter begins with a summary diagram which maps out the areas covered by the chapter. There are detailed summary diagrams at the start of each main section of the chapter. You can use the diagrams during revision as a basis for your notes.

- After the main summary diagram there is an introduction, which sets the chapter in context. This is followed by learning objectives, which show you what you will learn as you work through the chapter.

- Throughout the Course Book, there are special aids to learning. These are indicated by symbols in the margin:

Signposts guide you through the book, showing how each section connects with the next.

Definitions give the meanings of key terms. The *glossary* at the end of the book summarises these.

Activities help you to test how much you have learned. An indication of the time you should take on each is given. Answers are given at the end of each chapter.

Topics for discussion are for use in seminars. They give you a chance to share you views with your fellow students. They allow you to highlight holes in your knowledge and to see how others understand concepts. If you have time, try 'teaching' someone the concepts you have learned in a session. This helps you to remember key points and answering their questions will consolidate your knowledge.

Examples relate what you have learned to the outside world. Try to think up your own examples as you work through the Course Book.

Chapter roundups present the key information from the chapter in a concise format. Useful for revision.

- The wide **margin** on each page is for your notes. You will get the best out of this book if you interact with it. Write down your thoughts and ideas. Record examples, question theories, add references to other pages in the Course Book and rephrase key points in your own words.

- At the end of each chapter, there is a **chapter roundup** and a **quick quiz** with answers. Use these to revise and consolidate your knowledge. The chapter roundup summarises the chapter. The quick quiz tests what you have learned (the answers often refer you back to the chapter so you can look over subjects again).

- At the end of the Course Book, there is a glossary of definitions and an index.

Part A

Strategy Formulation

Chapter 1 :
OBJECTIVES

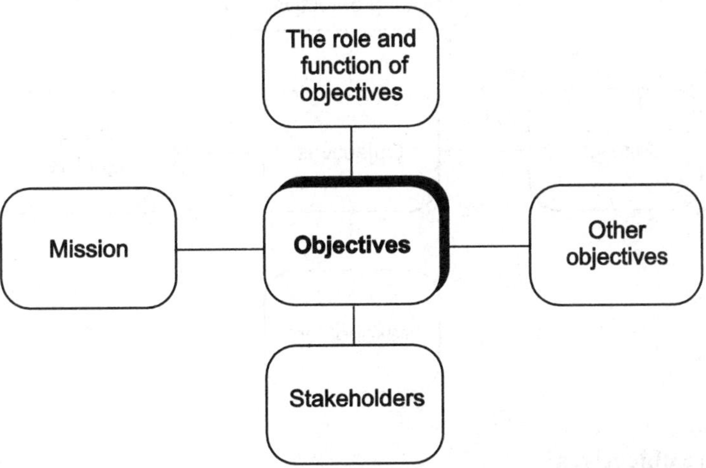

Introduction

Clear objectives are vital to the strategic formulation process. In this opening chapter we look in detail at their **functions**, and see that there is a hierarchy of objectives.

We then examine the process of **setting** objectives. Next we turn our attention to **types** of objective – mission, corporate objectives, functional objectives and individual objectives.

The views of **stakeholders** also need to be taken into account: a strategy affects different stakeholders in different ways.

Your objectives

In this chapter you will learn about the following.

(a) The importance of objectives in the formulation of strategy, and the functions that they fulfil

(b) The hierarchy of objectives within an organisation

(c) The stages involved in setting meaningful objectives

(d) The purpose of a mission and the possible components of an organisation's mission statement

(e) The differences between corporate, functional and individual objectives and examples of each

(f) The influence of stakeholders on strategy formulation

1 THE ROLE AND FUNCTION OF OBJECTIVES

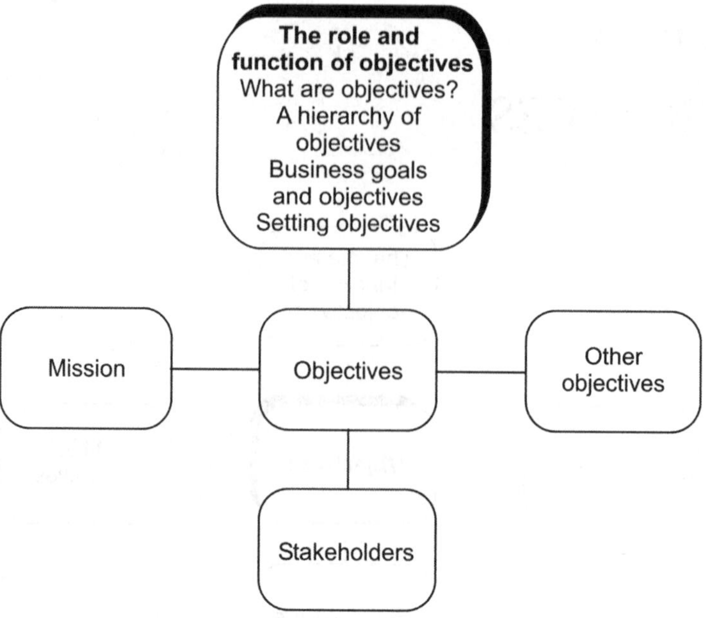

1.1 What are objectives?

Objectives are the **specific outcomes** that an organisation wishes to achieve by carrying out its activities.

Objectives are the anticipated end result of programmes of activity, and therefore have a central role in strategy formulation. The word **aims** is also sometimes used, although this tends to apply to vague statements of intent which cannot be defined. Another word with a similar meaning to objectives is **goals**.

Objectives should always be stated as precisely as possible, so that we can measure whether objectives have been achieved.

Objectives have several functions.

(a) They enable the overall objectives of the organisation to be **broken down** into clear statements of what needs to be done **at each level**.

(b) They provide **clear statements** of what action needs to be taken.

(c) They provide **a focus** for all activity.

(d) They provide **targets** for both individual and group achievement.

(e) They facilitate the **control** of actual performance.

(f) They provide a **basis for evaluating** how successfully the plans are being implemented.

Activity 1 **(10 minutes)**

List three likely consequences of operating an organisation where there are never any clear objectives.

We now go on to see that there is a hierarchy of objectives.

1.2 A hierarchy of objectives

Objectives can be illustrated as a hierarchy. The ones that affect the whole organisation are at the top of the **pyramid-style representation** shown in Figure 1.1 below.

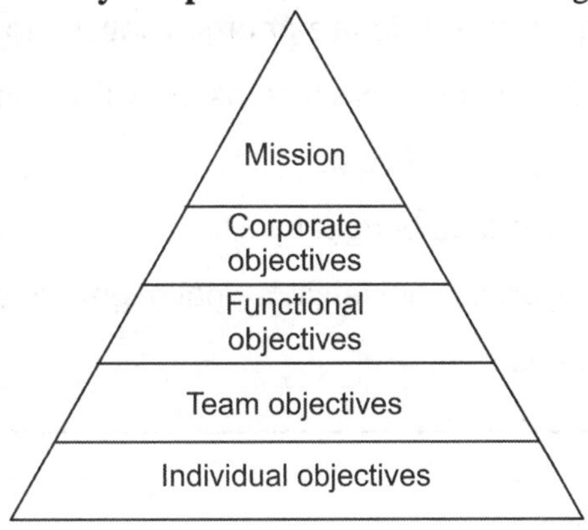

Figure 1.1: The objectives hierarchy

These objectives can be split into different categories.

(a) **Strategic objectives** such as the mission and corporate objectives affect the whole organisation and are normally long-term.

(b) **Functional objectives** relate to a department or section and will include most team objectives as well. These are typically medium-term.

(c) **Individual objectives** relate to particular people and to their work. Most of these, but by no means all, will involve short-term activities.

The pursuit of collective or corporate objectives is a central reason for an organisation's existence. **All objectives should relate to the core objectives of the organisation as a whole.** If they do not, then either they are not relevant or the corporate objectives are wrongly stated.

Activity 2 **(10 minutes)**

Write down some realistic objectives for your study programme.

(a) Long-term (by the end of the academic year)

(b) Medium-term (by the end of the current term)

(c) Short-term (by the end of the next week)

Try to place these into a hierarchy to see how they relate to each other.

1.3 Business goals and objectives

Definitions

Mintzberg (1999) defines *goals* as 'the intentions behind decisions or actions, the states of mind that drive individuals or organisations to do what they do.'

(a) **Operational goals** can be expressed as objectives. Here is an example.

(i) An operational goal: 'Cut costs'

(ii) The objective: 'Reduce budget by 5%'

(b) **Non-operational goals** A university's goal might be to 'seek truth'.

Not all goals can be measured.

Primary and secondary objectives

Some objectives are more important than others. In the hierarchy of objectives, there is a **primary corporate objective** and other **secondary objectives** which should combine to ensure the achievement of the overall corporate objective. We look at these in Section 3.

For example, if a company sets itself an objective of growth in profits, as its primary aim, it will then have to develop strategies by which this primary objective can be achieved. Secondary objectives might then be concerned with sales growth, continual technological innovation, customer service, product quality, efficient resource management or reducing the company's reliance on debt capital.

EXAMPLE

British Airways publicity once indicated the following corporate goals. What do you think of it? Which is most important? Would they have changed after the events of September 11 2001 and the subsequent turmoil in the airline industry?

- Safety and security
- Strong and consistent financial performance
- Global reach
- Superior service
- Good value for money
- Healthy working environment
- Good neighbourliness

Long- and short-term objectives

Objectives may be long-term and short-term. A company that is suffering from a recession in its core industries and making losses in the short-term might continue to have a long-term primary objective of achieving a growth in profits, but in the short-term its primary objective might be survival.

Financial objectives

For business in the UK, the primary objective is concerned with the **return to shareholders**.

(a) A satisfactory return for a company must be sufficient to **reward shareholders adequately** in the long run for the risks they take. The reward will take the form of **profits,** which can lead to **dividends** or to **increases in the market value** of the shares.

(b) The size of return which is adequate for ordinary shareholders will vary according to the **risk** involved.

There are different ways of expressing a financial objective in quantitative terms. Financial objectives would include the following.

- Profitability
- Return on investment (ROI) or return on capital employed (ROCE)
- Share price, earnings per share, dividends
- Growth

Multiple objectives

A firm might identify several objectives.

- Scope for growth and enhanced **corporate wealth**
- Maintaining a policy of paying attractive but not over-generous **dividends**
- Maintaining an acceptable level of **borrowing**

Corporate objectives and unit objectives

Here are some examples of corporate and unit objectives.

(a) **Corporate objectives**. These objectives should relate to the key factors for business success.

- Profitability
- Market share
- Growth
- Cash-flow
- Customer satisfaction
- The quality of the firm's products
- Human resources

(b) **Unit objectives**. Examples are as follows.

(i) From the business world:

- Increasing the number of customers by 10%
- Reducing the number of rejects by 50%
- Producing monthly reports more quickly, within five working days of the end of each month

(ii) From the public sector:

- Responding more quickly to emergency calls
- Reducing the length of time a patient has to wait for an operation

Technological goals

Technological goals might be stated as follows.

(a) A commitment to **product design and production methods** using current and new technology.

(b) A commitment to improve current products through research and development work.

(c) A commitment to a particular level of quality.

Product-market goals

Goals for products and markets will involve the following type of decisions.

(a) **Market leadership**. Whether the organisation wants to be the market leader, or number two in the market etc.

(b) **Coverage**. Whether the product range needs to be expanded.

(c) **Positioning**. Whether there should be an objective to shift position in the market – eg from producing low-cost for the mass market to higher-cost specialist products.

(d) **Expansion**. Whether there should be a broad objective of 'modernising' the product range or extending the organisation's markets.

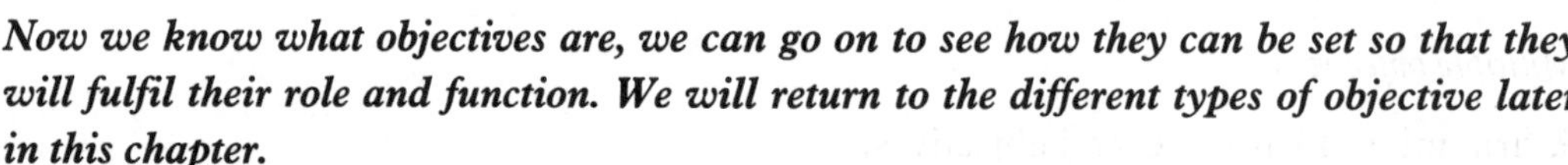

Now we know what objectives are, we can go on to see how they can be set so that they will fulfil their role and function. We will return to the different types of objective later in this chapter.

1.4 Setting objectives

The objectives set by an organisation are likely to have far-reaching consequences and it is therefore important that they are carefully and systematically agreed. This is normally done **collectively**. At the very least they should be agreed with the relevant people before being finalised.

Setting objectives is a stage-by-stage process:

1	**Agree the objectives**	'What do we want to achieve?'
2	**Prioritise the objectives**	'How important are they?'
3	**Define the activities and tasks**	'What has to be done to achieve the objective?'
4	**Agree standards of performance**	'How will we be able to tell that the tasks have been completed to a satisfactory standard?'
5	**Allocate roles**	'Who should perform the required tasks?'
6	**Set and timetable performance criteria**	'At what stages during the fulfilment of the objective will we be able to identify that things are being done to standard and to plan?'

Definitions

- **Standards** are the agreed quality measures that are used to judge whether a task has been satisfactorily completed.
- **Performance criteria** are the individual standards of performance that help to judge that work is being done satisfactorily.

A useful way to think of the criteria for setting objectives is to use the mnemonic **SMART**. Objectives should always be:

Specific	with regard to what is intended
Measurable	based upon performance criteria that can be used to judge whether the objectives are being achieved according to plan
Agreed	with the people responsible for achievement
Realistic	relevant to the needs of the organisation and the people involved, and capable of being achieved within the time and resources available
Timetabled	set to a timetable that will give signposts for fulfilment and a final date for completion

EXAMPLE

Setting objectives for a marketing project

Nina and Hansa are beginning a project to market sets of garden tools locally. They intend to sell a small set for £10.00, with a profit of £2.50 per set, and need to identify realistic objectives. They plan to look at advertising rates for the local newspaper and get population figures from the library. They will relate their promotional budget to expected sales and profit, and they plan to set a timescale.

1 *Agree the objectives*

   These might be:

   (a) To target 3,000 people through door-to-door leaflets or inserts in the free paper by a certain date

   (b) To provide media coverage of promotions through advertisements in local newspapers and radio in accordance with the programme

   (c) To limit costs to £4,000 – £5,000, according to their budget

2 *Prioritise the objectives*

   Previous experience should indicate the likely effectiveness of the different forms of promotion and the costs involved and hence, in terms of effort and timing, it may be possible to prioritise (a) and (b). Costings are always likely to influence priorities, however. They will need to ask, 'How many households can we cover at what cost using each of the media?'

3 *Define the activities and tasks*

   Nina and Hansa will break down the activities and tasks required to achieve the objectives, first by area of activity, and then into the main tasks within each area. This will provide a picture of the type and volume of work required.

4 *Agree standards of performance*

   Next they will set standards for the quality of work that has to be done (the style of promotional material and the effectiveness of the way the marketing is carried out). These standards are more important to some activities than others. In the case of

marketing, the public image of the organisation and its products is of paramount importance and safeguards will be needed so as to ensure that the marketing does not project a substandard image of the organisation.

5 *Allocate roles*

Once they have set both the tasks and the standards, Nina and Hansa will allocate roles and responsibilities to ensure that the tasks will be carried out in a coordinated fashion without duplication or gaps. Marketing relies upon a series of activities that fit together as a marketing plan, thereby ensuring maximum impact and, eventually, sales.

6 *Set and timetable performance criteria*

In this stage a timetable for action should be drawn up.

(a) What tasks need to be done

(b) Who should do them

(c) Who is responsible for overseeing the work

(d) What can be done to check that the work is satisfactory and the results are acceptable

The process outlined in this example clearly goes beyond objective setting, and covers planning for the implementation of the marketing project. This is because if objectives are to be set realisitically, the planner will need to know in detail about the **tasks** that need to be done, the **resources** that are available and the **time** in which everything has to happen.

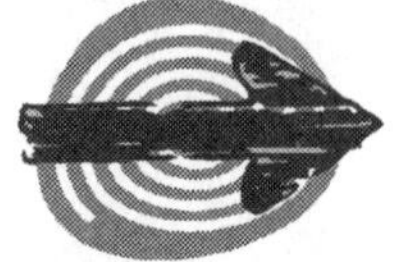

Next we need to look more closely at specific types of objective. We start with the mission, an objective that relates to the whole organisation.

2 MISSION

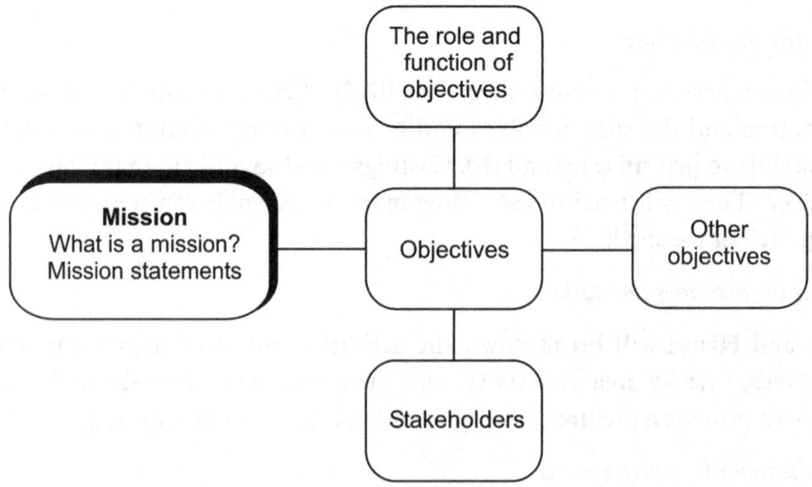

2.1 What is a mission?

As we already know, a mission describes an organisation's basic function in society, but originally the term was used to describe specific journeys made to discover somewhere or something, or to spread knowledge and belief (such as the journeys made by missionaries to spread religion).

EXAMPLE

The US attempt to place a man on the moon was a mission that succeeded. The National Aeronautics and Space Administration (NASA) adopted the mission 'To put a man on the moon by 1969'. Everyone connected with the programme in any capacity whatever was therefore working towards this collective mission. In July 1969 Neil Armstrong took 'One small step for man, and one giant leap for mankind' and the mission succeeded.

The concept of a **central guiding purpose** is more suited to some organisations than to others.

Activity 3 **(30 minutes)**

Write a short mission statement for each of the following:

1 An electronics company

2 A university or a college

3 A local authority day centre for the elderly

4 A charity for the homeless

5 A charity for conservation of the countryside

Explain briefly how the nature and content of the mission statement may be different in different sorts of organisations.

2.2 Mission statements

Although many organisations do not have a clearly defined mission, they are becoming increasingly common, especially in larger organisations, and are usually set out in the form of a mission statement. This written declaration of an organisation's central mission is a useful concept that can:

(a) Provide a ready **reference point** against which to make decisions

(b) Help guard against there being different (and possible misleading) **interpretations** of the organisation's stated purpose

(c) Help to present a **clear image of the organisation** for the benefit of customers and the general public

Most missions statements will address some of the following aspects.

(a) The **identity** of the persons for whom the organisation exits; such as shareholders, customers, and staff and other employees

(b) The **nature of the firm's business**: such as the products it makes or the services it provides, and the markets it produces for

(c) Ways of **competing**; such as reliance on quality, innovation, technology and low prices; commitment to customer care; policy on acquisition versus organic growth; and geographical spread of its operations

(d) **Principles of business**; such as commitment to suppliers and staff; social policy, for example, on non-discrimination or environmental issues

(e) **Commitment to customers**

A number of questions need to be considered when a mission statement is being formulated.

- ***Who is to be served and satisfied?***
- ***What need is to be satisfied?***
- ***How will this be achieved?***

Private sector organisations (such as Tesco and Kodak) traditionally seek to make a profit, but increasingly companies try to project other images too, such as being environmentally friendly, being a good employer, or being a provider of friendly service.

> **The purpose of Motorola is to honourably service the needs of the community by providing products and services of superior quality at a fair price to our customers.**

Public sector organisations (such as local councils, colleges and hospitals) provide services and increasingly seek to project quality, value for money, green issues, concern for staff (equal opportunities) and so on as missions.

> **We at the Leicester Royal Infirmary will work together to become the best hospital in the country, with an outstanding local and national reputation for out treatment, research and teaching.**
> **We will give to each patient the same care and consideration we would give to our family.** *(Leicester Royal Infirmary)*

Voluntary and community sector organisations cover a wide range of organisations including charities, trades unions, pressure groups and religious organisations. They usually exist either to serve a particular need or for the benefit of their membership. Their mission statements are likely to reflect the particular interests they serve (and perhaps the values of their organisation).

> **To achieve the conservation of nature and ecological processes by:**
>
> - **Preserving genetic species and ecosystem diversity**
> - **Ensuring that the use of renewable natural resources is sustainable both now and in the longer term, for the benefit of all life on earth**
> - **Promoting actions to reduce, to a minimum, pollution and the wasteful exploitation and consumption of resources and energy**
>
> *(The World Wide Fund for Nature)*

The mission may be a very simple statement such as that of the Royal Lifeboat Institute:

The preservation of life from shipwreck

(Royal National Lifeboat Institution)

FOR DISCUSSION

What important features are mission statements of the following organisations likely to include?

(a) An international aid organisation that seeks to combat famine worldwide

(b) A trading company (which is a subsidiary company of the above) and raises funds through shops for the charity's work

(c) A high street bank

(d) A district council

(e) A company specialising in designing and manufacturing innovative microchips

A mission covers the whole organisation. We will now go on to look at other types of objective that are likely to be found within an organisation.

3 OTHER OBJECTIVES

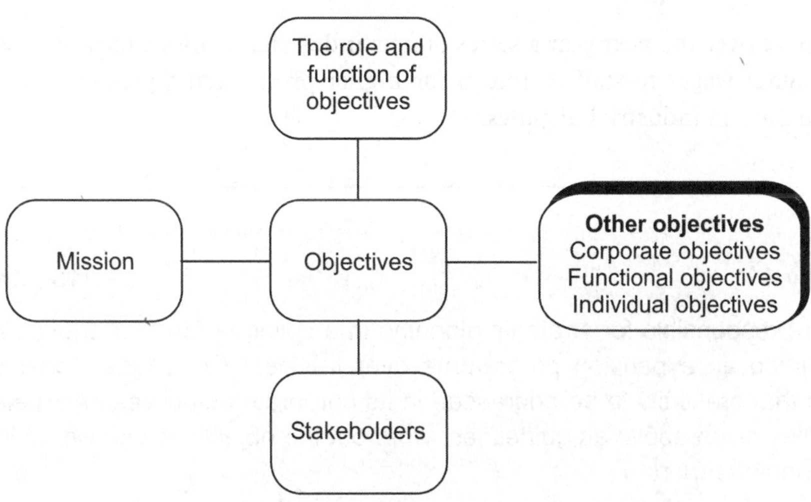

3.1 Corporate objectives

Once an organisation has defined its mission, senior management should agree a series of corporate objectives. These are strategic objectives that outline the expectations of the organisation; they should be **explicit, quantifiable** and **capable of being achieved.** If they are achieved, the organisation's mission should have been fulfilled. The strategic planning process (which we will look at in more detail in Part B of this course book) is concerned with how to achieve such objectives.

Corporate objectives should relate to those factors that determine an organisation's success. These are typically the following.

- Market share
- Growth
- Profitability
- Cash-flow
- Survival
- Growth in payments to shareholders
- Customer satisfaction
- Quality of products/services
- Industrial relations

EXAMPLE

Possible corporate objectives

'To **increase market share** within the country to 35% of all sales by the end of the next financial year. This is to be achieved through a combination of product development and intensive marketing.'

'To **increase the profitability** of the company by 12% over last year's figures through improved production methods, increased sales, and increased profit margin per sale.'

'To **ensure survival** of the organisation by investigating areas that fit within the mission, yet provide opportunities for additional activity and income.'

'To **invest 5% of profits** for each of the next three years in the development of new and improved product ranges.'

'To **negotiate** over the next year a series of new industrial relations measures, which will provide higher wages to staff in return for higher productivity, greater staff flexibility and a reduction in industrial disputes.'

Activity 4 **(15 minutes)**

You are responsible for strategic planning in a college of further education that is planning an expansion programme over the next five years. Consider the issues that are likely to be addressed in its corporate objectives and, using the examples given above as guidelines, write out the objectives you would include in a planning report.

Subsidiary or secondary objectives

As we have seen, whatever primary objective or objectives are set, **subsidiary objectives** will then be developed beneath them.

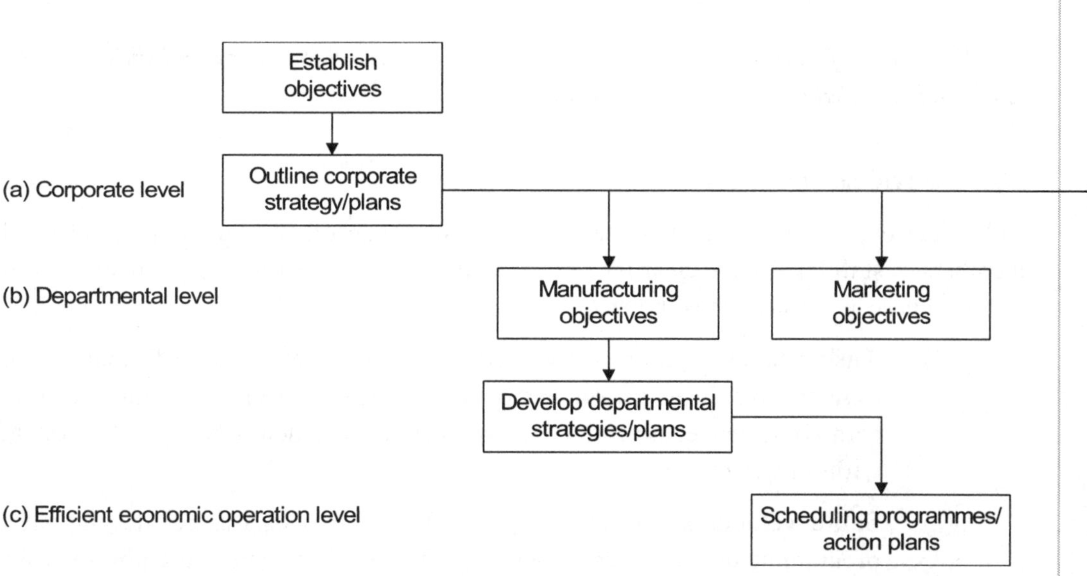

Figure 1.2: Secondary objectives

The overall objectives of the organisation will indicate different requirements for different functions.

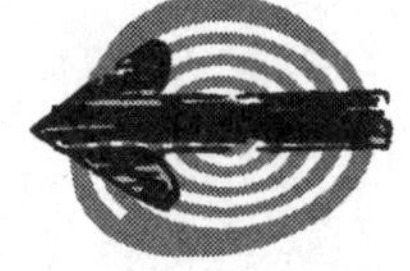

Corporate objectives are normally long-term or medium-term. We are now going to look at functional objectives, which deal with the shorter-term.

3.2 Functional objectives

Functional objectives are specific to individual units of an organisation, and are often associated with the **tactical** or **operational aspects** of an organisation's activities. They might relate to a department, a section or a team, depending upon the size of the organisation and the way that it is structured. Here are some typical examples of functional objectives.

(a) From the commercial world:

(i) Increasing the number of customers by x% (sales department)

(ii) Reducing the number of rejects by 50% (production department)

(iii) Producing monthly reports more quickly, within five working days of the end of each month (management accounting department)

(b) From the public sector:

(i) Increasing the number of places at nursery schools by x% (education department)

(ii) Responding more quickly to calls (ambulance service, fire service)

(c) From the voluntary sector:

(i) Raising £x from various sources

(ii) Increasing membership by x%

(iii) Implementing and maintaining an effective equal opportunities programme

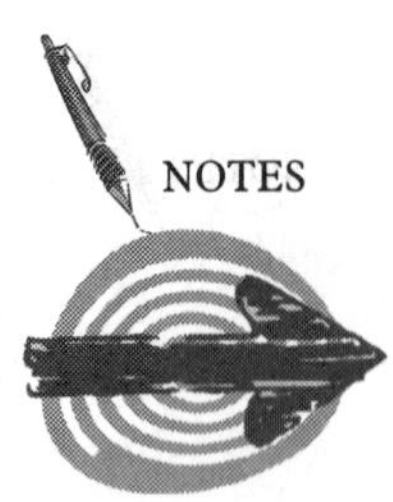

The final type of objective that we are going to look at relates to an individual's own work and is called an individual objective.

3.3 Individual objectives

Individual objectives are easier to set for some jobs than others, but it is useful if all members of staff have some clear idea of what they are expected to achieve over a given period. There are basically two types.

(1) **Task-related objectives** deal only with aspects of work performance (for example 'to reduce operating errors by 20% from the end of the month' or 'to gain competence in product knowledge and the new stock control system within three months').

(2) **Self-development objectives** may either be part of a career development programme or be associated with the fulfilment of personal ambitions (for example 'to obtain a certain qualification' or 'to improve communication or assertion skills').

There are a number of guidelines you can use to ensure that individual objectives are set and used correctly.

(a) They should always be **discussed and agreed** with the individual to which they relate, perhaps as part of a staff appraisal scheme, where performance is measured against previously agreed objectives.

(b) They should be **achievable** within the capabilities and defined responsibilities of the individual.

(c) There should be sufficient **time, resources and support** to allow the objectives to be fulfilled.

(d) They should **link** clearly to other work plans and objectives.

(e) They should be **measurable** by the individual concerned so that individuals can assess their own progress.

(f) Progress made should be **recorded** in some appropriate way.

(g) Progress made should be **discussed** periodically with the person concerned, and the objectives **revised** if necessary.

Activity 5 **(15 minutes)**

An organisation in your area, uses 'self-directed training' and asks all managers to ask themselves the question: 'Where do I expect to be in two years?'. The training programme gives all employees the opportunity to direct their careers.

Suppose that you have recently left college and started a job as a management trainee. You are due to have an interview with the training officer who has asked you for a short memo setting out (a) your personal objectives for the next year and (b) a statement of where you expect to be in two years.

Write the memorandum.

4 STAKEHOLDERS

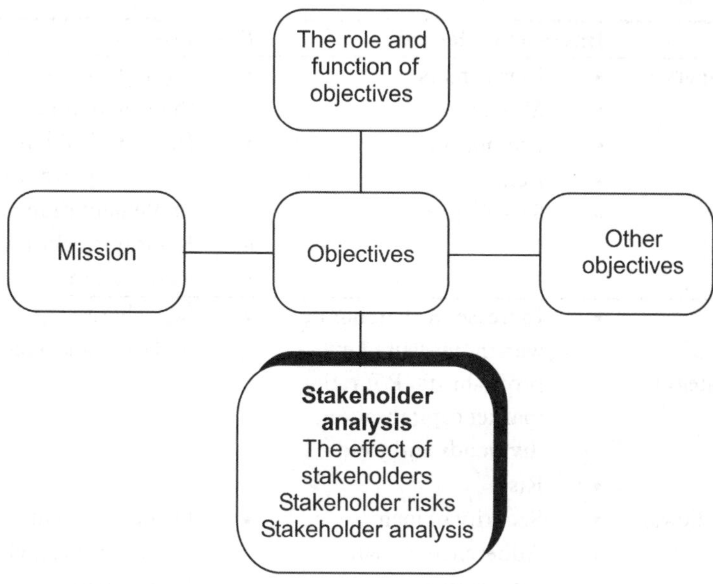

4.1 The effect of stakeholders

The evaluation techniques discussed assume that managers are **free to choose** organisational objectives and **able to** implement them **autonomously**.

Sometimes stakeholders have sufficient power to influence management's choice of strategy. There are two aspects of **stakeholder risk**.

(a) Strategic options pose varying degrees of risk to the **interests** of the different stakeholders.

(b) **Stakeholders may respond** in such a way as to reduce the attractiveness of the proposed strategy.

There are three broad types of stakeholder in an organisation, as we have seen.

(a) **Internal stakeholders** such as employees and management

(b) **Connected stakeholders** such as shareholders, customers, suppliers and financiers

(c) **External stakeholders** including the community, government and pressure groups

NOTES

4.2 Stakeholder risks

Stakeholder	Interests to defend	Response risk
Internal managers and employees	• Jobs/careers • Money • Promotion • Benefits • Satisfaction	• Pursuit of systems goals rather than shareholder interests • Industrial action • Negative power to impede implementation • Refusal to relocate • Resignation
Connected Shareholders (corporate strategy)	• Increase in shareholder wealth, measured by profitability, P/E ratios, market capitalisation, dividends and yield • Risk	• Sell shares (eg to predator) or replace management
Bankers (cash-flows)	• Security of loan • Adherence to loan agreements	• Denial of credit • Higher interest charges • Receivership
Suppliers (purchase strategy)	• Profitable sales • Payment for goods • Long-term relationship	• Refusal of credit • Court action • Wind down relationships
Customers (product market strategy)	• Goods as promised • Future benefits	• Buy elsewhere • Sue
External Government	• Jobs, training, tax	• Tax increases • Regulation • Legal action
Interest/pressure groups	• Pollution • Rights • Other	• Publicity • Direct action • Sabotage • Pressure on government

How stakeholders relate to the management of the company depends very much on what **type of stakeholder** they are – internal, connected or external – and on the **level in the management hierarchy** at which they are able to apply pressure. Clearly a company's management will respond differently to the demands of, say, its shareholders and the community at large.

4.3 Stakeholder analysis

Stakeholder analysis is important for the development of knowledge and understanding about other organisations in the firm's environment. The first step is to list all stakeholders, and then position them on a **stakeholder map**. This indicates the main relationships and patterns of interdependence between stakeholders.

Such maps not only show directly related stakeholders, but also include all those that indirectly assist the business in achieving its objectives. The likely effect that any proposed strategy will have on these various groups (that is, **support** or **resistance**) can then be assessed.

There are two primary **stakeholder roles**, following the idea of internal, connected and external stakeholders described above.

(i) **Performance role** – directly involved with adding value (eg manufacturer, wholesaler, retailer).

(ii) **Support role** – banks, consultancies, government supporting the 'performing' members.

Activity 6 **(20 minutes)**

Ticket and Budget International is a large multinational firm of accountants. The firm provides audit services, tax services, and consultancy services for its many clients. The firm has a strong Technical Department which designs standardised audit procedures. The firm has recently settled a number of expensive law suits for negligence (which it has 'contested vigorously') out of court, without admitting liability. The Technical Department is conducting a thorough review of the firm's audit procedures. The firm has just employed a marketing manager. The marketing manager regards an audit as a 'product', part of the entire marketing mix. The marketing manager is held in high regard by the firm's senior partner. The marketing director and the senior partner have unveiled a new strategic plan, drawn up in conditions of secrecy, which involves a tie-up with an advertising agency. The firm will be a 'one-stop shop' for business services and advice to management on any subject. Each client, or 'customer' will have a dedicated team of auditors, consultants and advertising executives. A member of staff may be a member of a number of different teams.

What are some of the stakeholders (internal and external) in this proposed change?

Activity 7 **(10 minutes)**

Identify some 'performance' and 'support' organisations that are connected with your organisation, or one with which you are familiar.

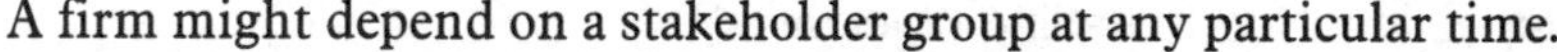

A firm might depend on a stakeholder group at any particular time.

(a) A firm with persistent cash-flow problems might depend on its bankers to provide it with money to stay in business at all.

(b) In the long-term, any firm depends on its customers.

The degree of dependence or reliance can be analysed according to these criteria.

(a) **Disruption**. Can the stakeholder disrupt the organisation's plans (eg a bank withdrawing overdraft facilities)?

(b) **Replacement**. Can the firm replace the relationship?

(c) **Uncertainty**. Does the stakeholder cause uncertainty in the firm's plans? A firm with healthy positive cash-flows and large cash balances need not worry about its bank's attitude to a proposed investment.

EXAMPLE

In practice, when thinking about the significance of particular stakeholders, companies must:

- Identify the stakeholders
- Identify what their particular interests are
- Consider the importance of developing and maintaining relationships with them

Chapter roundup

- Objectives are of central importance to planning because they are the end result of programmes of activity.
- Objectives form an interrelated hierarchy.
- Objectives need to be set systematically. Standards of performance must be incorporated into them.
- The mission is the overriding objective of any organisation. It is often made public in the form of a mission statement.
- Corporate, functional and individual objectives need to be set as part of the strategic planning process.
- Different stakeholder groups have a different assessment of the risk a strategy poses to their interests. Some are able to exercise power over management.

Quick quiz

1 Why are objectives so important in the planning process?

2 What are the functions of objectives?

3 What makes up the hierarchy of objectives?

4 What are the stages involved in setting objectives?

5 What does the mnemonic SMART refer to in objective setting?

6 What is a mission?

7 What are the possible features of a mission statement?

8 Differentiate between corporate, functional and individual objectives, giving examples of each.

Answers to quick quiz

1 Objectives are the anticipated end result of programmes of activity; without them there would be no specific goals to aim for, and now way of measuring achievement of plans.

2 Objectives have several functions; they allow, at various levels, the overall objectives of the organisation to be broken down into clear statements of what needs to be done at each level; they provide clear statements of what action needs to be taken; they provide a focus for all activity; they provide targets for both individual and group achievement; they facilitate the control of actual performance; and they provide a basis for evaluating how successfully the plans are being implemented.

3 Strategic objectives such as the mission and corporate objectives; functional objectives which relate to a department or section; and individual objectives which relate to a person.

4 Agree the objectives, prioritise the objectives, define the activities and tasks, agree standards of performance, allocate roles set and timetable performance criteria.

5 Specific, Measurable, Agreed, Realistic, Timetabled.

6 A mission describes an organisation's basic function in society.

7 A mission statement will: provide a ready reference point against which to make decisions; help guard against there being different (and possibly misleading) interpretations of the organisation's stated purpose; help to present a clear image of the organisation for the benefit of customers and the general public.

8 Corporate objectives affect the whole organisation and are normally long-term. For example: 'to achieve a market share of 20% in five years'.

  Functional objectives relate to a department or section and are typically medium-term. For example: 'to train all staff to Level 3 by the end of the next financial year'.

  Individual objectives relate to a person and their work. Most of these – but not all – will involve short-term activities like completing the quarterly stock check by the end of the week.

Answers to activities

1 The consequences will include confusion, duplication, wastage, delays, lack of motivation and conflict.

2 Your long-term objective might been to pass the year with distinction; your medium-term objective may be to finish all assignments on time and to have done all the course reading; in the short-term you probably want to complete this chapter and all its activities.

NOTES

3 You might have produced statements along the following lines.

1 To establish a market share of 20% and become the acknowledged leader for quality and innovation.

2 To enable every member of the community to maximise their potential for education and learning.

3 To provide facilities for day care and activities suited to clients' needs in a caring environment.

4 To provide shelter and care for the homeless and assistance with finding permanent accommodation.

5 To develop support and raise funds for practical conservation projects in the countryside in partnership with other interest groups.

The concept of a mission is often most relevant to private sector organisations that want to achieve, say, market-leading positions, offer the biggest product range, sell the best products, and so on.

Public sector organisations often stress the quality of the services they offer, but normally the concept is less relevant.

The suitability of the concept to the voluntary sector varies; it is unsuitable for some routine service providers but very good for campaigning, researching or member interest groups.

4 Corporate objectives for an FE college might relate to:

- An increase in student numbers
- An increase in courses provided
- An expansion of premises and facilities
- An improvement in the financial standing of the college

5 Individual objectives could be related either to work tasks that needed improving or to experience in any one of a number of areas. Alternatively, they could relate to personal development such as increased responsibility. You might have set out some ideas of how you could improve your management skills or a course you could take, in two years' time, you could expect to be something like an assistant manager of a store. You should have assessed your abilities and needs realistically and aimed for an attainable position. Ask someone to comment on your memo.

6 The Technical Department will almost certainly resist such a change as the proposals devalue audit to being one of many business services to management. An audit is undertaken for the benefit of shareholders. The Technical Department (the firm's technostructure (see Chapter 3)) is also powerful, as enforcement of the standards it will suggest should reduce professional negligence costs. The structure will thus exert a powerful influence over the strategy and business practices.

External influences include professional associations which have an influence on the profession as a whole. The marketing manager may also be misled as to the degree to which customers want a 'one-stop shop' for accounting and advertising services.

7 Your own research is needed for this one.

Chapter 2 : THE EXTERNAL ENVIRONMENT

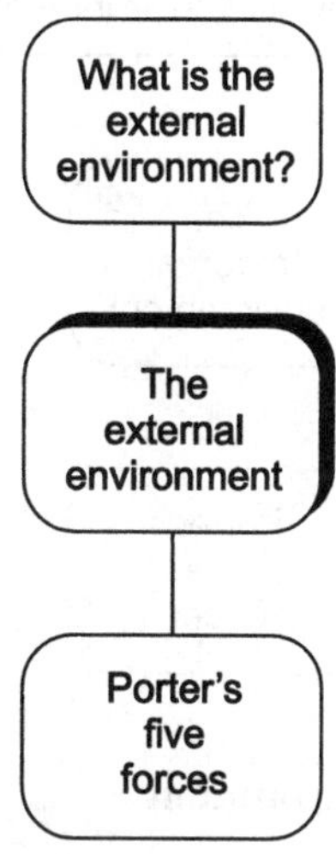

Introduction

Good planning will only occur if the planner has a detailed knowledge of both the internal and external environments within which the organisation operates. In this chapter we will examine the complex range of influences which need to be considered in the **external environment**.

An organisation has many interchanges within its environment. It draws **inputs** from it, and **outputs** goods and services to it. The environment is a major source of uncertainty.

An organisation is affected by general environmental trends, which can be usefully summarised in the PESTEL model.

Issues relating specifically to a particular industry reflect the **competitive environment,** and we discuss ***Porter's* five forces model** as a way of analysing it.

Your objectives

In this chapter you will learn about the following.

(a) The importance of the external environment to the strategy process

(b) The range of factors (PESTEL) in the external environment that may influence planning decisions, and the impact they may have

(c) *Porter's* five-forces model

1 WHAT IS THE EXTERNAL ENVIRONMENT?

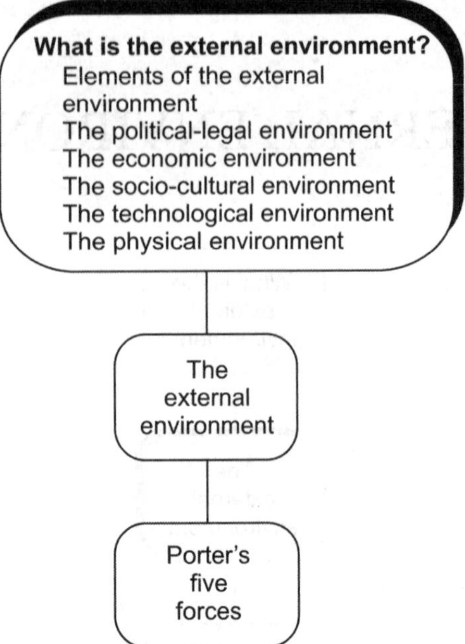

1.1 Elements of the external environment

FOR DISCUSSION

Take a look at any small local business: a shop, solicitor's office, garage, builder or any other you choose. You won't need to know the business in great detail, but each member of your group should choose a different type of business.

Look at its external environment. Look for the sources of business and what is affecting it, for example high property rents or unemployment, any legal constraints or technological changes. What might happen in the event of political change at the local council?

When you have made your notes on a business and its external enviornment, compare them and discuss what common factors you can identify.

Organisations do not exist in isolation; they depend on the **environment** in which they exist, **from** which they draw **materials and customers**, and **to** which they supply **goods and services**.

Good knowledge of the external environment can help to improve planning. Analysis of the external environment, and the trends which lead to changes in it, can identify **threats** and **opportunities** more quickly, decrease the likelihood of major surprises and shorten the firm's reaction time to events.

The external environment can be split into three elements, although these are often interrelated in practice.

- The physical environment
- The social environment
- The competitive environment

The physical and social environments can be further divided into **PESTEL factors**.

- **P**olitical
- **E**conomic
- **S**ocio-cultural
- **T**echnological
- **E**nvironmental/ecological
- **L**egal

The interrelationship of the various aspects of the external environment is shown in Figure 2.1.

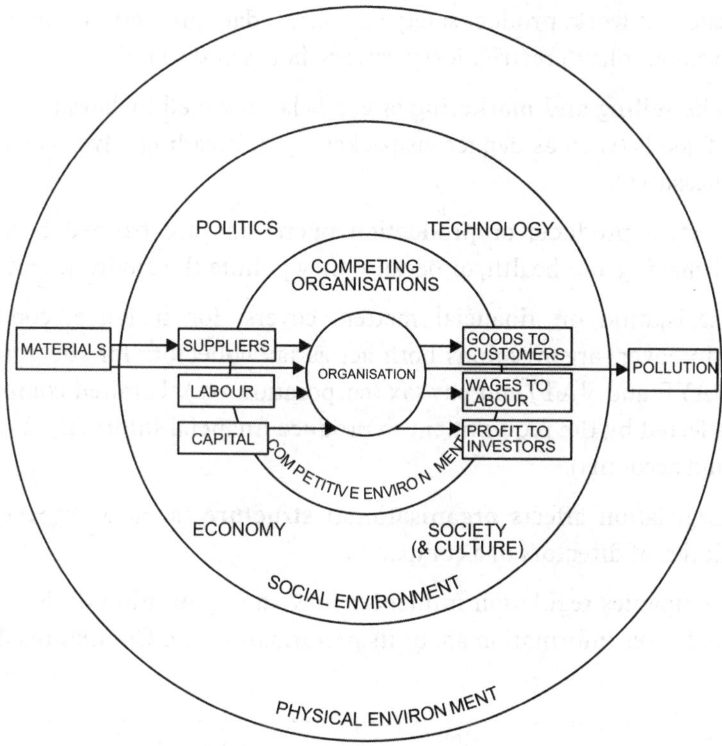

Figure 2.1: Aspects of the external environment

The first of the PESTEL (the 'P' and 'L' of the mnemonic) factors of the social environment that we consider is the political and legal environment.

1.2 The political-legal environment

Politics affects organisations in several ways: changes in political control can influence public priorities and funding arrangements. Organisations operate within a broad framework of **laws** which are set by Parliament, and therefore depend upon political considerations.

Criminal law will also affect an organisation. Examples of offences may include insider dealing, theft or even corporate manslaughter.

Of increasing importance are laws made by the **European Union (EU)**. Changes in EU and UK law are often predictable, but planners still need to consider the possible impact

of political changes. The government often publishes advance information about its plans for consultation purposes.

In general, the law affects how an organisation does its business (for example, the law of contract). More specific legal constraints affecting the management of an organisation can be categorised as follows.

(a) Employment law and trade union law affect **human resources** and how an organisation treats its employees. For example, a minimum wage now exists in the UK, and Working Time Regulations were a response to an EC Directive.

(b) Laws place restrictions on the **operations** of the organisation (health and safety at work, product safety standards, data protection, the introduction of tachographs to restrict lorry drivers' hours and so on).

(c) The **selling and marketing** of goods is restricted by laws on the description of goods (such as dangerous packaging, misleading advertising, weights and measures).

(d) Certain products or production operations are banned because they are damaging and health, or because they pollute the environment.

(e) Legislation on financial matters covers, for instance, consumer credit. Moreover, organisations both act as tax collectors for the government (via PAYE and VAT) and pay tax (corporation tax). Limited companies are also affected by the requirement to produce financial information (annual report and accounts).

(f) Legislation affects **organisational structure** (such as by establishing the duties of directors of a company).

(g) Companies regulation influences how an organisation deals with its owners and gives information about its performance (the **Companies Acts**).

EXAMPLE

The National Lottery (or 'Lotto') in the UK is one of the most highly regulated lotteries in the world. Under the terms of its licence, Camelot (the operator) is required to operate the lottery in an efficient and socially responsible way, protecting players and the integrity of the lottery, and to ensure that it generates the maximum amount of money for the 'Good Causes' which are designated by Parliament:

- The Community Fund
- The Millennium Commission
- The Sports Council
- The Heritage Lottery Fund
- The Arts Council
- New Opportunities Fund

The National Lottery Commission regulates the operation of the lottery. It has the right to award and revoke the operating licence, determine the number of games that can be offered and to carry out compliance audits (such as making sure there are no sales to under-16s).

Camelot's strategic objectives are clear:

(i) Deliver target returns to good causes in a socially responsible way
(ii) Increase the number of players and total sales
(iii) Maximise player and retailer satisfaction
(iv) Retain the trust and support of the general public
(v) Deliver healthy returns for shareholders

However, it sees the regulatory regime in which it operates (there are over 2,000 regulations) as a barrier to a rapid response to an increasingly competitive market. Unequal tax regimes are a prime concern. The tax on bingo has been abolished, and it seems likely that regulation over competitors to the Lottery will be further reduced. Camelot believes that the only way to achieve a more effective balance between its own commercial requirements and the needs of customers is to allow it greater self regulation.

Legislation is created by the government, but legislation is not the only way in which political influence can affect organisations. Changes in political control can also affect the following.

- Areas receiving special assistance
- Subsidies and other financial incentives to attract businesses
- The way public-sector organisations are run
- Levels of investment in both public and private sectors

Government policy affects the whole **economy**, and governments are responsible for enforcing and creating a **stable framework** in which business can be done. A report by the World Bank indicated that the quality of **government policy is important in providing** three things.

- **Physical** infrastructure (eg transport)
- **Social** infrastructure (education, a welfare safety net, law enforcement, equal opportunities)
- **Market** infrastructure (enforceable contracts, policing corruption)

Political risk

The political risk in a decision is the risk that political factors will invalidate the strategy and perhaps severely damage the firm. Examples are wars, political chaos, corruption and nationalisation.

A **political risk checklist** is outlined below. Companies should ask the following six questions.

1. How **stable** is the host country's political system?
2. How **strong** is the host government's commitment to specific rules of the game, such as ownership or contractual rights, given its ideology and power position?
3. How **long** is the government likely to remain in **power?**
4. If the present government is **succeeded,** how would the specific rules of the game change?
5. What would be the effects of any expected **changes** in the specific rules of the game?
6. In light of those effects, what **decisions and actions should be taken now**?

We shall now examine the economic environment and its effect on organisations.

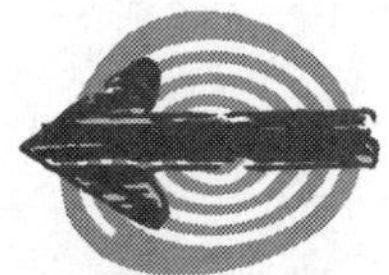

1.3 The economic environment

The state of the economy affects all organisations, both commercial and non-commercial. The rate of growth in the economy is a measure of the overall change in demand for goods and services, and growth is an indictor of increased demand.

Economic influences on an organisation operate at various levels.

(a) **Regional economic influences**
The organisation's local geographical environment is important, as this may be characterised by growth or decay. The economic future of the area will affect the availability of labour, disposable income of local consumers, unemployment, crime levels, subsidies, the provision of roads and other services.

(b) **National economic influences**
Strategic planners will be interested in the prospects for national economic growth, inflation, interest rates, exchange rates, unemployment, public expenditure, overseas trade and taxation levels. These are factors over which an organisation has no direct control.

(c) **International economic influences**
These include economic growth rates, inflation, interest and wage rates, protectionism and economic agreements.

Definitions

1 **Protectionism** is the imposition of tariffs, quotas or other barriers to trade to restrict the inflow of imports, in order to protect domestic producers from overseas competition.

2 **Tariffs** are taxes imposed on an imported good.

3 **Quotas** are limits that are imposed on the quantity of a particular good that is imported.

The **forecast state of the economy** will influence the planning process for organisations which operate within it. In times of boom and increased demand and consumption, the overall planning problem will be to **identify** the demand. Conversely, in times of recession, the emphasis will be on cost-effectiveness, continuing profitability, survival and competition.

Key issues for the UK economy

(a) The **service sector** accounts for most output. Services include activities such as restaurants, tourism, nursing, education, management consultancy, computer consulting, banking and finance. Manufacturing is still important, especially in exports, but it employs fewer and fewer people.

(b) The **housing market** is a key factor for people in the UK. Most houses are owner-occupied, and most people's wealth is tied up in their homes. UK borrowers generally borrow at variable rates of interest, so are vulnerable to changes in interest rates.

(c) **Tax and welfare.** Although headline rates of tax have fallen, people have to spend more on private insurance schemes for health or pensions. The government aims to target welfare provision on the needy and to reduce overall welfare spending by getting people into work.

(d) **Productivity**. An economy cannot grow faster than the underlying growth in productivity, without risking inflation. UK manufacturing productivity is still lower than that of its main competitors, but in services the UK is relatively efficient.

National influences must be viewed within the context of international influences. Although international influences might seem irrelevant to the small- or medium-sized business, they have an important influence on the future of any organisation with plans to trade abroad.

Factor	Impact
Exchange rates	Cost of imports, selling prices and value of exports; cost of hedging against fluctuations
Characteristics of overseas markets. Different rates of economic growth and prosperity, tax etc.	Desirable overseas markets (demand) or sources of supply.
Capital, flows and trade	Investment opportunities, free trade, cost of exporting

Next we turn to the social-cultural environment which, although a less obvious influence than many other sectors of the external environment, can have a substantial impact on organisations.

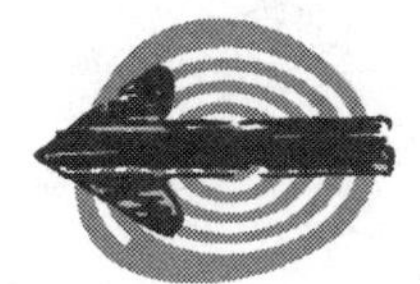

1.4 The socio-cultural environment

Social and cultural factors affect the make-up of the **population** and the **lifestyle** of society. The social and cultural environments are constantly changing. Trends identified can assist planners with their task.

Demography

Definition

Demography is the study of population and population trends.

One of the most important influences on an organisation is the **change in population** numbers and composition. The following demographic factors are especially important.

- The rate of growth or decline in national and regional populations
- Changes in the age distribution of the population
- The concentration of population in certain geographical areas

Demographic change has implications

(a) The services and products an organisation's customers will want and the size of demand for certain products

(b) The location of demand

(c) Recruitment (a falling birth-rate will mean that sixteen to twenty years later, there will be a decline in the number of young people entering the workforce)

(d) The wealth of the workforce (who sustain and support the ageing population)

Activity 1 **(15 minutes)**

The following demographic trends are taking place in the UK.

(a) There are fewer young people available to join the labour force.

(b) The total labour force is gradually ageing.

(c) The proportion of people over retirement age is growing.

What are the likely effects of these trends on the provision of goods and services?

Cultural changes

Each society has a certain culture (its own attitudes and way of doing things) and within each society there are many cultural groups, based on, for example:

- Ethnicity or race
- Religion
- Social class
- Membership of organisation

Significant cultural changes over the past few decades have included changing attitudes to debt, greater equality between the sexes and a blurring of sexual roles and the decline of participation in organised religion.

Subculture	Comment
Class	People from different social classes might have different values reflecting their position of society.
Ethnic background	Some ethnic groups can still be considered a distinct cultural group.
Religion	Religion and ethnicity are related.
Geography or region	Distinct regional differences might be brought about by the past effects of physical geography (socio-economic differences etc). Speech accents most noticeably differ.
Age	Age subcultures vary according to the period in which individuals were socialised to an extent, because of the great shifts in social values and customs in this century. ('Youth culture'; the 'generation gap' etc).

Subculture	Comment
Sex	Some products are targeted directly to women or to men.
Work	Different organisations have different corporate cultures, in that the shared values of one workplace may be different from another.

Activity 2 **(20 minutes)**

Club Fun is a UK company which sells packaged holidays. It offers a standard 'cheap and cheerful' package to resorts in Spain and, more recently, to some of the Greek islands. It has been particularly successful at providing holidays for the 18 to 30 age group.

What do you think the implications are for Club Fun of the following developments?

- A fall in the number of school leavers
- The fact that young people are more likely now to go into higher education
- Holiday programmes on TV which feature a much greater variety of locations
- Greater disposable income among the 18 to 30 age group

Social change and social trends

Changes in the nature, attitudes and habits of society should be considered during the planning process.

(a) Rising standards of living may result in wider ownership of consumer and luxury goods.

(b) Society's attitude to business many change. Issues such as environmental protection and ethical conduct towards customers and employees have recently emerged.

(c) Changes in the workforce itself (such as a switch from 'blue collar jobs' to 'white collar jobs' and an expansion in leisure time) influence how an organisation operates.

Business ethics

The ethical environment incorporates **justice**, respect for the **law** and a **moral code**. The conduct of an organisation, its management and employees is increasingly measured against ethical standards by the customers, suppliers and other members of the public with whom they deal.

Activity 3 **(30 minutes)**

The Heritage Carpet Company is a London-based retailer which imports carpets from Turkey, Iran and India. The company was founded by two Europeans who travelled independently through these countries in the 1970s. The company is the sole customer for carpets made in a number of villages in each of the source countries. The carpets are hand woven. Indeed, they are so finely woven that the process requires that children be used to do the weaving, thanks to their small fingers. The company believes that it is preserving a 'craft', and the directors believe that this is a justifiable social objective. Recently a UK television company has reported unfavourably on child exploitation in the carpet weaving industry. There were reports of children working twelve hour shifts in poorly lit sheds and cramped conditions, with consequent deterioration in eyesight, muscular disorders and a complete absence of education. The examples cited bear no relation to the Heritage Carpet Company's suppliers but there has been a spate of media attention. The regions in which the Heritage Carpet Company's supplier villages are found are soon expected to enjoy rapid economic growth.

What social and ethical issues are raised for the Heritage Carpet Company?

In most organisations managers aim to make a profit. At the same time, modern ethical standards impose a duty to guard, preserve and enhance the value of the organisation for the good of all associated with it, including the general public.

A manager may encounter numerous ethical problems in practice.

- Product quality and liability
- Bribery
- Competitive behaviour
- Treatment of employees (such as health and safety and equality issues)
- Environmental issues

FOR DISCUSSION

Virgin Atlantic took legal action against British Airways, claiming that BA had competed unethically by stealing information, planting inaccurate and derogatory stories in the press, refusing to allow Virgin to operate a normal aircraft service and initiating an unethical price war. In 2007 the two companies continued to be accused of unethical and now illegal practices related to price fixing. The airlines were found to be agreeing the amount they would charge in relation to fuel surcharges for both passenger fares and cargo. When Virgin lawyers blew the whistle on the illegal activities they escaped prosecution in the UK and US. BA however was fined £121.5m by the Office of Fair Trading and a further $300m (£147m) by the US Department of Justice.

The fact that a company as prestigious as BA was openly challenged in this way raises some interesting issues.

(a) What effect might this have had on the business world in general, and the way that business competition is planned and organised?

(b) What sorts of company might be particularly sensitive to these types of challenge?

The next of the PESTEL factors to consider is the technological environment.

1.5 The technological environment

Of the many factors which impact on an organisation, technological change probably has the most rapid, persistent and profound effect, influencing the following.

(a) The **type of products or services** that an organisation makes and sells. Home computers, compact discs, satellite dishes and microchips have only relatively recently appeared on the market.

(b) The **way in which products are made**. Modern labour-saving production equipment can now be used.

(c) The **way in which services are provided**. Relatively recent developments include cash dispensers and point of sale terminals at cash desks.

(d) The **way in which markets are identified**. Database systems of analysis are increasingly used.

(e) The **way in which employees are mobilised.** Technology has a major effect on working methods and skill requirements. IT encourages 'delayering' of organisational hierarchies, homeworking and better communication.

(f) **The means and extent of communications with external clients**. The financial sector is rapidly going electronic - call centres are now essential to stay in business, PC banking is here, and the Internet and interactive TV feature in business plans.

Definition

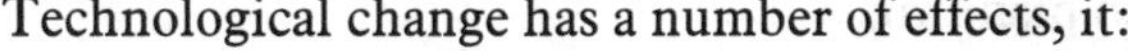

> A **database** is a large file of data which is held on a computer and which can be analysed to provide useful information.

Technological change has a number of effects, it:

(a) Can cut production **costs** and other costs of sale. This offers organisations the possibility of reducing the sales price, thereby assisting in any 'price wars'.

(b) Assists the development of better **quality** products and services.

(c) Aids the **development** of products and services that did not previously exist.

(d) Provides products or services to customers more **quickly** or **effectively** than before.

(e) Can **free staff** from repetitive work (or can put them out of work!).

(f) Creates more **flexible forms of work,** such as working from home.

An organisation that operates in an environment where the pace of technological change is very fast must be flexible enough to adapt to any change quickly, and must plan for **change and innovation,** perhaps by spending heavily on **research and development**.

Activity 4 **(30 minutes)**

During the early years of the recording industry, the disc gramophone record became established as the medium for producing sound recordings. During the 1970s cassette tapes looked set to change this because of their portability and convenient size, as well as their suitability for in-car systems. Despite this, the vinyl disc held off the challenge.

With the introduction of compact discs (CDs) during the 1980s and 90s, however, the vinyl disc seems to have become a collector's item. Even singles were sold on compact disc. The main markets for tapes (for use in personal stereos and cars) were taken over by compact discs, and later DVDs and music downloaded from the internet transformed the market.

1 Think about the effect of technological and economic change in this area, then write down briefly the factors that gave the CD dominance in the market of the time.

2 If you were thinking about taking over an audio shop, what other expected future developments and commercial opportunities might you be interested in?

Despite its benefits, technology also has disadvantages. These include job losses, negative social effects, environmental pollution and the use of non-renewable natural resources. However, technology is often the only way of dealing with the problems it creates.

The next aspect we shall consider is the environmental/ecological aspect.

1.6 The physical environment

Although the physical environment is often taken for granted, there are several reasons why it should be taken into account when planning.

Natural conditions such as the weather, floods and earthquakes can have an enormous effect on an organisation's operations.

The **natural environment** determines the supply of many **raw materials,** and technological progress and market changes can make it possible – and worthwhile – to exploit new sources of supply.

EXAMPLE

North Sea oil could not have been accessed without the experience in deep sea drilling gained in South American waters, and it might not have been tapped for many years if the price of oil had not been forced up fourfold in both 1973 and 1979.

The physical environment presents organisations with **logistical** problems (such as which transportation network to use) or opportunities (such as access to suitable markets). For example, should a company in Aberdeen continue to serve its Belgian market by sea, or use rail freight through the Channel Tunnel? Can improved transport enable it to sell to the South of France?

Some aspects of the physical environment are under the control of other organisations; for example new buildings require planning permission from local authorities, and **environmental legislation** is increasing. This has to be taken into account in the analysis of the political environment.

Organisations with a poor ecological record can be exposed to bad publicity, legal proceedings and regulation. Following the Exxon-Valdez oil spill of 1989, oil companies were required to invest in new double-hulled ships to reduce the risk of spills in accidents. BP was subject to a criminal and civil investigation by the US Government after the April 2010 Deepwater Horizon oil rig explosion, and its market value dropped sharply.

EXAMPLE

When the Brent Spar oil rig was going to be dumped in the North Sea, the public outcry and consumer boycott of petrol stations forced a change of mind by the company.

Activity 5 **(15 minutes)**

List ways in which an organisation could benefit from the growing public interest in environmental issues.

We shall now look at the competitive environment, the final aspect of the external environment that we will be considering.

2 PORTER'S FIVE FORCES

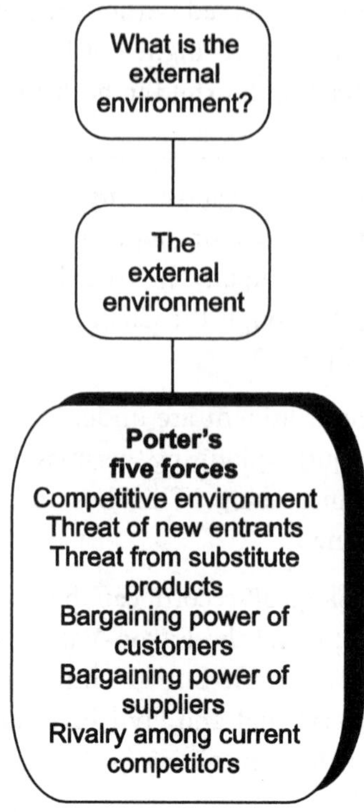

2.1 The competitive environment

The final external influence upon the organisation is the **competitive environment**. The competitive strategy of an organisation and the need to secure particular competitive advantage over competitors is becoming increasingly important, and hence an appraisal of the competitive environment is vital before plans are laid.

Definition

Competitive advantage is a factor which enables an organisation to compete successfully with its main competitors on a sustained basis.

Michael Porter (1996), suggests that the following five basic competitive forces influence the state of competition in any industry, and collectively determine the profit potential of the industry as a whole.

***Porter*: Five competitive forces**

1. The threat of **new entrants** into the industry
2. The threat of **substitute products** or services (for example, taking the Eurostar train from London to Paris is a substitute for flying there)

3 The **bargaining power of customers** (who may demand better quality at a lower price)

4 The **bargaining power of suppliers** (who may charge higher prices)

5 The **rivalry** amongst current competitors in the industry (which can lead to price wars, new product development and special offers)

In any industry, a knowledge of these factors should give a clear picture of the competitive environment and hence the competitive opportunities and threats.

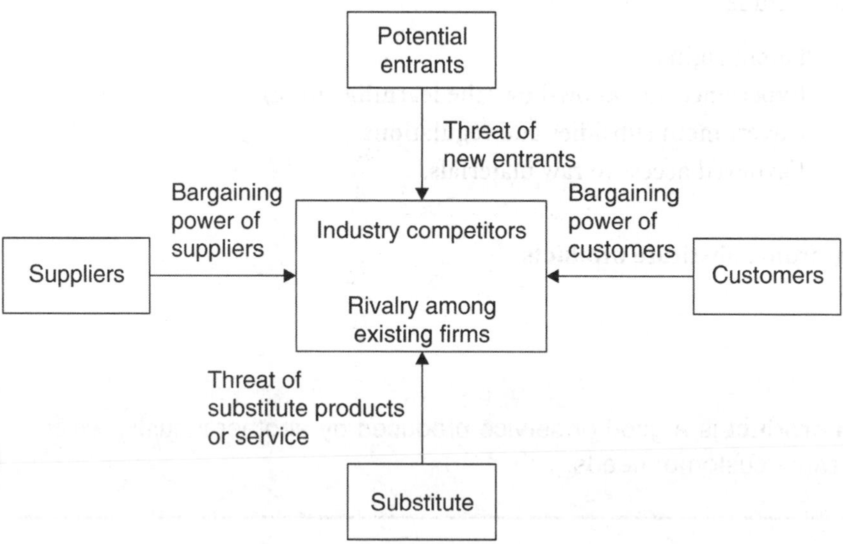

Figure 2.2: The five competitive forces

2.2 The threat of new entrants

A new entrant into an industry will bring extra capacity and more competition. The strength of this threat is likely to vary from industry to industry and depends on two things.

- The strength of the **barriers to entry**. Barriers to entry discourage new entrants.
- The likely **response of existing competitors** to the new entrant.

Barriers to entry

(a) **Scale economies.** If the market as a whole is not growing, the new entrant has to capture a large slice of the market from existing competitors, and this is expensive.

(b) **Product differentiation.** Existing firms in an industry may have built up a good brand image and strong customer loyalty over a long period of time. A few firms may promote a large number of brands to crowd out the competition.

(c) **Capital requirements.** When capital investment requirements are high, the barrier against new entrants will be strong, particularly when the investment would possibly be high-risk.

(d) **Switching costs.** Switching costs refer to the costs (time, money, convenience) that a customer would have to incur by switching from one

NOTES

supplier's products to another's. Although it might cost a **consumer** nothing to switch from one brand of frozen peas to another, the potential costs for the **retailer or distributor** might be high.

(e) **Access to distribution channels**. Distribution channels carry a manufacturer's products to the end-buyer. New distribution channels are difficult to establish, and existing distribution channels hard to gain access to.

(f) **Cost advantages of existing producers, independent of economies of scale** include:

- Patent rights
- Experience and know-how (the learning curve)
- Government subsidies and regulations
- Favoured access to raw materials.

2.3 The threat from substitute products

Definition

A **substitute product** is a good or service produced by another industry which satisfies the same customer needs.

EXAMPLE

Passengers have several ways of getting from London to Paris, and the pricing policies of the various industries transporting them there reflect this.

(a) 'Le Shuttle' carries cars in the Channel Tunnel. Its main competitors come from the ferry companies, offering a substitute service. Therefore, you will find that Le Shuttle sets its prices with reference to ferry company prices, and vice versa.

(b) Eurostar is the rail service from London to Paris/Brussels. Its main competitors are not the ferry companies but the airlines. Prices on the London-Paris air routes fell with the commencement of Eurostar services, and some airlines have curtailed the number of flights they offer.

2.4 The bargaining power of customers

Customers want better quality products and services at a lower price. Satisfying this want might force down the profitability of suppliers in the industry. Just how strong the position of customers will be depends on a number of factors.

- How much the **customer buys**
- How **critical** the product is to the customer's own business
- **Switching costs (ie the cost of switching supplier)**

- Whether the products are **standard items** (hence easily copied) or specialised
- The **customer's own profitability:** a customer who makes low profits will be forced to insist on low prices from suppliers
- Customer's **ability to bypass** the supplier (or take over the supplier)
- The **skills** of the customer **purchasing staff,** or the price-awareness of consumers
- When **product quality** is important to the customer, the customer is less likely to be price-sensitive, and so the industry might be more profitable as a consequence

2.5 The bargaining power of suppliers

Suppliers can exert pressure for higher prices. The ability of suppliers to get higher prices depends on several factors.

- Whether there are just **one or two dominant suppliers** to the industry, able to charge monopoly or oligopoly prices
- The threat of **new entrants** or substitute products to the **supplier's industry**
- Whether the suppliers have **other customers** outside the industry, and do not rely on the industry for the majority of their sales
- The **importance of the supplier's product** to the customer's business
- Whether the supplier has a **differentiated product** which buyers need to obtain
- Whether **switching costs** for customers would be high

2.6 The rivalry among current competitors in the industry

The **intensity of competitive rivalry** within an industry will affect the profitability of the industry as a whole. Competitive actions might take the form of price competition, advertising battles, sales promotion campaigns, introducing new products for the market, improving after sales service or providing guarantees or warranties. Competition can stimulate demand, expanding the market, or it can leave demand unchanged, in which case individual competitors will make less money, unless they are able to cut costs.

Factors determining the intensity of competition

(a) **Market growth.** Rivalry is intensified when firms are competing for a greater market share in a total market where growth is slow or stagnant.

(b) **Cost structure.** High fixed costs may be a barrier to competing on price, out in the short run any contribution from sales is better than none at all.

(c) **Switching.** Suppliers will compete if buyers switch easily (eg Coke vs Pepsi).

(d) **Capacity.** A supplier might need to achieve a substantial increase in output capacity, in order to obtain reductions in unit costs.

(e) **Uncertainty**. When one firm is not sure what another is up to, there is a tendency to respond to the uncertainty by formulating a more competitive strategy.

(f) **Strategic importance**. If success is a prime strategic objective, firms will be likely to act very competitively to meet their targets.

(g) **Exit barriers** make it difficult for an existing supplier to leave the industry. These can take many forms.

  (i) Fixed assets with a low **break-up value** (eg there may be no other use for them, or they may be old)

  (ii) The cost of **redundancy payments** to employees

  (iii) If the firm is a division or subsidiary of a larger enterprise, the **effect of withdrawal on the other operations** within the group

  (iv) The **reluctance of managers** to admit defeat, their loyalty to employees and their fear for their own jobs

  (v) **Government pressures** on major employers not to shut down operations, especially when competition comes from foreign producers rather than other domestic producers

---

EXAMPLE

In January 2006 the UK opened up its postal services monopoly to competition. By the end of 2006, PostComm the industry regulator had licensed just seventeen competitors. At this time The Royal Mail retained a 97% market share of the £4.65bn regulated addressed letters market. Within the UK 87% of mail is generated by businesses and of which the key industries include: financial services, publishing (magazines), public sector and home shopping (delivery of items purchased). Companies who have switched postal delivery suppliers have tended to be financial services organisations that mail in bulk.

Barriers to entry for new market entrant include large set-up costs associated with entering the postal network market and the existing economies of scale established by the Royal Mail to use part of their infrastructure. In 2006, only 0.7% of all mail was delivered entirely by postal operators, and it was forecasted that by 2010 still only 2.2% of mail would be delivered without the assistance of The Royal Mail.

Briefly put into the context of *Porter's* five forces indicates that within this industry there is very little competition:

(i) Bargaining power of customers – very low due to the monopoly powers within the industry

(ii) Bargaining power of suppliers – this is also very low

Adapted from *PostComm Competitive Market Review 2006*

Activity 6 **(45 minutes)**

The tea industry is characterised by oversupply, with a surplus of about 80,000 tonnes a year. Tea estates swallow capital, and the return is not as attractive as in industries such as technology or services. Tea cannot be stockpiled, unlike coffee, keeping for two years at most. Tea is auctioned in London and prices are the same in absolute terms as they were fifteen years ago. Tea is produced in Africa and India, Sri Lanka and China. Because of the huge capital investment involved, the most recent investments have been quasi-governmental, such as those by the Commonwealth Development Corporation in ailing estates in East Africa. There is no simple demarcation between buyers and sellers. Tea-bag manufacturers own their own estates, as well as buying in tea from outside sources.

Tea prices have been described in India at least as being 'exceptionally firm...

The shortage and high prices of coffee have also raised demand for tea which remains the cheapest of all beverages in spite of the recent rise in prices.

Demand from Russia, Poland, Iran and Iraq are expected to rise.'

(a) Carry out a five forces analysis.

(b) Thinking ahead, suggest a possible strategy for a tea-grower with a number of estates which has traditionally sold its tea at auction.

FOR DISCUSSION

One of the main features of contemporary shopping is the trend towards out-of-town shopping areas, which have been pulling customers away from town centres and local shops by offering lower prices and easier access for motorists.

Consider the situation in your town. What has happened in the High Street to the mix of businesses: how many are empty and how many are charity shops? If the town and local shops are to hold on to a reasonable share of trade, how can they achieve competitive advantage over out-of-town shopping areas?

Chapter roundup

- The organisation's environment is a source of uncertainty, depending on how complex or dynamic it is. General factors (PESTEL) affect all organisations.
- The main reason for examining the external environment is to identify any opportunities or threats which exist for the organisation.
- Relevant PESTEL (political, economic, socio-cultural, technological, environmental and legal) factors need to be identified and monitored by every organisation.
- The physical environment is important for logistical reasons, as a source of resources, and because of increasing regulation.
- The economic environment affects firms at national and international level; both in the general level of economic activity and in particular variables (eg exchange rates).
- The law impinges on organisations, defining what they can or cannot do.
- Political change is a source of environmental uncertainty.
- The social and cultural environment features long-term social trends and people's beliefs and attitudes (eg concern with ecological issues).
- The competitive environment is of major importance, and is structured by five forces: barriers to entry, substitute products, the bargaining power of customers, the bargaining power of suppliers and competitive rivalry.

Quick quiz

1 How can a good knowledge of the external environment help in planning?

2 How can the physical environment affect organisations?

3 What are the main legal controls affecting management?

4 In what ways is the economic environment important to organisational planning?

5 How can social changes affect organisations?

6 How do demographic factors affect organisations?

7 How do cultural issues influence planning decisions?

8 In what ways can ethical issues affect the management of organisations?

9 How can technological change influence planning in organisations?

10 What are the five key competitive forces that influence any industry?

Answers to quick quiz

1 Identify threats and opportunities more quickly, speed up reaction times, decrease the likelihood of major surprises

2 By its requirement for raw materials, logistical problems and the ecological effects of its operations.

3 Those which govern employment, operations, marketing, finance, structure and relations with stakeholders.

4 Local, regional, national and international changes like growth rates, employment and inflation all affect the market, and provide threats and opportunities to the organisation.

5 Demographic, cultural and social factors affect the market and labour force.

6 They affect the demand for services and products, the location of demand, wealth and income for spending and saving, and the size and composition of the workforce.

7 Cultural issues affect attitudes to work, the roles of the sexes, attitudes to debt, leisure demands and ethical attitudes.

8 Management has to take account of its treatment of customers and employees; attitudes in relation to product quality; the environment; working conditions; and all aspects of business behaviour.

9 It affects products, production, marketing, selling and the organisation of work. All of these have to be considered in planning.

10 *Porter's* five forces are the threat of new entrants, substitute products, the bargaining powers of suppliers and customers and rivalry amongst current competitors.

Answers to activities

1 (a) Fewer young people joining the labour force means that there will be less disposable income in this age group. This may result in a fall in the demand for certain music, mobile phones, clothes and so on.

(b) This will help to shift purchasing power to an older market.

(c) This will increase the products and services purchased by this group.

(d) There will be a need for care and service provision for this category of older, non-working people.

2 The firm's market is shrinking. Moreover, the increasing proportion of school leavers going into higher education may mean there are fewer who can afford Club Fun's packages, although a higher disposable income in the wider population might compensate for this trend. Some may choose destinations other than Club Fun's resorts if they view attractive alternatives publicised on television.

3 This is a case partly about management and partly about self-interest and business ethics. The adverse publicity, although indirect, could rebound badly. Potential customers might be put off. Economic growth in the area may mean that parents will be able to send their children to school. The Heritage Carpet Company could demonstrate a socially responsible attitude by demonstrating

its preservation of a craft, paying fair wages, limiting hours worked by children and reinvesting some of its profits in the villages. This could be laid down in a 'code of ethics' to reassure customers. Alternatively, it could not import child-made carpets at all. (This policy, however, would be unlikely to help communities in which child work is an economic necessity.)

4 CDs and DVDs transformed the recording industry for several reasons.

(a) They were smaller and easy to transport and store.

(b) They could store a huge amount of material.

(c) Individual tracks could be accessed accurately in a way that was not possible with records and tapes.

They were supported by the development of rewritable CDs for computer data storage which could be applicable for music at an affordable price.

Enthusiasts will continue to collect records, tapes and DVDs; there may be a specialist opening here worth considering, as meanwhile the market opens up to the possibility of digital downloads and MP3 players.

5 There are a number of possible ways of benefiting:

(a) Specifically using/selling environmentally friendly products and saying so
(b) Publicly supporting environmental causes
(c) Targeting environmentally conscious people as a potential market
(d) Conducting research into environmental issues
(e) Encouraging recycling

6 (a) Barriers to entry are high. There are plenty of substitute products (coffee), competitive rivalry is high because of the difficulty of stockpiling products. Customer bargaining power is high, but supplier power is low: all it needs is capital, the right sort of land and labour.

(b) Williamson and Major has begun to switch from selling tea at auction to consumer marketing. The firm is aiming to build up its own brand image in the UK and Germany, by offering – by mail order – unblended, specialist teas from its Indian estates. It advertised via Barclays Premier Card magazine; replies were used to set up a customer database. When the company's Earl Grey tea was recommended on BBC2's Food and Drink, these existing customers were targeted with a letter and a sample.

Chapter 3 :
INTERNAL ANALYSIS

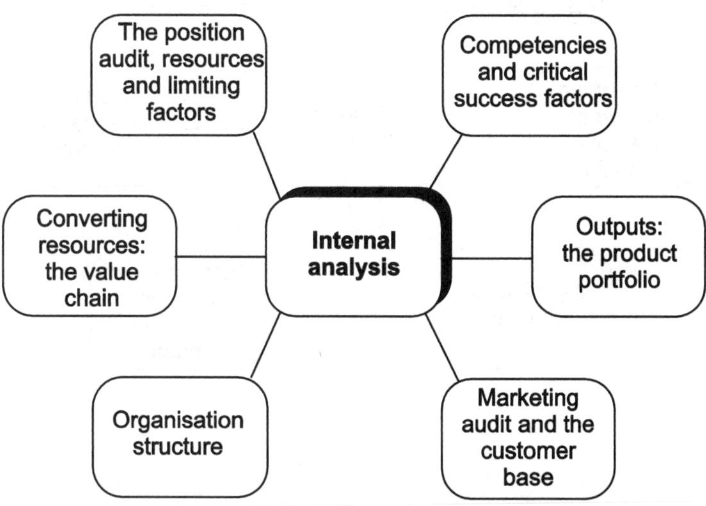

Introduction

In this chapter we examine some of the key aspects of the organisation's current **position**. A **resource audit** identifies any gaps in resources and limiting factors on organisational activity. **Value chain** analysis identifies how the business adds value to the resources it obtains, and how it deploys these resources to satisfy customers. A **competence** is a skill which the organisation has which can ensure a fit between the environment and the organisation's capability.

We then review the organisation's current outputs, its **product portfolio.**

Organisation structure is also a strategic issue, and describes how the organisation controls its work through its '**strategic architecture**'.

The purpose of all this activity is the customer, and a review of the **customer base** should identify trends and developments.

Your objectives

In this chapter you will learn about the following.

(a) The importance of the internal environment to the strategy process

(b) Those components of the internal environment that need to be examined in order to assess the current capabilities of an organisation

(c) Models such as the Boston matrix, the value chain and the 7S-framework

1 THE POSITION AUDIT, RESOURCES AND LIMITING FACTORS

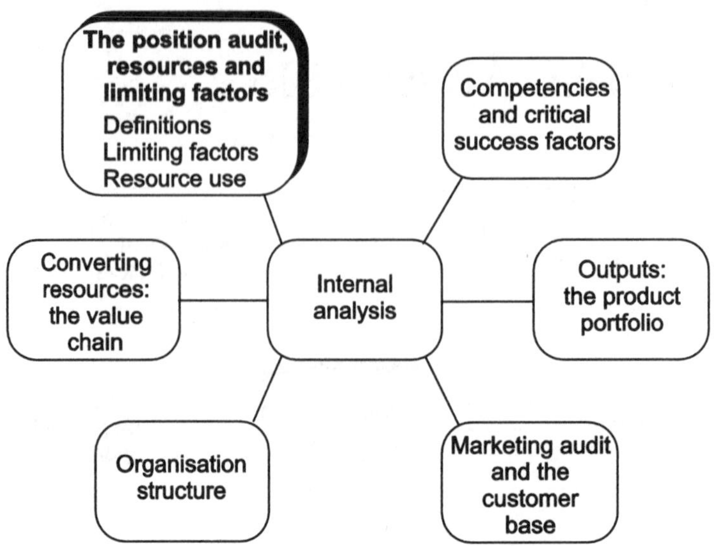

1.1 Definitions

Position audit is part of the planning process which examines the current state of the entity. A wide range of factors is examined. Here are some examples.

- Resources of tangible and intangible assets
- Products, brands and markets
- Operating systems such as production and distribution
- Internal organisation
- Current results
- Financial resources

A **resource audit** is a review of all aspects of the resources the organisation uses, including both physical and financial resources and systems.

Resources are of no value unless they are organised into systems, and so a resource audit should go on to consider how well or how badly resources have been utilised, and whether the organisation's systems are effective and efficient.

Resource	Example
Material inputs	Source, suppliers, waste, new materials, cost, availability, future provision
Human resources	Number, skills, wage costs, proportion of total costs, efficiency, labour turnover, industrial relations
Management	Size, skills, loyalty, career progression, structure
Fixed assets	Age, condition, cost utilisation rate, value, replacement, technologically up-to-date?
Working capital	Credit and turnover periods, cash surpluses/deficits
Finance	Short-term and long-term, gearing levels
Intangible assets	Patents, goodwill, brands
Organisation	Culture and structure
Knowledge	Ability to generate and disseminate ideas, innovation

1.2 Limiting factors

Every organisation operates under resource **constraints**.

Definition

A **limiting factor** or key factor is one which at any time may limit the activity of an entity, often where there is shortage or difficulty of supply.

Examples

- A shortage of production capacity
- A limited number of key personnel, such as salespeople with technical knowledge
- A restricted distribution network
- Too few managers with knowledge about finance, or overseas markets
- Inadequate research design or resources to develop new products or services
- A poor system of strategic intelligence
- Lack of money
- A lack of adequately trained staff

Once the limiting factor has been identified, the planners have two courses of action.

- In the short-term, make best use of the resources available
- Try to reduce the limitation in the long-term

1.3 Resource use

Resource use is concerned with the efficiency with which resources are used, and the effectiveness of their use in achieving the planning objectives of the business.

Definitions

Effectiveness is the measure of achievement and is assessed by reference to goals.

Economy is reduction or containment of cost. There will normally be a trade off between effectiveness and economy. Efficiency means being effective at minimum cost or controlling costs without losing operational effectiveness.

Efficiency is therefore a combination of effectiveness and economy.

2 COMPETENCIES AND CRITICAL SUCCESS FACTORS

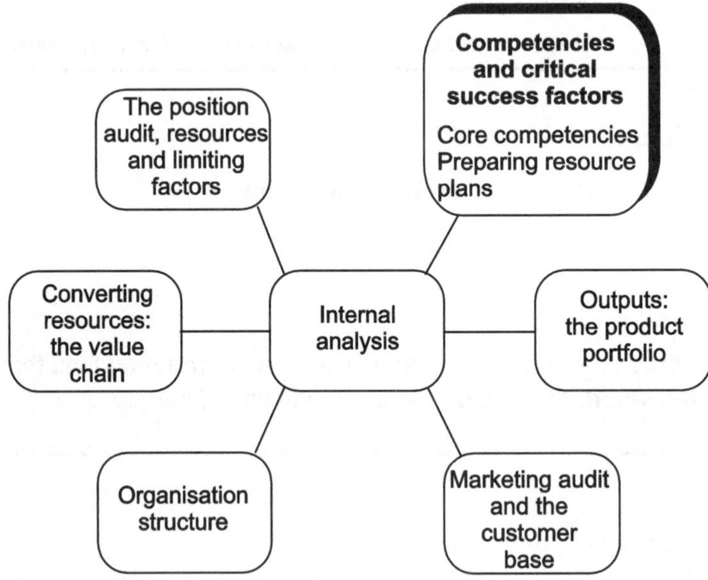

2.1 Core competencies

A strategic approach involves identifying a firm's **competencies**. These competences develop in a variety of ways.

- **Experience** in making and marketing a product or service
- The talents and potential of individuals in the organisation
- The **quality of co-ordination**

Definition

The **distinctive competence** of an organisation is what it does well, or better, than its rivals.

EXAMPLE: Nike

Hamel and Prahalad (1994) use the example of Nike, whose core competence is not in the actual manufacture of their athletic equipment, which they outsource, but rather in branding and design, product development, endorsement by leading athletes, merchandising and distribution. These competencies can add the 'wow' factor to an otherwise unremarkable pair of running shoes, on sale in many markets, and are difficult for a competitor to copy immediately.

Professional service firms

Whereas Nike is a consumer branding product, professional service firms are dependent on their staff. They may include partnerships in law, accounting, advertising systems and so on.

Professional service firms in part depend on 'star' performers who can, if they leave, take their clients with them. Staff may want to pursue their own personal ambitions, not the firm's.

What *really* is the competence of a professional service firm? The skills of its staff? Or, at a deeper level, the firm's ability to attract good staff, and to motivate them to act in the interests of the firm as a unity?

Tests for identifying a core competence

(a) **It provides potential access to a wide variety of markets**. GPS of France developed a core competence in 'one-hour' processing, enabling it to process films and build reading glasses in one hour.

(b) **It contributes significantly to the value enjoyed by the customer**. For example, for GPS, the waiting time restriction was very important.

(c) **It should be hard for a competitor to copy.** This will be the case if it is technically complex, involves specialised processes, involves complex interrelationships between different people in the organisation or is hard to define.

In many cases, a company might choose to combine competencies.

2.2 Preparing resource plans

Competencies can be related to critical success factors.

Definitions

- **Critical success factors (CSFs)** are those factors on which the strategy is fundamentally dependent for its success.
- **Key tasks** are what must be done to ensure each critical success factor is satisfied.
- **Priorities** indicate the order in which tasks are completed.

NOTES

(a) Some CSFs are generic to the whole industry, others to a particular firm. The critical success factor to run a successful **mail order business** is speedy delivery.

(b) A CSF of a **parcel delivery service** is that it **must be quicker than the normal post.**

(c) Underpinning critical success factors are **key tasks.** If **customer care** is a CSF, then a key task, and hence a measure of performance, would include responding to enquiries within a given time period. There may be a number of key tasks - but some might be more important than others, or must come first in a sequence.

Activity 1 **(15 minutes)**

Draw up a list of four critical success factors for the strategy of any organisation with which you are familiar.

Relationship between competencies and CSFs

- A competence is what an organisation **has or is able to do**
- A **CSF** is what is **necessary to achieve an objective**

Competencies thus fulfil the CSF. In the examples quoted, a competence of faster delivery supports a CSF that a courier service must be faster than a competitor.

3 CONVERTING RESOURCES: THE VALUE CHAIN

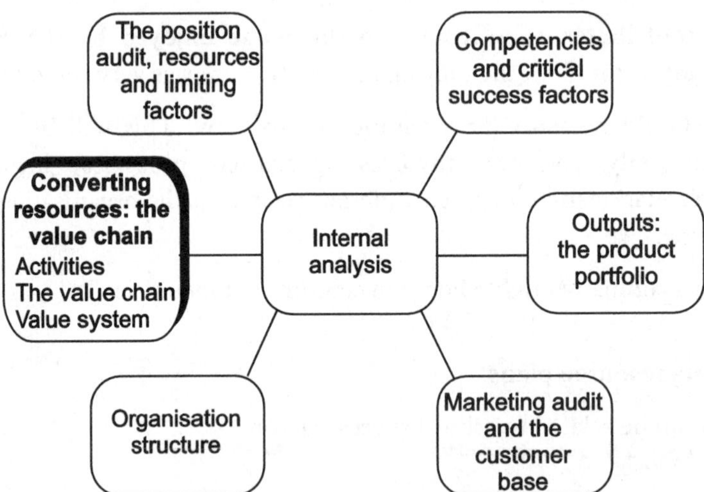

The **value chain** model of corporate activities, developed by *Michael Porter* (1996), offers a bird's eye view of the firm and what it does. Competitive advantage, says *Porter*, arises out of the way in which firms organise and perform **activities.**

3.1 Activities

Definition

> **Activities** are the means by which a firm creates value in its products. (They are sometimes referred to as value activities.)

Activities incur costs, and, in combination with other activities, provide a product or service which earns revenue.

Let us explain this point by using the example of a **restaurant**. A restaurant's activities can be divided into buying food, cooking it, and serving it (to customers). There is no reason, in theory, why the customers should not do all these things themselves, at home. The customer however, is not only prepared to **pay for someone else** to do all this but also **pays more than the cost of** the resources (food, wages and soon). The ultimate value a firm creates is measured by the amount customers are willing to pay for its products or services above the cost of carrying out value activities. A firm is profitable if the realised value to customers exceeds the collective cost of performing the activities.

(a) Customers **purchase value**, which they measure by comparing a firm's products and services with similar offerings by competitors.

(b) The business **creates value** by carrying out its activities either more efficiently than other businesses, or combine them in such a way as to provide a unique product or service.

> **Activity 2** **(15 minutes)**
>
> Outline different ways in which the restaurant can create value.

3.2 The value chain

Porter (1996) grouped the various activities of an organisation into a **value chain**.

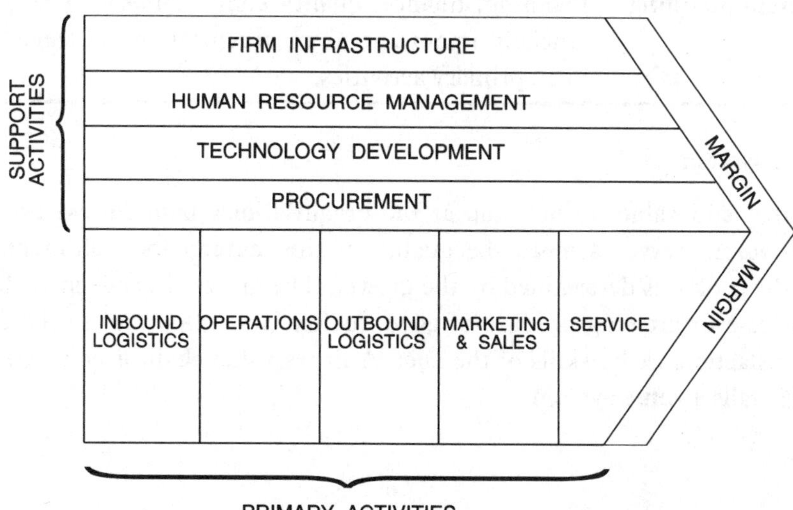

Figure 3.1: The value chain

(*Source: Michael Porter*, *Competitive Advantage*, 1996)

NOTES

The margin is the excess the customer is prepared to pay over the cost to the firm of obtaining resource inputs and providing value activities.

Primary activities are directly related to production, sales, marketing, delivery and service.

Activity	Comment
Inbound logistics	Receiving, handling and storing inputs to the production system: warehousing, transport, stock control and so on.
Operations	Convert resource inputs into a final product. Resource inputs are not only materials. People are a resource especially in service industries.
Outbound logistics	Storing the product and its distribution to customers: packaging, testing, delivery and so on.
Marketing and sales	Informing customers about the product, persuading them to buy it, and enabling them to do so: advertising, promotion and so on.
After sales service	Installing products, repairing them, upgrading them, providing spare parts and so forth.

Support activities provide purchased inputs, human resources, technology and infrastructural functions to support the primary activities.

Activity	Comment
Procurement	Acquire the resource inputs to the primary activities (eg purchase of materials, subcomponents equipment).
Technology development	Product design, improving processes and/or resource utilisation.
Human resource management	Recruiting, training, developing and rewarding people.
Management planning	Planning, finance, quality control: *Porter* believes they are crucially important to an organisation's strategic capability in all primary activities.

3.3 Value system

Activities that add value do not stop at the organisation's **boundaries**. For example, when a restaurant serves a meal, the quality of the ingredients – although they are chosen by the cook – is determined by the grower. The grower has added value, and the grower's success in growing produce of good quality is as important to the customer's ultimate satisfaction as the skills of the chef. A firm's value chain is connected to what *Porter* (1996) calls a **value system**.

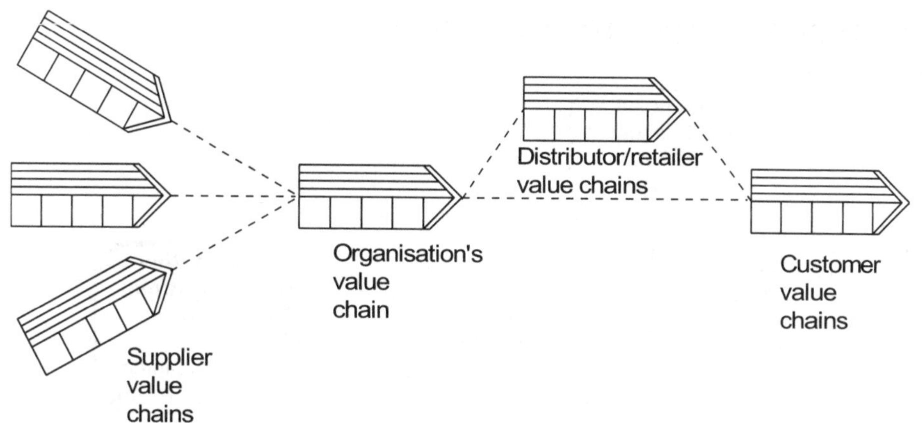

Figure 3.2: The value system
(Porter, 1996)

Using the value chain. A firm can secure competitive advantage in several ways.

- Invent new or better ways to do activities
- Combine activities in new or better ways
- Manage the linkages in its own value chain
- Manage the linkages in the value system

Activity 3 **(15 minutes)**

Sana Sounds is a small record company. Representatives from Sana Sounds scour music clubs for new bands to promote. Once a band has signed a contract with Sana Sounds it makes a recording. The recording process is subcontracted to one of a number of recording studio firms which Sana Sounds uses regularly. (At the moment Sana Sounds is not large enough to invest in its own equipment and studios.) Sana Sounds also subcontracts the production of records and CDs to a number of manufacturing companies. Sana Sounds then distributes the discs to selected stores, and engages in any promotional activities required.

What would you say were the activities in Sana Sounds' value chain?

4 OUTPUTS: THE PRODUCT PORTFOLIO

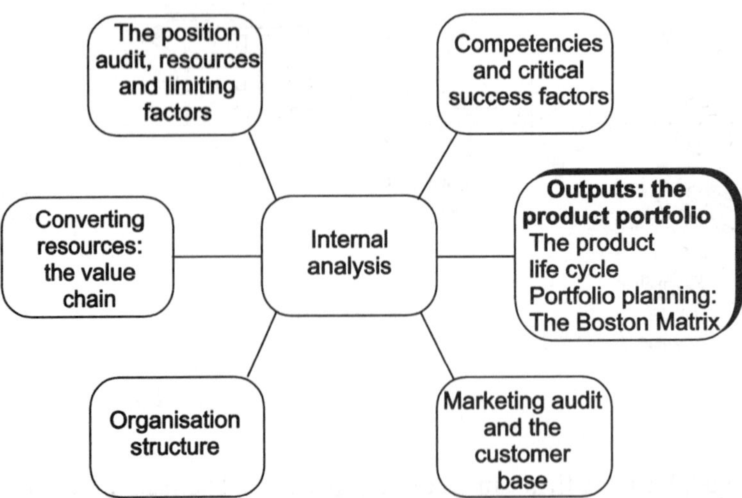

4.1 The product life cycle

Many firms make a number of different products or services. Each product or service has its own financial, marketing and risk characteristics. The combination of products or services influences the attractiveness and profitability of the firm.

The profitability and sales of a product can be expected to change over time. The **product life cycle** is an attempt to recognise distinct stages in a product's sales history. Marketing managers distinguish between different aspects of the product.

(a) **Product class:** this is a broad category of product, such as cars, washing machines, newspapers' also referred to as the **generic product**.

(b) **Product form:** within a product class there are different forms that the product can take, for example five-door hatchback cars or two-seater sports cars; twin tub or front loading automatic washing machines; national daily newspapers or weekly local papers etc.

(c) **Brand:** the particular type of the product form (for example Ford Escort, Vauxhall Astra; *Financial Times*, *Daily Mail*, *The Sun*).

The product life cycle applies in differing degrees to each of the three cases. A product-class (eg cars) may have a long maturity stage, and a particular make or brand might have an erratic life cycle (eg Rolls Royce) or not. Product forms however tend to conform to the classic life cycle pattern.

In reviewing outputs, planners should assess products in three ways.

(a) The **stage of its life cycle** that any product has reached.

(b) The **product's remaining life**, ie how much longer the product will contribute to profits.

(c) How **urgent is the need to innovate,** to develop new and improved products?

4.2 Portfolio planning: the Boston Matrix

Portfolio planning analyses the current position of an organisation's products in their markets, and the state of growth or decline in each of those markets.

Definition

Market share: One entity's sale of a product or service in a specified market expressed as a percentage of total sales by all entities offering that product or service.

The **Boston Consulting Group (BCG)** developed a matrix based on research that classifies a company's products in terms of potential **cash generation** and **cash expenditure** requirements.

		Market share	
		High	*Low*
Market growth	*High*	Stars	Question marks
	Low	Cash cows	Dogs

Figure 3.3: The Boston matrix (Boston Consulting Group)

(a) **Stars**. In the short-term, these require capital expenditure in excess of the cash they generate, in order to maintain their market position, but promise high returns in the future.

(b) In due course, stars will become **cash cows**. Cash cows need very little capital expenditure and generate high levels of cash income. Cash cows can be used to finance the stars.

(c) **Question marks**. Do the products justify considerable capital expenditure in the hope of increasing their market share, or should they be allowed to die quietly as they are squeezed out of the expanding market by rival products?

(d) **Dogs**. They may be ex-cash cows that have now fallen on hard times. Dogs should be allowed to die or should be killed off. Although they will show only a modest net cash outflow, or even a modest net cash inflow, they are cash traps which tie up funds and provide a poor return on investment.

Activity 4 **(20 minutes)**

Juicy Drinks Ltd provides fruit juices to supermarket chains, which sell them under their own label. The traditional squeezed orange juice is performing well and although margins are low, there are sufficient economies of scale to do well in this market. Juicy Drinks has advanced production and bottling equipment and long-term contracts with some major growers. Recently the company conducted market tests on freshly squeezed pomegranate juice. In the taste tests consumers loved it, but the production process proved problematic, particularly because of the numerous small seeds. However, the company hopes to eliminate the production problems and expand its share of the growing exotic juice market.

What sort of products, according to the Boston classification, are described here?

5 ORGANISATION STRUCTURE

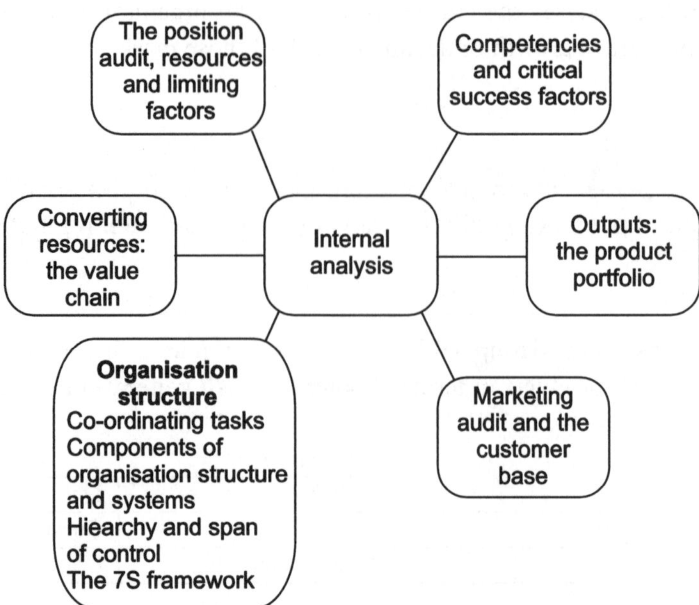

Organisation structure determines how work is allocated, directed and controlled, in order to achieve the goals of the organisation's strategy.

5.1 Co-ordinating tasks

Mintzberg (1997) suggests five methods of co-ordination.

(a) **Mutual adjustment.** People co-ordinate themselves.

(b) **Direct supervision.** One person is responsible for co-ordinating the work of others. This person issues instructions and monitors performance.

(c) **Standardisation of work processes.** The contents of work are 'specified or programmed' (eg standard procedures for carrying out an audit).

(d) **Standardisation of outputs**. Outputs in this instance can mean a set level of profits (or level of performance) but the work process itself is not designed or programmed.

(e) **Standardisation by skills and knowledge.** The kind of knowledge and training required to perform the work is specified. For example, doctors are trained in the necessary skills before being let loose on patients.

5.2 Components of organisation structure and systems

The **organisation structure** embodies mechanisms for co-ordinating work. *Mintzberg* (*The Structuring of Organisations,* 1997) believes that any organisation is based on the following principles.

- **Job specialisation** (the number of tasks in a given job, the division of labour)
- **Behaviour formalisation** (in other words, the standardisation of work processes)
- **Training** (to enforce work standardisation)

- **Indoctrination** of employees (in the organisation's culture)
- Unit **grouping** (eg organisation by function, geographical area, or product)
- Unit **size** (eg span of control)
- **Planning and control systems**
- **Liaison** and **communication** devices (networks, committees, matrix structures)

Mintzberg (1979) identifies five component parts, represented on what he calls an '**organigram**', as illustrated below.

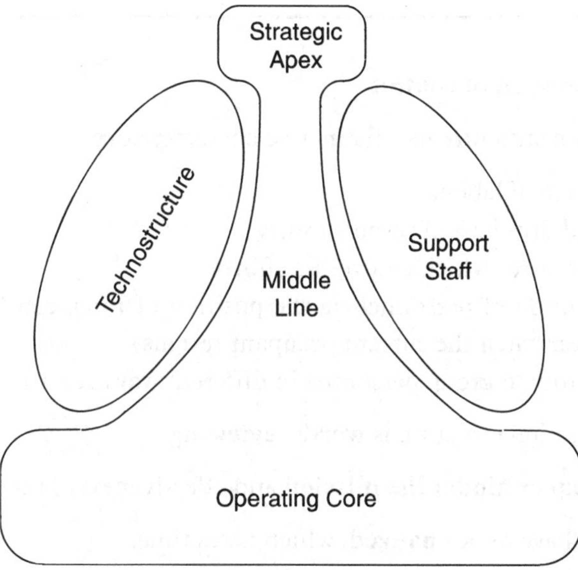

Figure 3.4: Mintzberg's organigram

Component	Comment
Operating core	People directly involved in production (ie in securing inputs and processing them into outputs and distributing those outputs), perhaps the **primary activities** of the value chain.
Strategic apex	Owner, board of directors. This component ensures that the organisation follows its mission and serves the needs of its owners. Its job is supervision, control, boundary management and strategy.
Middle line	People in this area administer the work done. The chain of formal authority runs from senior managers at the apex through middle managers to front line supervisors at the operating core. It converts the wishes of the strategic apex into the work of the operating core.

Component	Comment
Technostructure	Administrators and planners **standardise work**. Work-study analysts (eg engineers) standardise work processes by analysing and determining the most efficient method of doing a job. Planners (eg quality staff, accountants) standardise outputs. Personnel analysts standardise skills by arranging for training programmes.
Support staff	Ancillary services such as public relations, legal counsel, or the cafeteria do not plan or standardise production. They function independently of the operating core.

5.3 Hierarchy and span of control

A formal organisation structure has distinctive characteristics

- A division of labour
- Planned divisions of responsibility
- Power centres which control its efforts
- Substitution of personnel (ie the position of Financial Controller does not disappear when the current occupant resigns)
- The ability to group personnel in different ways according to work

The existing organisation structure is **worth reviewing**

(a) It can **help or hinder the mission** and effectiveness of the organisation.

(b) It might have to be **changed,** which takes time.

(c) It shapes the **deployment of value activities** and the management of the **linkages** between them.

(d) It **channels and filters information** from markets and personnel.

(e) It **is the arena for various political manoeuvrings** by management and other interest groups.

Definitions

The **scalar chain** (or chain of command) describes the organisation hierarchy, from the most junior to the most senior. A long scalar chain has many levels with many ranks between the most junior and the senior.

The **span of control** (unit size) refers to the number of subordinates working for a manager in the level immediately below the manager.

A **tall organisation** has a large number of management levels and small spans of control.

- These are held to be cumbersome and inflexible. They slow down communications and responsiveness to the market, and stifle initiative.
- They offer more secure **promotion paths**.

Flat organisations (few management levels) are becoming more popular, as they are supposed to be more flexible and responsive. They also save large costs in the form of management salaries.

- Information technology must be used in order to reduce the information processing function of middle management.
- Front line employees must accept much more responsibility. This is called **empowerment.**

Delayering is the removal of management layers. Many large organisations have shed large numbers of managerial staff in this way.

The **informal organisation** is those work and social relationships that exist outside the formal organisation structure. The informal organisation depends on individual personalities and, unlike the formal organisation structure, is affected when someone leaves.

- Certain individuals might have a **significant influence** outside of their formal authority (eg if one of the directors gets on particularly well with the MD).
- An inefficient formal organisation structure might force employees to rely on the informal organisation to get work done.

5.4 The Seven S framework

Mintzberg and Quinn (1999) have studied the organisation and conclude that successful **organisational change** (and therefore successful strategy implementation) arises from the following interdependent (and interacting) factors.

- Structure
- Strategy
- Systems
- Style
- Skill
- Staff
- Superordinate goals

All these elements must pull together if a strategy, however carefully planned, is to work. It can be presented on a diagram that demonstrates this interconnectedness.

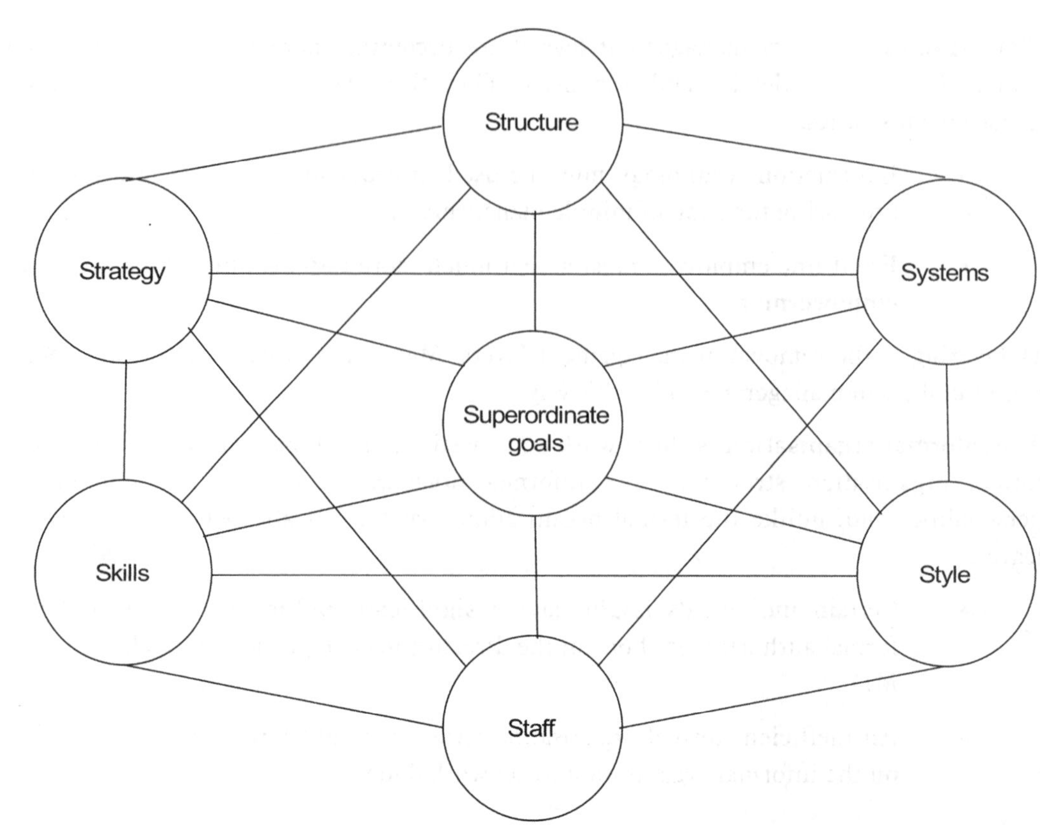

Figure 3.5: The 7S framework
(Source: Mintzberg & Quinn, The Strategy Process, 1999)

- **Structure** — How does the organisation actually work? Which parts are important in focussing on what the organisation does best?
- **Strategy** — We have already defined what this is. It is clearly an important influence on organisational design, as it is the organisation's plan as to how it is going to create value.
- **Systems** — Both formal and informal procedures. One of the most important is the management information system, which provides data (sales figures, customer data and so on) on which to base decisions.
- **Style** — This refers to patterns of management action and behaviour that guide the thinking of the organisation. It also incorporates elements of corporate culture.
- **Staff** — The development of managers to take the company forward is vital. Quinn calls this 'the socialisation process' of a company. Staff should be considered as a pool of resources to be developed and allocated. Staff on the 'front line' are especially vital within service sectors.
- **Skills** — We often characterise companies by what they do best. A particular skill of the Amazon Internet bookshop is speed of delivery, for example.
- **Superordinate goals** — These are the main values of the business. 'Superordinate' literally means 'of higher order', and such goals go beyond conventional objectives, and may indicate the overall future direction in which management is headed.

EXAMPLE

In 2002 a *'mega-merger'* took place between IT giants Hewlett Packard and Compaq. At the time, the merger led to much speculation about whether it would be a positive move. It took nearly five years for independent consultants IDC to declare that the merger had been a success. A 'massive integration effort' had to be completed before the new combined company could meet new profit and revenue levels in an increasingly competitive marketplace. The overall integration involved a range of elements to facilitate its success. Within the 7s framework these included:

Structure – a merged organisation with a re-organised management structure and fewer HP staff

Strategy – To remain relevant within the sectors they competed in and to commit to infrastructure software development (eg OpenView) and away from a resilience on IT commodities

Systems – New combined working systems and practices would need to be developed

Style – Cultural change to infuse Compaq's faced-paced style and increase HP's *'business velocity'*

Skill – a need for new skills bases with the development of the infrastructure software market

Staff – a critical issue within the merger as management changes took place and a reduction in HP workforce size

Superordinate goals – *'The merger accomplished what it set out to do in the first place, providing the critical mass and reach needed to ensure a long-term role in an industry undergoing a fundamental transition'* To remain competitive in a turbulent industry.

Adapted from Jaques. R (2006) Five Years on: HP Compaq Merger declared a success. Vnunet.com 08 Nov 2006

6 MARKETING AUDIT AND THE CUSTOMER BASE

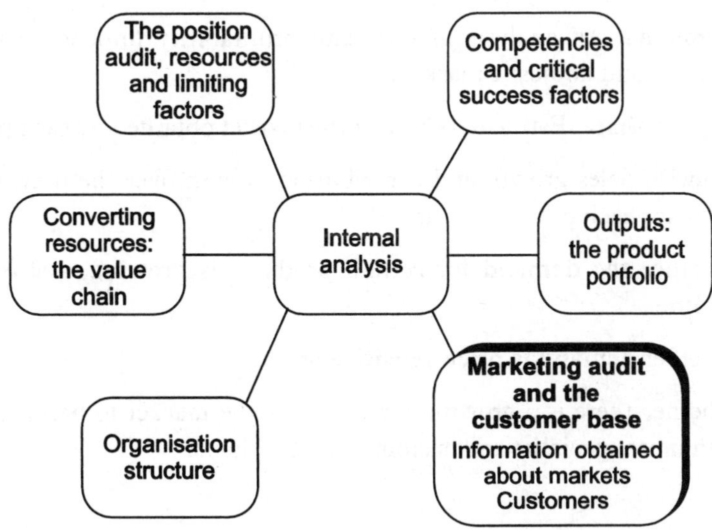

A **marketing audit** involves a review of an organisation's products and markets, the marketing environment, and its marketing system and operations. The profitability of each product and each market should be assessed, and the costs of different marketing activities established.

Definition

6.1 Information obtained about markets

(a) **Size of the customer base**. Does the organisation sell to a large number of small customers or a small number of big customers?

(b) **Size of individual orders.** The organisation might sell its products in many small orders, or it might have large individual orders. Delivery costs can be compared with order sizes.

(c) **Sales revenue and profitability.** The performance of individual products can be compared. Here is an example.

Product group	**Sales revenue**		**Contribution to profits**	
	£'000	% of total	£'000	% of total
B	7,500	35.7	2,500	55.6
E	2,000	9.5	1,200	26.7
C	4,500	21.4	450	10.0
A	5,000	23.8	250	5.6
D	2,000	9.5	100	2.2
	21,000	100.0%	4,500	100.0%

An imbalance between sales and profits over various product ranges can be potentially dangerous. In the figures above, product group A accounts for 23.8% of turnover but only 5.6% of total contribution, and product group D accounts for 9.5% of turnover but only 2.2% of total contribution.

(d) **Segments.** An analysis of sales and profitability into, for instance, export markets and domestic markets

(e) **Market share.** Estimated share of the market obtained by each product group

(f) **Growth.** Sales growth and contribution growth over the previous four years or so, for each product group

(g) Whether the **demand** for certain products is **growing, stable or likely to decline**

(h) Whether **demand is price sensitive** or not

(i) Whether there is a growing tendency for the market to become **fragmented,** with more specialist and custom-made products.

6.2 Customers

Many firms, especially in business-to-business markets, sell to a relatively small number of customers. **Key customer analysis** calls for seven main areas of investigation.

(a) **Key customer identity** (name, location, size, product market)

(b) **Customer history:** order size and frequency, reasons for purchase, key decision makers

(c) **Relationship of customer to product**

  (i) Are the products purchased to be resold? If not, why are they bought?
  (ii) Do the products form part of the customer's service/product?

(d) **Relationship of customer to potential market**

  (i) What is the size of the customer in relation to the total end-market?
  (ii) Is the customer likely to expand, or not? Diversify? Integrate?

(e) **Customer attitudes and behaviour**

  (i) What interpersonal factors affect sales by the firm and by competitors?
  (ii) Does the customer also buy competitors' products?
  (iii) To what extent may purchases be postponed?
  (iv) What emotional factors exist in buying decisions?

(f) **The financial performance of the customer**

How successful is the customer in his own markets?

(g) The profitability of selling to the customer

  (i) What profit/contribution is the organisation making on sales to the customer, after discounts and selling and delivery costs?

  (ii) What would be the financial consequences of losing the customer?

  (iii) Is the customer buying in order sizes that are unprofitable to supply?

  (iv) What is return on investment in plant used?

  (v) What is the level of inventory required specifically to supply these customers?

  (vi) Are there any other specific costs involved in supplying this customer, such as technical and test facilities, R & D facilities, special design staff?

  (vii) What is the ratio of net contribution per customer to total investment on both a historic and replacement cost basis?

Not all customers are as important as others. The checklist overleaf can help identify the most important.

Strategic importance evaluation guide		*High*	*Medium*	*Low*	*N/A*
1	Fit between customer's needs and our capabilities, at present and potentially.				
2	Ability to serve customer compared with our major competitors, at present and potentially.				
3	'Health' of customer's industry, current and forecast.				
4	'Health' of the customer, current and forecast.				
5	Customer's growth prospects, current and forecast.				
6	What can we learn from this customer?				
7	Can the customer help us attract others?				
8	Relative significance: how important is the customer compared with other customers?				
9	What is the profitability of serving the customer?				

Chapter roundup

- A position audit reviews the organisation's current position.
- Resource audits identify physical human and material resources and how they are deployed into a distinctive competence, something the company does uniquely well.
- The value chain describes those activities of the organisation which add value to purchased inputs. Primary activities are involved in the production of goods and services. Support activities provide necessary assistance. Linkages are the relationships between activities.
- Managing the value chain, which includes relationships with outside suppliers, can be a source of strategic advantage.
- The product life cycle concept holds that products have a life cycle, and that a product demonstrates different characteristics of profit and investment at each stage in its life cycle. It enables a firm to examine its portfolio of goods and services as a whole.
- The Boston classification classifies products in terms of their capacity for growth within the market and the market's capacity for growth as a whole. A firm should have a balanced portfolio of products.

Chapter roundup (cont'd)

- Organisation structure indicates how value activities are co-ordinated within the organisation. Organisations are characterised by formal division of labour, hierarchies of authority (scalar chains) and networks of authority and power.
- The Seven S framework outlines the internal interdependent factors that contribute towards successful strategy implementation.
- It is not only important to understand the customer base as a whole, but to be able to identify those that are the most important in terms of profitability.

Quick quiz

1 What is a limiting factor?

2 What is a competence?

3 What is the significance of the value chain?

4 Distinguish between product class, product form and brand.

5 List the stages of the product life cycle.

6 What are stars, cash cows, question marks, and dogs?

7 Describe *Mintzberg's* five component parts of the organisation.

8 What is meant by scalar chain?

9 What is the informal organisation?

10 What are the elements of the Seven S framework?

11 What information might be gained from a marketing audit?

12 What is key customer analysis?

Answers to quick quiz

1 A factor which may limit the activity of an entity, often being one where there is a shortage of supply.

2 That which the organisation does well, or better than its rivals.

3 It gives us a view of the firm and what it does, and the way in which it organises and performs activities. If the customer pays more than the cost of these activities, the firm is profitable. The company should always try to combine its activities in new or better ways.

4 Product class: a broad category; product form: a style within a category; brand: a particular type of a particular style.

5 Introduction, growth, maturity, decline.

6 Elements of the Boston matrix. See Section 4.2.

7 Strategic apex; middle line; operating core; technostructure and support staff.

NOTES

8 It is the chain of command describing the organisation hierarchy between junior and senior.

9 Those work and social relationships that exist outside the formal organisation structure.

10 Structure, strategy, systems, style, skills, staff, superordinate goals.

11 A marketing audit reviews an organisation's products and markets, the market environment and the marketing system and operations, to give information about such factors as customer orders, market share and advertising effectiveness.

12 Customer identity, history, relationship to product, relationship to potential market, attitudes and behaviour, financial performance and profitability of selling to customer.

Answers to activities

1 The answer to this activity depends on your own research.

2 Here are some ideas. Each of these options is a way of organising the activities of buying, cooking and serving food in a way that customers will value.

(a) It can become more efficient, by automating the production of food, as in a fast food chain.

(b) The chef can develop commercial relationships with growers, so he or she can obtain the best quality fresh produce.

(c) The chef can specialise in a particular type of cuisine (eg, Nepalese, Korean).

(d) The restaurant can be sumptuously decorated for those customers who value atmosphere and a sense of occasion, in addition to a restaurant's purely gastronomic pleasures.

(e) The restaurant can serve a particular type of customer (eg, celebrities).

3 Sana Sounds is involved in the record industry from start to finish. Although recording and CD manufacture are contracted out to external suppliers, this makes no difference to the fact that these activities are part of Sana Sounds' own value chain. Sana Sounds earns its money by managing the whole set of activities. If the company grows then perhaps it will acquire its own recording studios.

4 (a) Orange juice is a cash cow

(b) Pomegranate juice is a question mark, which the company wants to turn into a star.

Chapter 4 :
STRATEGIC POSITIONING I

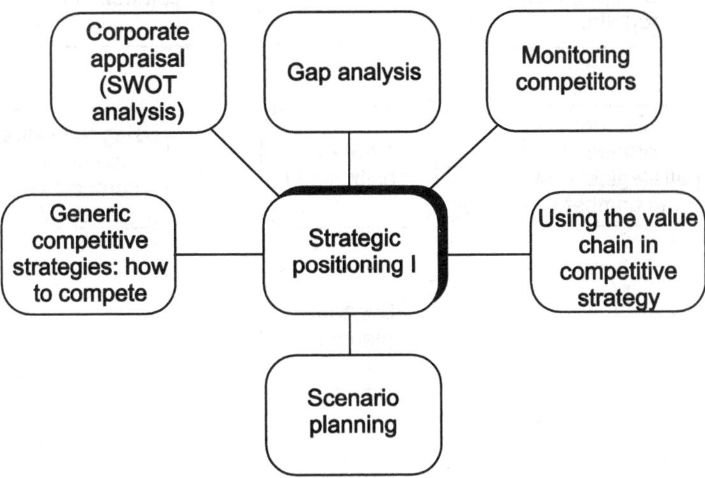

Introduction

Once the internal and external analyses are complete, the next task is to develop strategies. **SWOT analysis** is a way of identifying the extent to which an organisation has managed to obtain a fit with the environment: it identifies internal **strengths** and **weaknesses**, and external **opportunities** and **threats**. Strategies are developed to exploit strengths and opportunities, and to mitigate threats and weaknesses. **Gap analysis** is a technique of quantifying the extent to which new strategic projects are necessary. We can identify three basic strategic decisions.

How you compete: competitive strategy. Taking the **industry scenario** into account, it should be possible to identify the best way of competing. The value chain, which we encountered earlier, can be used here. **Where** you compete will be discussed in the next chapter.

Your objectives

In this chapter you will learn about the following.

(a) Approaches to strategy formulation

(b) SWOT analysis and gap analysis

(c) Competitor analysis and the choice of competitive strategy

(d) Using the value chain in competitive strategy

1 CORPORATE APPRAISAL (SWOT ANALYSIS)

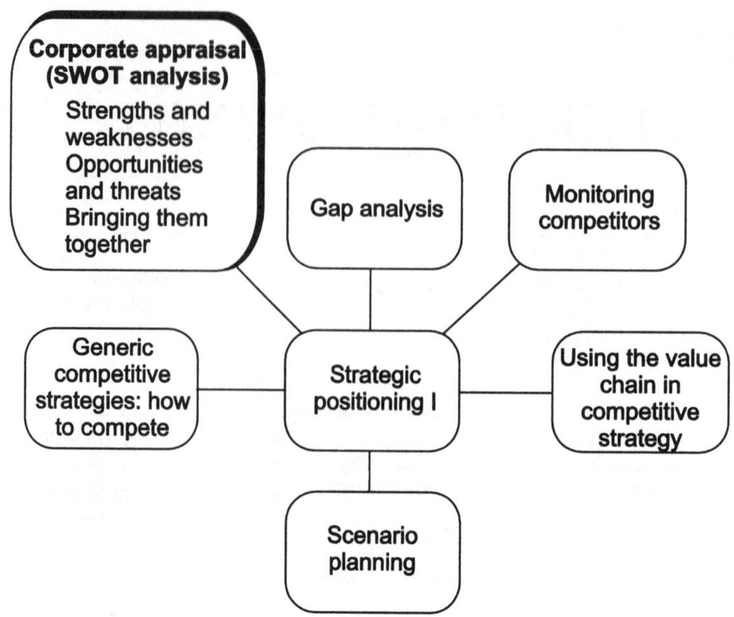

Definition

> **Corporate appraisal (SWOT)**: a critical assessment of the strengths and weaknesses, opportunities and threats in relation to the internal and environmental factors affecting the entity in order to establish its condition prior to the preparation of a long-term plan.

1.1 Strengths and weaknesses

A strengths and weaknesses analysis establishes strengths that should be exploited and weaknesses which should be improved. It therefore covers the results of the position audit, which we looked at in the previous chapter.

1.2 Opportunities and threats

- What opportunities exist in the business environment?
- What is their inherent profit-making potential?
- What is the organisation's ability to exploit the worthwhile opportunities?
- What threats might arise?
- How will competitors be affected?
- How will the company be affected?

The opportunities and threats might arise from PESTEL and competitive factors.

1.3 Bringing them together

EXAMPLE

STRENGTHS	WEAKNESSES
£10 million of capital available	Heavy reliance on a small number of customers
Production expertise and appropriate marketing skills	Limited product range, with no new products and expected market decline. Small marketing organisation.
THREATS	**OPPORTUNITIES**
A major competitor has already entered the new market	Government tax incentives for new investment. Growing demand in a new market, although customers so far relatively small in number.

This company is in imminent danger of losing its existing markets and must diversify its products and markets. The new market opportunity exists to be exploited, and since the number of customers is currently small, the relatively small size of the existing marketing force would not be an immediate hindrance.

A strategic plan could be developed to buy new equipment and use existing production and marketing to enter the new market, with a view to rapid expansion. Careful planning of manpower, equipment, facilities, research and development would be required and there would be an objective to meet the threat of competition so as to obtain a substantial share of a growing market. The cost of entry at this early stage of market development should not be unacceptably high.

Effective SWOT analysis does not simply require a categorisation of information, it also requires some **evaluation of the relative importance** of the various factors under consideration.

(a) These features are only of relevance if they are **perceived to exist by the consumers.** Listing corporate features that internal personnel regard as strengths/weaknesses is of little relevance if they are not perceived as such by the organisation's consumers.

(b) In the same vein, threats and opportunities are conditions presented by the external environment and they should be independent of the firm.

The SWOT can be used in guiding strategy formulation as shown in the diagram below.

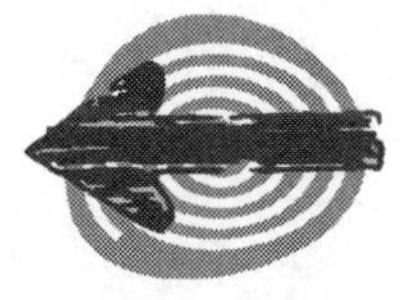

NOTES

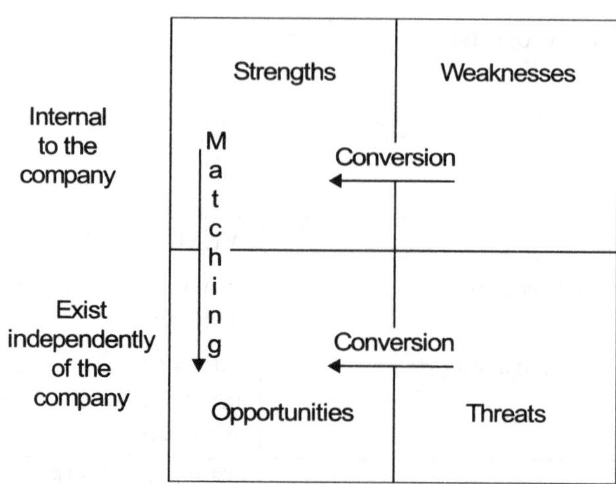

Figure 4.1: Using SWOT

This diagram demonstrates that strengths and opportunities should be matched, while threats and weaknesses should be converted into opportunities and strengths respectively wherever possible.

Match strengths with market opportunities

Strengths which do not match any available opportunity are of limited use while opportunities which do not have any matching strengths are of little immediate value.

Conversion

This requires the development of strategies which will convert weaknesses into strengths in order to take advantage of some particular opportunity, or converting threats into opportunities which can then be matched by existing strengths.

EXAMPLE

A rare success story occurred in Hamilton, south of Glasgow, Scotland, where a branch of Safeway, the UK supermarket chain, had opened in the early 1990s. Lightbody of Hamilton, a local baker with twenty local branches and four generations of experience, initially took Safeway on, sparking a price war which saw the price of a loaf of bread dive to 25p. Lightbody could not sustain these prices, or the loss of customers following the supermarket's opening. History is full of small shopkeepers losing out to the national companies, and it was almost inevitable that in 1995 Lightbody would give up baking bread.

This story does have an unusual twist. The MD used the proceeds from the sale of the bakeries to build a speciality cake factory to supply the very supermarkets that had originally put him out of business. The company launched with sales of 150,000 cakes a week to the supermarket giants, and hit revenues of £50m in 2006 (from £3.3m in 1997). By 2007, with a host of industry awards (such as The Customer Focus Award (The Bakery Industry Awards 2006)) the company had joined forces with Finsbury Food Group to continue to grow within the global market. Product ranges expanded significantly with a range of successful branded cakes such as Thornton's, Famous Grouse and a whole collection of licensed characters (including Disney) to supplement their large novelty cake range and retailer branded cereal and cake bars.

When compared to the situation in the early 1990s, the company is now in a far stronger position. The icing on top of the cake is that their original biggest threat, Safeway, has since been acquired by Morrisons. 'In the face of tough choices, Lightbody's strategic decision proved the turning point in the business'.

Sources: Blin (2001)
www bakeryawards.co.uk

What questions might have been asked by Lightbody following an environmental analysis of the competition represented by Safeway, when trying to decide what strategy to pursue?

Activity 1 **(30 minutes)**

Hall Faull Downes Ltd has been in business for 25 years, during which time profits have risen by an average of 3% per annum, although there have been peaks and troughs in profitability due to the ups and downs of trade in the customers' industry. The increase in profits until five years ago was the result of increasing sales in a buoyant market, but more recently, the total market has become somewhat smaller and Hall Faull Downes has only increased sales and profits as a result of improving its market share.

The company produces components for manufacturers in the engineering industry.

In recent years, the company has developed many new products and currently has 40 items in its range compared to 24 only five years ago. Over the same five-year period, the number of customers has fallen from twenty to nine, two of whom together account for 60% of the company's sales.

Give your appraisal of the company's future, and suggest what it is probably doing wrong.

2 GAP ANALYSIS

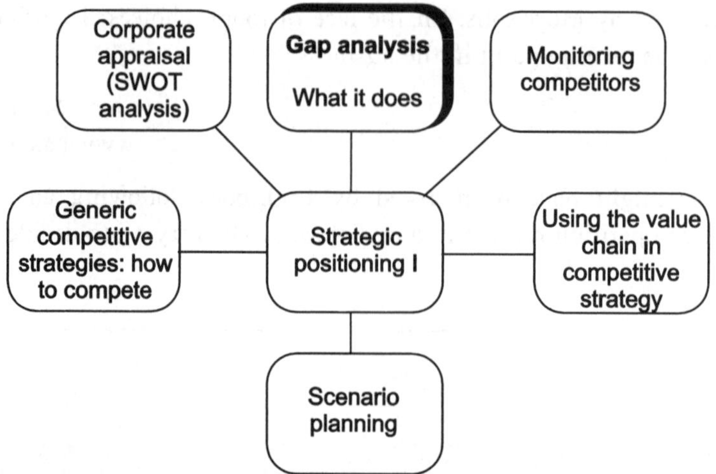

Definitions

- **Forecasting** is the identification of relevant factors and quantification of their effect on an entity as a basis for planning.
- **Gap analysis** is the comparison of an entity's ultimate objective with the sum of projections and already planned projects.

2.1 What it does

Gap analysis compares two things.

(a) The organisation's **targets** for achievement over the planning period

(b) What the organisation would be **expected to achieve** if it carried on in the current way with the same products and selling to the same markets, with no major changes to operations. This is called an $\mathbf{F_0}$ **forecast.**

This difference is the **gap**. New strategies will have to be developed which will close this gap, so that the organisation can expect to achieve its targets over the planning period.

Errors in the forecast

Forecasts can never be completely accurate – they might be misleading in cases of environmental turbulence. But in stable environments they are valid, if adjusted for error. Errors can be accounted for in two ways.

(a) Estimating **likely variations**: for example, 'in 2004 the forecast profit is £5 million with possible variations of plus or minus £2 million'.

(b) Providing a **probability distribution** for profits: for example, 'in 2004 there is a 20% chance that profits will exceed £7 million, a 50% chance that they will exceed £5 million and an 80% chance that they will exceed £2 million. Minimum profits in 2004 will be £2 million'.

The gap could be filled by new **product-market growth strategies**, as demonstrated in the following diagram.

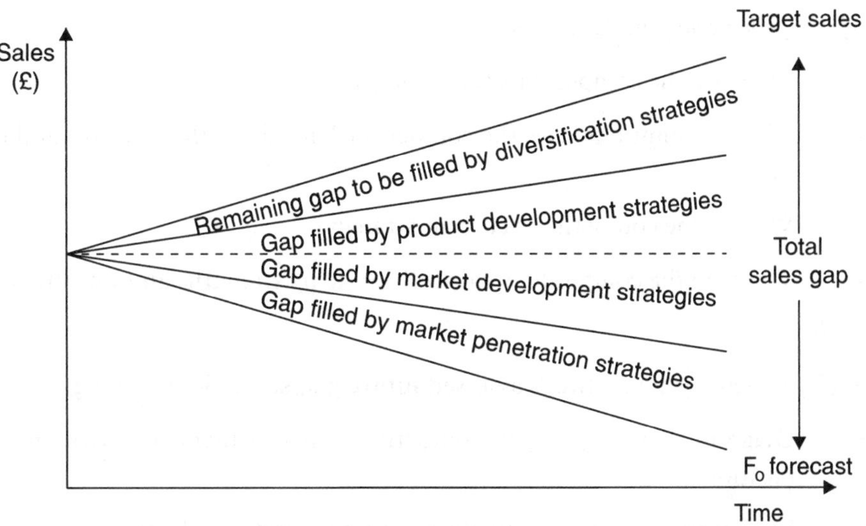

Figure 4.2: Strategies for closing the gap

Activity 2 **(15 minutes)**

Gap analysis can be used to model a variety of factors in addition to sales and profit. How do you think you could use gap analysis for manpower?

3 MONITORING COMPETITORS

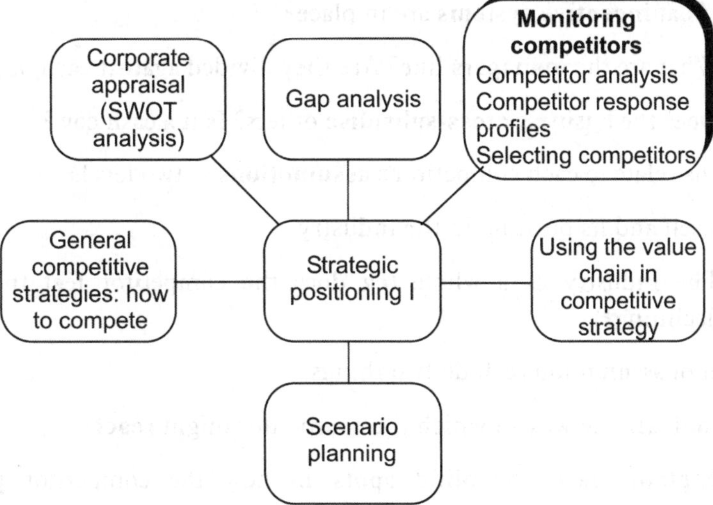

3.1 Competitor analysis

The purpose of analysing competitors is to try and assess what they will do. This will enable the organisation to respond accordingly. Competitive advantage is about **relative** competitive position.

NOTES

Aspects of competitor analysis: key questions

- What are the competitor's future goals?
- What assumptions does the competitor hold about the industry and its place in it?
- What is the competitor's current strategy?
- What are the competitor's capabilities (ie its strengths and weaknesses)?

Future goals

The firm, by reviewing competitor's assessed **future goals**, can do two things.

- Diagnose how happy the competitor's management are with the current position.
- Predict the competitor's likely response to strategic changes.

Useful information about the competitor's goals

- What are the business's **stated financial goals**?
- What **trade-offs** are made between long-term and short-term objectives?
- What is the competitor's **attitude to risk**?
- Do **managerial beliefs** (eg that the firm should be a market leader) affect its goals?
- **Organisation structure**: what is the relative status of each department?
- What **incentive systems** are in place?
- What are the **managers** like? Are they divided against each other?
- Does the business **cross-subsidise** others? Is it a cash cow?

Other questions relate to each competitor's **assumptions** at two levels.

- Itself and its position in the industry
- The industry as a whole (eg does the competitor feel the industry is declining?)

An assessment of assumptions can do two things.

- **Indicate the way** in which the competitor might **react**
- **Explain biases or blind spots** in how the competitor perceives the environment

Useful information about competitor assumptions

- What does a competitor **believe** to be its relative position (in terms of cost, product quality etc) in the industry?
- Is there a strong '**emotional' bond** with particular products and markets?
- Do **cultural or regional differences** influence the way managers think?
- What does the competitor believe about the **future demand** for the industry?

- Does the competitor accept the industry's '**conventional wisdom**'?
- **Career analysis** of key managers. An accountant in charge is likely to have different priorities from a marketer.

Current strategy

All aspects of the competitor's current strategy should be analysed.

- Products
- Distribution
- Marketing and selling
- Operations
- Research and engineering
- Overall costs
- Financial strengths
- Organisation
- General managerial skills
- Managerial ability

Capabilities

There are two main aspects of the competitor's capabilities.

- Core or distinctive competences
- Ability to expand in a particular market
    - Is the competitor hampered by a lack of production capacity?
    - Does it need to raise capital externally?
    - Is it capable of adapting to change?
    - Can it survive a prolonged battle?

3.2 Competitor response profiles

All these are combined in a **competitor response profile**. This should indicate two things.

(a) The **competitor's vulnerability,** for example, to environmental forces, competitors' actions or downturn in sales.

(b) **The right battleground on which to fight**. For example, a firm may invade a competitor's position in a weak market, or in a low-priority product range. Japanese companies initially competed in the small car market, before moving to promote luxury models like the Lexus.

A **competitor intelligence system** needs to be set up.

(a) Contents

(i) Financial statements
(ii) Information from common customers and suppliers
(iii) Inspection of a competitor's products
(iv) Information from former employees
(v) Job advertisements

(b) Processing

The data needs to be compiled, catalogued, for easy access, analysed (eg summarised, ranked by reliability, extrapolating data from financial reports) and communicated to the strategist.

FOR DISCUSSION

What might these sources tell an organisation about a competitor's plans?

3.3 Selecting competitors

Selecting a competitor can be a strategic decision.

(a) Attack 'bad' competitors (who are long-term threats). A bad competitor is intensely committed to the market, faces high exit barriers, has no other business and is highly focused.

(b) Maintain position relative to 'good' competitors (who do not represent a long-term threat). Good competitors may not be as committed to the market, may be quite happy for matters to tick over, or do not depend on the market for survival.

Strategic benefits of competitors

(a) They increase the possible sources of competitive advantage (eg by enhancing the ability to differentiate by serving unattractive segments)

(b) They improve the industry structure (eg by increasing demand)

(c) They aid market development (eg they share costs, help standardise technologies)

(d) They deter entry by newcomers

4 GENERIC COMPETITIVE STRATEGIES: HOW TO COMPETE

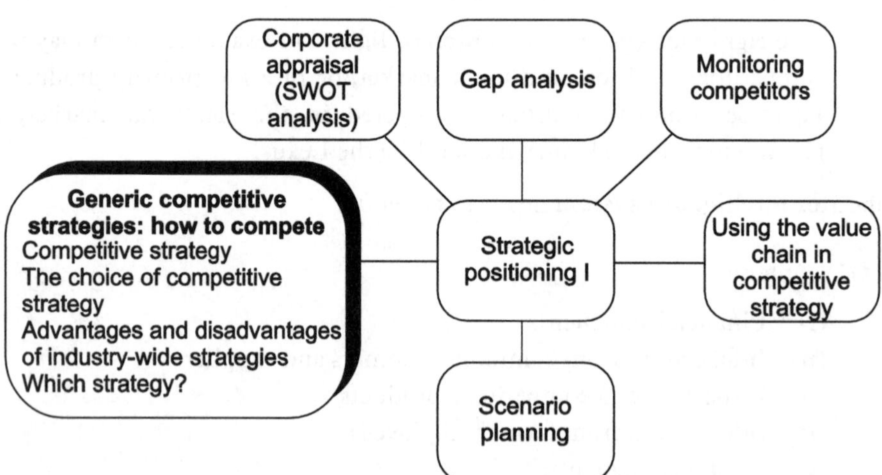

4.1 Competitive strategy

Competitive advantage is anything which gives one organisation an edge over its rivals. *Porter* (1996) argues that a firm should adopt a competitive strategy which is intended to achieve some form of competitive advantage for the firm.

Definition

> **Competitive strategy** means 'taking offensive or defensive actions to create a dependable position in an industry, to cope with ... competitive forces and thereby yield a superior return on investment for the firm. Firms have discovered many different approaches to this end, and the best strategy for a given firm is ultimately a unique construction reflecting its particular circumstances.' (*Porter, 1996*)

4.2 The choice of competitive strategy

Porter believes there are three **generic strategies** for competitive advantage.

Definitions

> (a) **Cost leadership** means being the lowest cost producer in the industry as a whole.
>
> (b) **Differentiation** is the exploitation of a product or service which the industry as a whole believes to be unique.
>
> (c) **Focus** involves a restriction of activities to only part of the market (a segment) through:
>
> (i) Providing goods and/or services at lower cost to that segment (cost-focus);
>
> (ii) Providing a differentiated product or service to that segment (differentiation-focus)

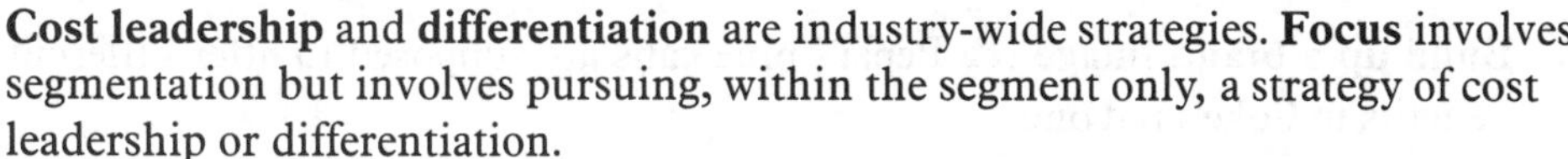

Cost leadership and **differentiation** are industry-wide strategies. **Focus** involves segmentation but involves pursuing, within the segment only, a strategy of cost leadership or differentiation.

Cost leadership

A cost leadership strategy seeks to achieve the position of lowest-cost producer in the **industry as a whole**. By producing at the lowest cost, the manufacturer can compete on price with every other producer in the industry, and earn the higher unit profits, if the manufacturer so chooses.

How to achieve overall cost leadership

(a) Set up production facilities to obtain **economies of scale**

(b) Use the **latest technology** to reduce costs and/or enhance productivity (or use cheap labour if available)

(c) In high technology industries, and in industries depending on labour skills for product design and production methods, exploit the **learning curve effect**. By producing more items than any other competitor, a firm can benefit more from the learning curve, and achieve lower average costs.

(d) Concentrate on **improving productivity**

(e) **Minimise overhead costs**

(f) **Get favourable access to sources of supply**

(g) **Relocate to cheaper areas**

EXAMPLE

Large out-of-town stores specialising in one particular category of product are able to secure cost leadership by economies of scale over other retailers. Such shops have been called category killers, an example of which is PC World.

Differentiation

A differentiation strategy assumes that competitive advantage can be gained through **particular characteristics** of a firm's products. Products may be divided into three categories.

(a) **Breakthrough products** offer a radical performance advantage over competition, perhaps at a drastically lower price (eg float glass, developed by Pilkington).

(b) **Improved products** are not radically different from their competition but are obviously superior in terms of better performance at a competitive price (eg microchips).

(c) **Competitive products** derive their appeal from a particular compromise of cost and performance. For example, cars are not all sold at rock-bottom prices, nor do they all provide immaculate comfort and performance. They compete with each other by trying to offer a more attractive compromise than rival models.

How to differentiate

(a) **Build up a brand image** (eg Pepsi's blue cans are supposed to offer different benefits to Coke's red ones).

(b) **Give the product special features** to make it stand out.

(c) **Exploit other activities of the value chain.**

4.3 Advantages and disadvantages of industry-wide strategies

Advantages	Cost leadership	Differentiation
New entrants	Economies of scale raise entry barriers	Brand loyalty and perceived uniqueness are entry barriers
Substitutes	Firm is not so vulnerable as its less cost-effective competitors to the threat of substitutes	Customer loyalty is a weapon against substitutes
Customers	Customers cannot drive down prices further than the next most efficient competitor	Customers have no comparable alternative

Suppliers	Flexibility to deal with cost increases	Higher margins can offset vulnerability to supplier price rises
Industry rivalry	Firm remains profitable when rivals go under through excessive price competition	Brand loyalty should lower price sensitivity

Disadvantages	**Cost leadership**	**Differentiation**
	Technological change will require capital investment, or make production cheaper for competitors	Sooner or later, customers become price sensitive
	Competitors can learn via imitation	Customers may no longer need the differentiating factor
	Cost concerns ignore product design or marketing issues	
	Increase in input costs can reduce price advantages	Imitation narrows differentiation

Focus (or niche) strategy

In a **focus strategy**, a firm concentrates its attention on one or more particular segments or niches of the market, and does not try to serve the entire market with a single product.

EXAMPLE: NICHE MARKETS

Consultants Booz Allen Hamilton have warned that it is no longer sufficient to segment markets but rather to invest in mature markets more targeted to micro-differentiated products and services. They refer to niche marketing but unlike previous definitions they mean narrow, not small. Niche today means something more than a small exclusive group. 'Niching' looks for differences within a similar group, then finds opportunities for customisation to appeal to the interests of each niche.

Technology has been an enabling factor particularly among some of the companies that Booz Allen Hamilton identify as benefiting from niching namely; Crocs, Red Bull, Hewlett-Packard and Hallmark.

The business journal *The Economist* argues that the definition of a flourishing economy today is one rich with niches.

Adapted from Lindsay, M. (2007) 'Today's niche marketing is about narrow, not small'. Advertising Age 6.4.07, Vol 78, Issue 23, pp.30 – 32

There are different types of focus strategy.

(a) A **cost-focus strategy:** aim to be a cost leader for a particular segment. This type of strategy is often found in the printing, clothes manufacture and car repair industries.

(b) A **differentiation-focus strategy:** pursue differentiation for a chosen segment. Luxury goods are the prime example of such a strategy.

Advantages of a focus strategy

(a) A niche is more secure and a firm can insulate itself from competition
(b) The firm does not spread itself too thinly

Drawbacks of a focus strategy

(a) The firm sacrifices economies of scale which would be gained by serving a wider market.

(b) Competitors can move into the segment, with increased resources (eg the Japanese moved into the US luxury car market, to compete with Mercedes and BMW).

(c) The segment's needs may eventually become less distinct from the main market.

4.4 Which strategy?

Although there is a risk with any of the generic strategies, Porter (1996) argues that a firm must pursue one of them. A **stuck-in-the-middle** strategy is almost certain to make only low profits. **Focus** probably has fewer difficulties, as it ties in very neatly with market segmentation. In practice most companies pursue this strategy to some extent, by designing products/services to meet the needs of particular target markets.

Activity 3 **(15 minutes)**

The MD of Hermes Telecomm plc is reviewing corporate strategy. Hermes has invested a great deal of money in establishing a network which competes with that of Telecom UK, a recently privatised utility. Initially, Hermes concentrated its efforts on business customers in South East England, especially the City of London, where it offered a lower cost service to that supplied by Telecom UK. Recently, Hermes has approached the residential market (ie domestic telephone users) offering a lower cost service on long-distance calls. Technological developments have resulted in the possibility of a cheap mobile telecommunication network, using microwave radio links. The franchise for this service has been awarded to Gerbil phone, which is installing transmitters in town centres and stations.

Required

What issues of competitive strategy have been raised in the above scenario, particularly in relation to Hermes Telecommunications plc?

5 USING THE VALUE CHAIN IN COMPETITIVE STRATEGY

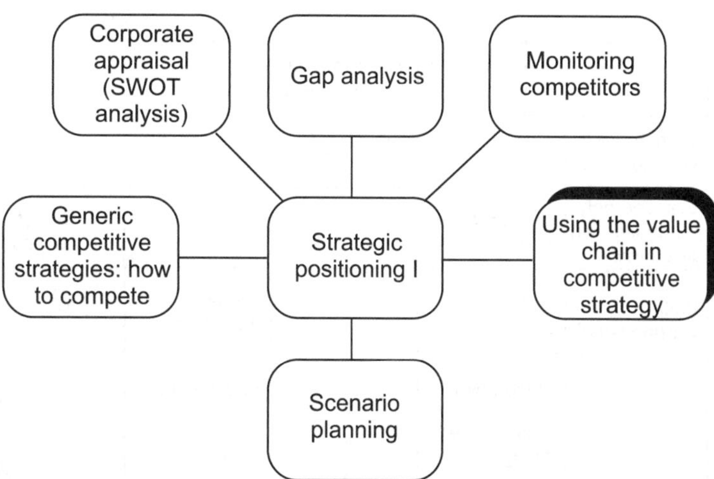

The value chain can be used to design a competitive strategy, by deploying the various activities strategically. The examples below are based on two supermarket chains, one concentrating on low prices, the other differentiated on quality and service. See if you can tell which is which.

(a)

Firm infrastructure	Central control of operations and credit control				
Human resource management	Recruitment of mature staff	Client care training	Flexible staff to help with packing		
Technology development		Recipe research	Electronic point of sale	Consumer research & tests	Itemised bills
Procurement	Own label products	Prime retail positions		Adverts in quality magazines & poster sites	
	Dedicated refrigerated transport	In store food halls Modern store design Open front refrigerators Tight control of sell-by dates	Collect by car service	No price discounts on food past sell-by dates	No quibble refunds
	INBOUND LOGISTICS	OPERATIONS	OUTBOUND LOGISTICS	MARKETING & SALES	SERVICE

Figure 4.3 (a): Quality foods value chain

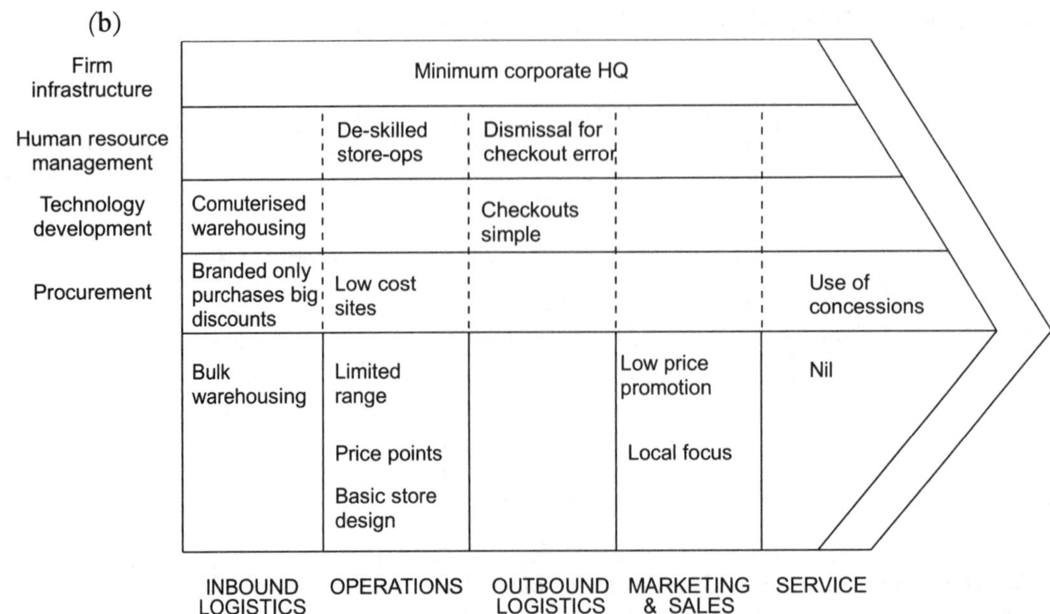

Figure 4.3 (b): Discount supermarket value chain

The two supermarkets represented are based on the following.

(a) The value chain in 4.3(a) is based on Marks and Spencer foods, which seeks to differentiate on quality and service. Hence the no quibble refunds, the use of prime retail sites, and customer care training.

(b) The value chain in 4.3(b) is similar to that of Lidl, a 'discount' supermarket chain which sells on price, pursuing a cost leadership, or perhaps more accurately, a cost-focus strategy. This can be seen in the limited product range and its low-cost sites.

6 SCENARIO PLANNING

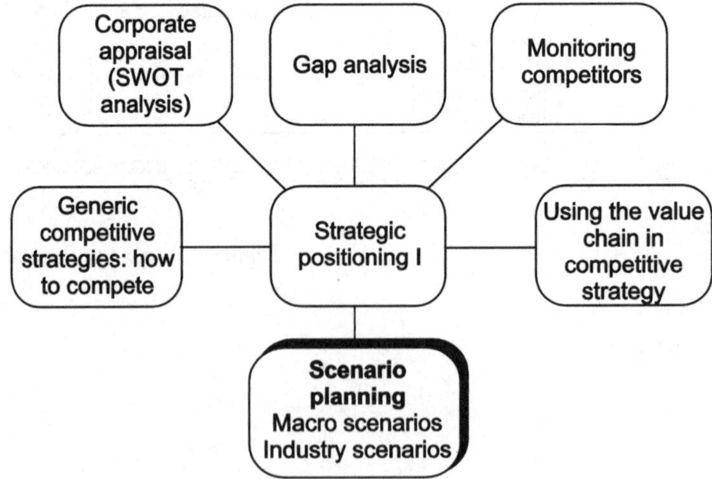

Because the environment is so complex, it is easy to become overwhelmed by the many factors.

Firms therefore try to model the future and the technique is **scenario planning**.

Definition

> A **scenario** is 'an internally consistent view of what the future might turn out to be'.

6.1 Macro scenarios

Macro scenarios use macro-economic or political factors, creating alternative views of the future environment (eg global economic growth, political changes, interest rates). Macro scenarios developed because the activities of oil companies (which are global and at one time were heavily influenced by political factors) needed techniques to deal with uncertainties.

Steps in scenario planning

Step 1 **Decide on the drivers for change**

- Environmental analysis helps determine key factors
- At least a ten year time horizon is needed, to avoid simply extrapolating from the present
- Identify and select the important issues

Step 2 **Bring drivers together into a viable framework**

- This relies almost on an ability to make patterns out of 'soft' data, so is the hardest
- Items identified can be brought together as mini-scenarios

Step 3 **Produce seven to nine mini-scenarios**

Step 4 **Group mini-scenarios into two or three larger scenarios containing all topics**

- This generates most debate and is likely to highlight fundamental issues
- The scenarios should be complementary and equally likely

Step 5 **Write the scenarios**

- The scenarios should be written-up in the form most suitable for managers
- Most scenarios are qualitative in nature

Step 6 **Identify issues arising**

- Determine the most critical outcomes
- Role play can be used to test what the scenarios mean to key staff involved

6.2 Industry scenarios

Porter believes that the most appropriate use for scenario analysis is if it is restricted to an industry. An **industry scenario** is an internally consistent view of

an **industry's** future structure. Different competitive strategies may be appropriate to different scenarios.

Using scenarios to formulate competitive strategy

(a) A strategy built in response to only **one scenario is risky**, whereas one supposed to cope with them **all might be expensive**.

(b) Choosing scenarios as a basis for decisions about competitive strategy.

Approach	Comment
Assume the most probable	This choice puts too much faith in the scenario process and guesswork. A less probable scenario may be one whose **failure** to occur would have the **worst** consequences for the firm.
Hope for the best	A firm designs a strategy based on the scenario most attractive to the firm: wishful thinking.
Hedge	The firm chooses the strategy that produces **satisfactory** results under **all** scenarios. **Hedging, however, is not optimal**. The **low risk** is paid for by a **low reward**.
Flexibility	A firm taking this approach plays a 'wait and see' game. It is safer, but sacrifices first-mover advantages.
Influence	A firm will try and influence the future, for example by influencing demand for related products in order that its favoured scenario will be realised in events as they unfold.

Chapter roundup

- The SWOT analysis combines the results of the environmental analysis and the internal appraisal into one framework for assessing the firm's current and future strategic fit, or lack of it, with the environment. It is an analysis of the organisation's strengths and weaknesses, and the opportunities and threats offered by the environment.
- Gap analysis quantifies what a firm must do to reach its objectives. Any gap between the firm's objectives and the forecast results of continuing with other activities must be met somehow.
- The purpose of analysing competitors is to try and assess what they will do
  - Future goals
  - Assumptions
  - Strategy
  - Capabilities
- Competitive strategy involves a choice between being the lowest cost producer (cost leadership), making the product different from competitors' products in some way (differentiation) or specialising on a segment of the market (focus, by addressing that segment by a strategy of cost leadership or differentiation). *Porter* believes that a firm must choose one of these or be stuck-in-the-middle.
- The value chain can be used as a tool to devise competitive strategies.
- Industry scenarios can be used to analyse the industry environment.

- Successful scenario building requires that the likely responses of competitors can be assessed.

Quick quiz

1 Define corporate appraisal.

2 How can it be used to guide strategy formulation?

3 What is gap analysis?

4 Why carry out an analysis of competitors?

5 What information might be contained in a competitor intelligence system?

6 List three generic strategies for competitive advantage.

7 What is required for a successful cost leadership strategy?

8 How do you differentiate?

9 What are the drawbacks of a focus strategy?

Answers to quick quiz

1 A corporate appraisal is a critical assessment of the strengths and weaknesses, opportunities and threats facing an organisation in both its internal capabilities and environmental factors.

2 It can be used to match strengths with available market opportunities, and to convert weaknesses into strengths or threats into opportunities.

3 Gap analysis compares an organisation's ultimate objective with the sum of the forecast for current activities and planned projects.

4 To try and assess what they will do, to enable the organisation to respond accordingly.

5 Financial statements
Information from common customers and suppliers
Inspection of a competitor's products
Information from former employees
Job advertisements

6 Cost leadership; differentiation; focus

7 Economics of scale, latest technology, exploit the learning curve effect, improve productivity, minimise overheads, access to supplies, relocation.

8 Build up a brand image
Give the product special features
Exploit other activities in the value chain

9 Sacrificing economies of scale
Competitors can move in
Segment itself may become less distinct

Answers to activities

1 A general interpretation of the facts as given might be sketched as follows.

(a) **Objectives**: the company has no declared objectives. Profits have risen by 3% per annum in the past, which has failed to keep pace with inflation but may have been a satisfactory rate of increase in the current conditions of the industry. Even so, stronger growth is indicated in the future.

(b)

Strengths	**Weaknesses**
Many new products developed Marketing success in increasing market share	Products may be reaching the end of their life and entering decline New product life cycles may be shorter Reduction in customers Excessive reliance on a few customers Doubtful whether profit record is satisfactory
Threats	**Opportunities**
Possible decline in the end-product Smaller end-product market will restrict future sales prospects for Hall Faull Downes	None identified

(c) **Strengths**: the growth in company sales in the last five years has been as a result of increasing the market share in a declining market. This success may be the result of the following.

(i) Research and development spending
(ii) Good product development programmes
(iii) Extending the product range to suit changing customer needs
(iv) Marketing skills
(v) Long-term supply contracts with customers
(vi) Cheap pricing policy
(vii) Product quality and reliable service

(d) **Weaknesses**:

(i) The products may be custom-made for customers so that they provide little or no opportunity for market development.

(ii) Products might have a shorter life cycle than in the past, in view of the declining total market demand.

(iii) Excessive reliance on two major customers leaves the company exposed to the dangers of losing their custom.

(e) **Threats**: there may be a decline in the end-market for the customers' product so that the customer demands for the company's own products will also fall.

(f) **Opportunities**: no opportunities have been identified, but in view of the situation as described, new strategies for the longer term would appear to be essential.

(g) **Conclusions**: the company does not appear to be planning beyond the short-term, or is reacting to the business environment in a piecemeal fashion. A strategic planning programme should be introduced.

(h) **Recommendations**: the company must look for new opportunities in the longer-term.

   (i) In the short-term, current strengths must be exploited to continue to increase market share in existing markets and product development programmes should also continue.

   (ii) In the longer-term, the company must diversify into new markets or into new products and new markets. Diversification opportunities should be sought with a view to exploiting any competitive advantage or synergy that might be achievable.

   (iii) The company should use its strengths (whether in R & D, production skills or marketing expertise) in exploiting any identifiable opportunities.

   (iv) Objectives need to be quantified in order to assess the extent to which new long-term strategies are required.

2 (a) The forecast would start with current manpower levels, and would be projected into the future assuming natural wastage, no training and no new appointments.

(b) The organisation would have to assess its needs in terms of manpower numbers and skills.

(c) Strategies to fill the gap would include recruitment and training programmes.

3 (a) Arguably, Hermes initially pursued a cost-focus strategy, by targeting the business segment.

(b) It seems to be moving into a cost leadership strategy over the whole market although its competitive offer, in terms of lower costs for local calls, is incomplete.

(c) The barriers to entry to the market have been lowered by the new technology. Gerbil phone might pick up a significant amount of business.

NOTES

Chapter 5 :
STRATEGIC POSITIONING II

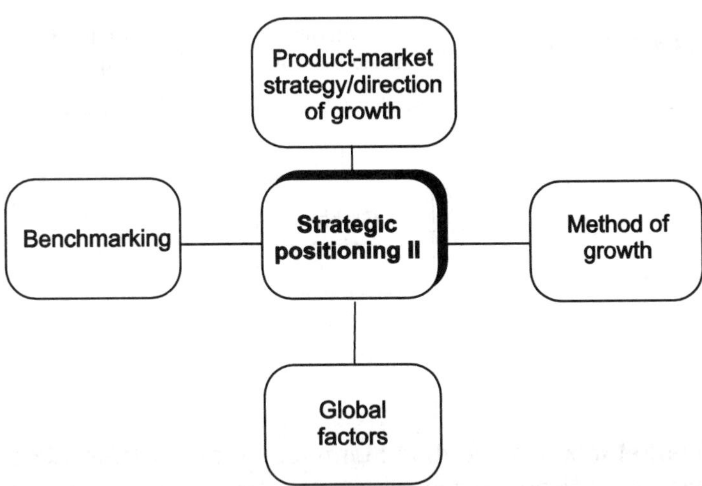

Introduction

This brief chapter continues with the theme of strategic positioning begun in Chapter 4. It starts with a consideration of **where you compete** – this decision relates to the products sold and the markets they are sold in: *Ansoff's* model (1987).

The decision as to the **method of growth** relates to whether a firm grows by its own efforts (organic growth) or acquires other businesses (acquisition). This is covered in more detail in Chapter 9 when we consider strategy selection.

The chapter continues with a consideration of the **global factors** impacting on business strategy and global business decisions. *Porter's* (1998) theory of **competitive advantage of nations** is relevant here.

Finally, this chapter looks at **benchmarking,** which is the process by which a firm compares itself with others to see where it might improve its processes to improve in turn its competitive position.

Your objectives

In this chapter you will learn about the following.

(a) A brief introduction to the *Ansoff* matrix of product-market strategies

(b) Method of growth

(c) The global factors which influence strategy formulation

(d) The uses and advantages of benchmarking

1 PRODUCT-MARKET STRATEGY: DIRECTION OF GROWTH

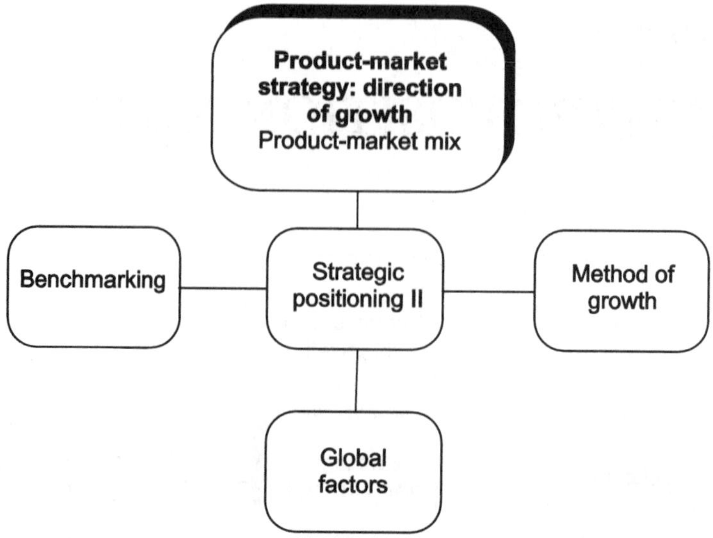

Definition

Product-market mix is a shorthand term for the products/services a firm sells (or a service which a public sector organisation provides) and the markets it sells them to.

1.1 Product-market mix

Ansoff (1987) drew up a **growth vector matrix**, describing a combination of a firm's activities in current and new markets, with **existing** and **new** products.

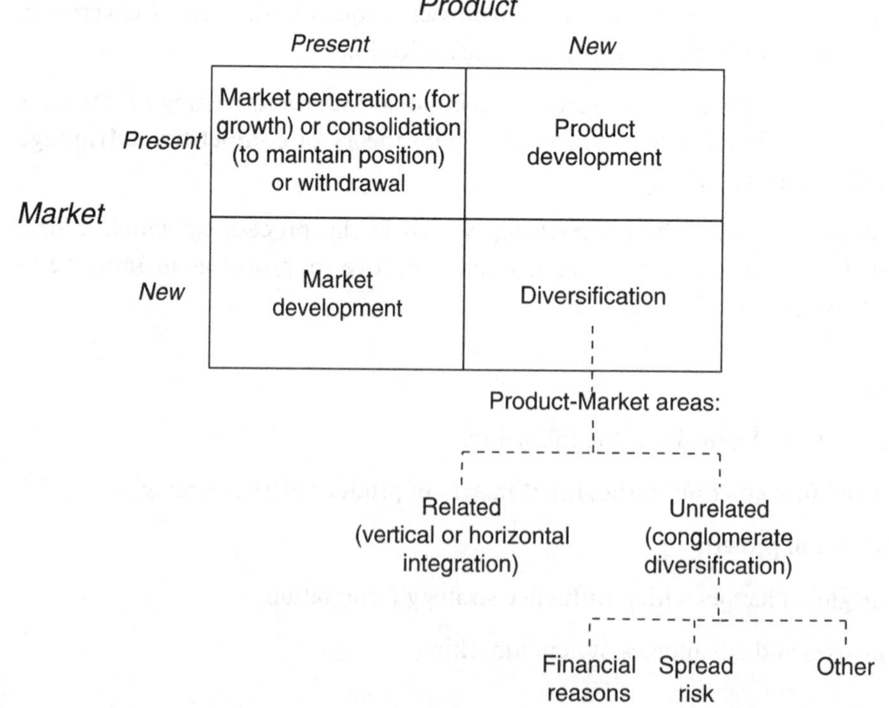

Figure 5.1: Ansoff's matrix

Current products and current markets: market penetration

The firm has four objectives.

(a) **Maintain or to increase its share** of current markets with current products, eg through competitive pricing, advertising, sales promotion

(b) **Secure dominance** of growth markets

(c) **Restructure a mature market** by driving out competitors

(d) **Increase usage by existing customers** (eg airmiles, loyalty cards)

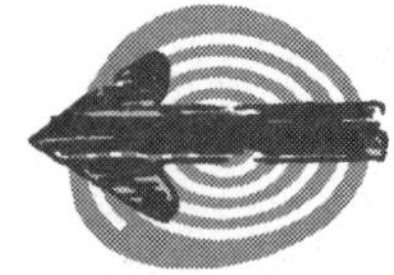

We elaborate on this in Chapter 9 of the Course Book when we consider strategy selection.

2 METHOD OF GROWTH

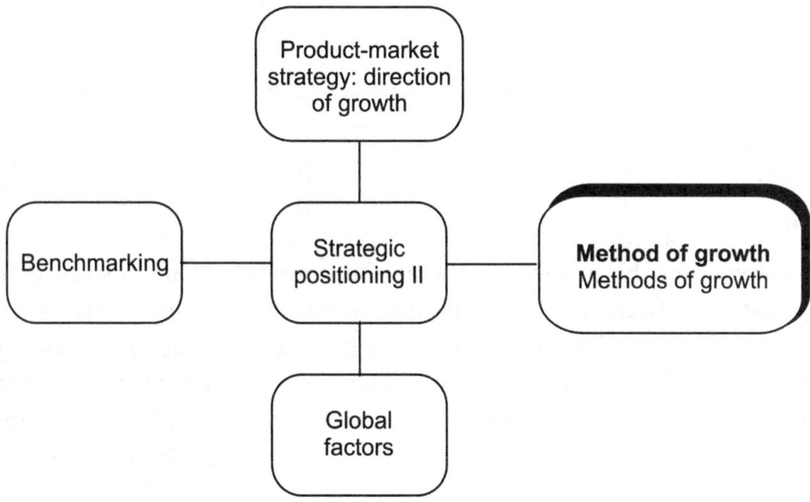

2.1 Methods of growth

- **Building up new businesses** from scratch and developing them
- **Acquiring** already existing businesses from their current owners
- **Merger** of two or more separate businesses
- Spreading the costs and risks by **joint ventures** or other forms of strategic alliance.

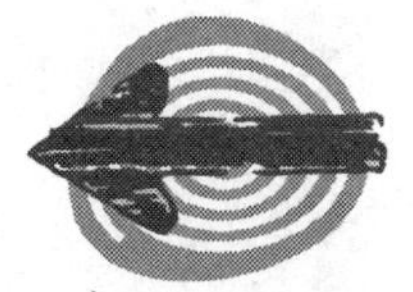

These are considered in more detail in Chapter 9.

3 GLOBAL FACTORS

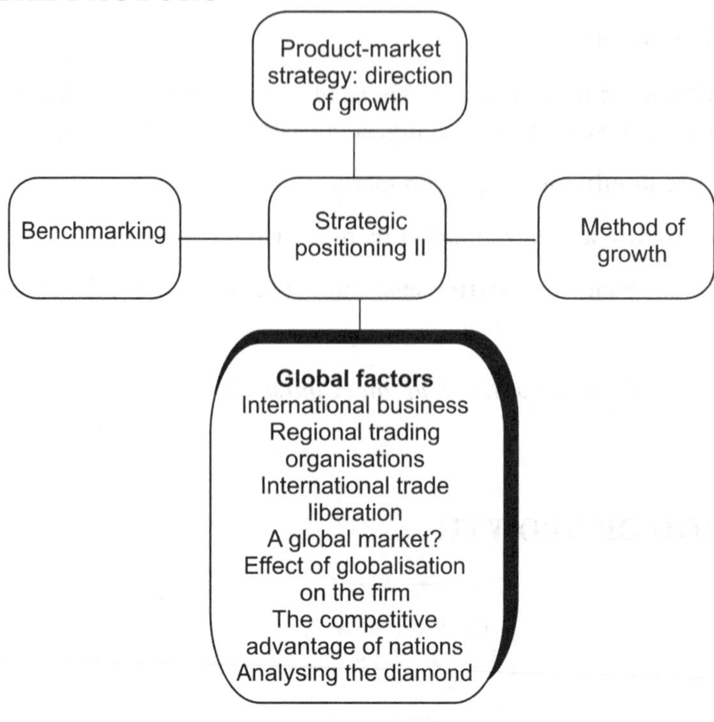

EXAMPLE

Software is conventionally thought to be a high-tech product made in wealthy first world countries. However, India has a flourishing software industry. Thanks to satellite technology, engineers in Bangalore can communicate almost instantaneously with counterparts in the US, Europe and Japan ... Many foreign high-tech companies believe India's engineers are hard to beat because they speak English, the language of international high-tech trade, and are trained at some of the best universities in the developing world.

3.1 International business

International business conditions affect several aspects of a company.

(a) The nature of the industry

(b) The various positions of different countries, the size and wealth of their markets and the prosperity and efficiency of their productive bases

(c) The management, by governments or international institutions, of the framework in which business is done

Many countries have limited or controlled their trading activities, with varying success. **Protectionist measures to restrict competition** from overseas include:

- **Quotas** on the number of items that can be imported (eg Japanese cars)
- **Import bans** (eg Brazil prohibited the import of cheap US-made computers)
- **Restrictions** on foreign ownership of certain industries (eg defence)
- **Tariffs**
- **Abuse of** quality control and technical **standards**

Also bear in mind that protectionist measures are not the only barrier to entry.

- Tax regimes
- Wage levels
- Infrastructure
- Language and culture
- Skills levels
- Prosperity

3.2 Regional trading organisations

Countries in various regions have entered into closer economic arrangements such as NAFTA (USA, Canada, Mexico), the EU, Mercosur (Brazil, Argentina, Uruguay, Paraguay and now Chile). The **EU** is the world's largest single market, but is unusual in that it features a common political decision-making process (Council of Ministers, Commission, Parliament) and a single currency.

The EU single market programme has involved areas as diverse as harmonising technical standards, opening up areas such as telecommunications to competition, consumer protection, mutual recognition of professional qualifications and so on.

3.3 International trade liberalisation

Since 1945, the major industrial, and now the developing, countries have sought to increase trade. Efforts to liberalise trade culminated in the founding of the **World Trade Organisation** (WTO) in 1995 as successor to the former General Agreement on Tariffs and Trade (GATT).

Most countries in the developed world are signatories and the WTO is an important influence over the trading environment.

(a) **The WTO has dispute resolution powers.** Aggrieved countries can take matters up with the WTO if they cannot be resolved bilaterally.

(b) **Membership** of the WTO requires **adherence to certain conditions** regarding competition in the home market. Consequently, certain countries such as China have yet to be admitted, despite intense political pressure.

(c) **Membership rules are slightly less onerous for developing countries,** which can maintain some protectionist measures.

3.4 A global market?

Some writers assert that with the WTO and free movement of capital the world has now become a **global market.**

Despite the real gains in liberalisation, globalisation in a full-blooded form is **not an accurate description** of the reality facing most businesses.

(a) **Depends on the industry.** Some services are still subject to **managed trade** (eg some countries prohibit firms from other countries from selling insurance) and there are some services which by their very nature can never be exported (eg haircuts are resolutely local).

(b) There is **unlikely ever to be a global market for labour,** given the disparity in skills between different countries, and restrictions on immigration. Companies can best respond by relocating, but this is perhaps not always a viable commercial option.

(c) **Depends on the market**

(i) **Upmarket luxury goods** may not be required or afforded by people in developing nations: while there is competition, it is limited to certain locations.

(ii) Some goods can be sold almost anywhere, but to limited degrees. Television sets are consumer durables in some countries, but still luxury or relatively expensive items in other ones. Goods, such as oil, are needed almost everywhere: arguably, the oil industry is truly global. There are relatively few companies serving the aerospace market, so this is also global in a way.

EXAMPLES

Global drivers (factors encouraging the globalisation of world trade) include the following.

(a) **Financial factors** eg Third world debt. Often the lenders require the initiation of economic reforms as a condition of the loan.

(b) **Country/continent** alliances, such as that between the UK and USA, which fosters trade and tourism.

(c) **Legal factors** such as patents and trade marks, which encourage the development of technology and design.

(d) **Stock markets** trading in international commodities.

(e) The level of **protectionist** measures.

3.5 Effect of globalisation on the firm

- Lower barriers to entry, hence incoming competition
- Opportunities to compete abroad via exports
- Opportunities to invest abroad
- Opportunities to raise finance from overseas sources of capital

---

EXAMPLES

Here are some of the changes that have happened in the world market place.

- **Globalisation of business** – increased competition and global customers
- **Science and technology** developments
- Mergers, acquisitions and **strategic alliances**
- Changing **customer values** and behaviour
- Increased **scrutiny** of business decisions by government and the public
- Increased **deregulation** and co-operation between business and government
- Changes in **business practices** - downsizing, outsourcing and re-engineering
- Changes in the **social and business** relationships between companies and their employees, customers and other stakeholders

---

3.6 The competitive advantage of nations

Michael Porter (1998) suggests that some nations' industries succeed more than others in terms of international competition. UK leadership in some industries (eg ship-building) has been overtaken by Japan and Korea.

Porter does not believe that countries or nations as such are competitive, but instead asks three questions.

(a) 'Why does a **nation become the home base** for successful international competitors in an industry?'

(b) 'Why are firms based in a particular nation able to create and **sustain competitive advantage** against the world's best competitors in a particular field?'

(c) 'Why is **one nation** often the home for **so many of an industry's world leaders**?'

Porter identifies determinants of national competitive as outlined in the diagram below. *Porter* refers to this as the **diamond**.

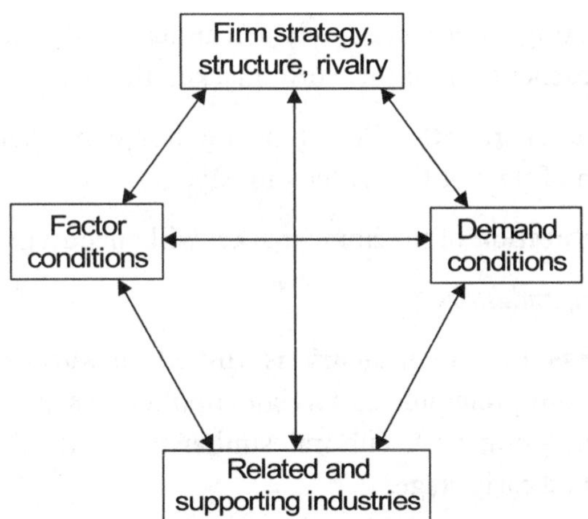

Figure 5.2: The diamond
(Source: Porter, The Competitive Advantage of Nations, 1998)

3.7 Analysing the diamond

Factor conditions are a country's endowment of inputs to production.

- Human resources (skills, price, motivation, industrial relations)
- Physical resources (land, minerals, climate, location relative to other nations)
- Knowledge (scientific and technical know-how, educational institutions)
- Capital (amounts available for investment, how it is deployed)
- Infrastructure (transport, communications, housing)

Porter distinguishes between basic and advanced factors.

(a) **Basic factors** are natural resources, climate, semiskilled and unskilled labour. Basic factors are inherited, or at best their creation involves little investment. Basic factors are **unsustainable** as a source of national competitive advantage. The wages of unskilled workers in industrial countries are undermined by even lower wages elsewhere.

(b) **Advanced factors** include modern digital communications, highly educated personnel (eg computer scientists), research laboratories and so forth. They are necessary to achieve high order competitive advantages such as differentiated products and proprietary production technology.

An abundance of factors is not enough. It is the efficiency with which they are deployed that matters. The former USSR has an abundance of natural resources and a fairly well educated workforce, but has been an economic catastrophe.

Demand conditions: the home market

The **home market determines how firms perceive, interpret and respond to buyer needs**. This information puts pressure on firms to innovate and provides a launch pad for global ambitions.

(a) There are **no cultural impediments** to communication.

(b) The **segmentation** of the home market shapes a firm's priorities: companies will be successful globally in segments which are similar to the home market.

(c) **Sophisticated and demanding buyers** set standards.

(d) **Anticipating buyer needs:** if consumer needs are expressed in the home market earlier than in the world market, the firm benefits from experience.

(e) The **rate of growth**. Slow growing home markets do not encourage the adoption of state of the art technology.

(f) **Early saturation** of the home market will encourage a firm to export.

Related and supporting industries

Competitive success in one industry is linked to success in related industries. Domestic suppliers are preferable to foreign suppliers, as 'proximity of managerial and technical personnel, along with cultural similarity, tends to facilitate free and open information flow' at an early stage.

Firm strategy, structure and rivalry

Structure. National cultural factors create certain tendencies to orientate business-people to certain industries. German firms, according to Porter, have a strong showing in industries with a high technical content.

Strategy. Industries in different countries have different **time horizons**, funding needs and so forth.

(a) **National capital markets** set different goals for performance. In some countries banks are the main source of capital not equity shareholders.

(b) When an industry faces difficult times, it **can either innovate within the industry**, to sustain competitive position or **shift resources from one industry to another**.

Domestic rivalry is important for several reasons.

- There can be no special pleading about unfair foreign competition.
- With little domestic rivalry, firms are happy to rely on the home market.
- Tough domestic rivals teach a firm about competitive success.

- Domestic rivalry forces firms to compete on grounds other than basic factors.
- Each rival can try a different strategic approach.

Having looked at the international context and the competitive advantage of nations, the next section rounds up the chapter with a technique that many companies are using to assess their performance: benchmarking.

4 BENCHMARKING

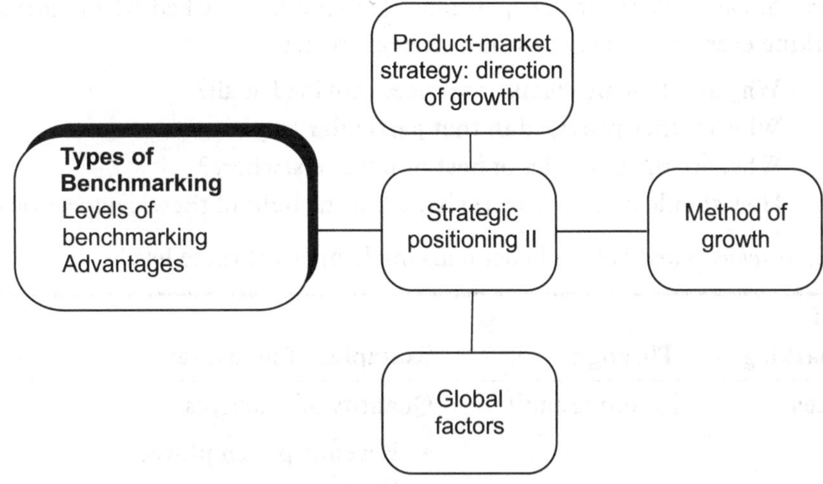

Definition

> **Benchmarking** is the establishment, through data gathering, of targets and comparators, through whose use relative levels of performance (and particularly areas of underperformance) can be identified. By the adoption of identified best practices it is hoped that performance will improve.

4.1 Types of benchmarking

Types of benchmarking include:

(a) **Internal benchmarking**. A method of comparing one operating unit or function with another within the same industry.

(b) **Functional benchmarking.** Internal functions are compared with those of the best external practitioners of those functions, regardless of the industry they are in (also known as operational benchmarking or generic benchmarking).

(c) **Competitive benchmarking**. Information is gathered about direct competitors.

(d) **Strategic benchmarking**. A type of competitive benchmarking aimed at strategic action and organisational change.

4.2 Levels of benchmarking

Benchmarking can be divided into stages.

- **Set objectives** and determine the areas to benchmark
- Establish **key performance measures**
- **Select organisations** to study
- **Measure** own and others' performance
- **Compare** performances
- Design and implement **improvement programme**
- **Monitor** improvements

Johnson and Scholes (2002) set out questions that should be asked when carrying out a benchmarking exercise as part of a wider strategic review.

- **Why** are these products or services provided at all?
- Why are they provided **in that particular way**?
- What are the examples of **best practice** elsewhere?
- How should activities be **reshaped** in the light of these comparisons?

According to *Johnson and Scholes* benchmarking happens at three levels.

Level of benchmarking	Through	Examples of measures
Resources	Resource audit	Quantity of resources • Revenue per employee • Capital usage
		Quality of resources • Qualifications of employees • Age of machinery • Uniqueness (eg patents)
Competencies in separate activities	Analysing activities	Sales calls per salesperson Output per employee Materials wastage
Competencies in linked activities	Analysing overall performances	Market share Profitability Productivity

When selecting an appropriate benchmark basis, companies should ask themselves:

(a) Is it possible and easy to obtain reliable competitor information?

(b) Is there any wide discrepancy between different internal divisions?

(c) Can similar processes be identified in non-competing environments and are these non competing companies willing to co-operate?

(d) Is the best practice example operating in a similar environmental setting?

(e) What is the timescale for the study?

(f) Which companies have similar objectives and strategies to ours?

4.3 Advantages

Benchmarking has the following advantages.

(a) **Position audit**. Benchmarking can assess a firm's existing position, and provide a basis for establishing standards of performance.

(a) The comparisons are **carried out by the managers** who have to live with any changes implemented as a result of the exercise.

(b) Benchmarking **focuses** on improvement in key areas and sets targets which are challenging but evidently 'achievable'.

(c) The sharing of information can be a **spur to innovation**.

EXAMPLE

A five-year research programme by Insead Business School identified the following five companies as likely to still be successful in 10 or 20 years' time.

- American International Group (AIG), the US insurer
- Heineken, the Dutch brewer
- Hewlett-Packard, the US electronics manufacturer
- JP Morgan, the US bank
- SGS Thomson, the Franco-Italian semiconductor maker

The underlying premise of the study, as reported in the *Financial Times*, is that success or failure depends on a complex series of actions. Companies were compared on twelve capabilities – customer orientation, technical resources, market strategy and so forth. An overall score for effectiveness was calculated.

The study showed how the best companies go about their business, and allowed others to diagnose their shortcomings. To quote the project leader when talking about IBM: 'There was a time when it was the best at customer orientation. If we had had this tool twenty years ago, we could have seen it going wrong.'

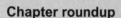

Activity 1 **(20 minutes)**

A company which manufactures and distributes industrial oils employs a team of sales people who work directly from home and travel around different regions in the country. Each member of the sales team has his or her own geographical area to cover and they visit clients on a regular basis.

The sales team staff are each paid a basic monthly salary. Each member of the team is set an identical target for sales to be achieved in the month. A bonus payment in addition to the basic salary is made to any member of the team who exceeds his or her monthly sales target.

Generally, experience has been that the members of the sales team succeed in improving on their targets each month sufficiently to earn a small bonus. However, the managers are unclear whether all the team members are achieving their maximum potential level of sales. Consequently, the managers are considering introducing a system of benchmarking to measure the performance of the sales team as a whole and its individual members.

Explain the objectives of benchmarking and how it may be used to assist the managers in evaluating operational performance.

Chapter roundup

- Product-market strategies determine which products should be sold in which markets, by market penetration, market development, product development and diversification.
- There are various methods of growth. Companies can grow organically, building up their own products and developing their own market.

  Alternatively, they may choose to acquire these ready-made by buying other companies, or use other means, such as joint ventures or franchising.
- To the extent that there is already a single global market depends on the goods and services involved. Global corporations are supposed to act independently of national considerations. Trade liberalisation and reduced technology costs might favour small businesses in the global market place.
- Globalisation means that domestic markets are less protected than previously, but there are new opportunities in foreign markets.
- Porter argues that the national origin of a company can be a factor in its competitive advantage. A country's advantage in an industry is gained from the way it manages the diamond ie the relationship between factor endowments (resources, human skills etc), competition and demand in the home market and related and supporting industries.
- Benchmarking is a technique by which a company tries to emulate or exceed standards achieved or processes adopted by another company, or industry generally an exemplar organisation.

Quick quiz

1. Draw *Ansoff's* growth vector diagram.
2. What are the effects of globalisation on a company?
3. What are the elements of *Porter's* diamond?
4. What are the *Johnson and Scholes'* three levels of benchmarking?

Answers to quick quiz

1 See Section 1.1

2 Lower barriers to entry, opportunities to compete and invest abroad, opportunities to raise finance from overseas sources of capital.

3 Factor conditions

Firm strategy, structure and rivalry

Demand conditions

Related and supporting industries

4 Resources

Competencies in separate activities

Competencies in linked activities

Answer to activity

1 The objectives and value of benchmarking are as follows.

(a) To keep up with industry best practice – perhaps to negate a competitor's operational competitive advantage.

(b) To enhance the efficiency and effectiveness of the function involved in the benchmarking exercise.

(c) To reduce the need to 'reinvent the wheel' – a firm can climb the learning curve to achieve best practice much quicker if it uses another firm's experience: of course a competitor or even a firm in the same industry is unlikely to be too helpful.

(d) As performance indicators to motivate managers: the benchmark standards are achievable, as other firms have achieved them.

In all these respects, benchmarking can be used for planning and control. As planning measures, they can be used to design systems and to assess the resources required to achieve a certain standard of performance. In evaluating operational performance, benchmarks can be used as the 'plan or standard' of a control system, and feedback can be used to see whether the plan has been met. Such non-financial performance indicators can be introduced ready-made into the strategic control system.

Problems with benchmarking in evaluating operational performance are as follows.

(a) The benchmark standards do not always take the use of resources into account.

(b) Managers will be satisfied when they have reached the benchmark standard and will be less motivated to exceed it.

(c) There may be better ways of enhancing performance (eg by exploiting different linkages in the value chain, outsourcing some value activities etc).

(d) It is based on copying industry leaders, rather than doing things in a different, more innovative way.

Many organisations have field sales forces organised on an area basis, and so this company is not unique. It can therefore learn from other companies as to the best way of managing and controlling its sales personnel. Benchmarking techniques can be used, for two types of information.

(i) The best way to design and run a field sales force (eg the optimum balance of salary and commission, the most appropriate way of designing and setting targets).

(ii) The performance of the sales team, as it is currently managed in the light of other field sales forces (in other words the content of the targets).

Part B

Strategic Planning

Chapter 6 : THE PLANNING FRAMEWORK

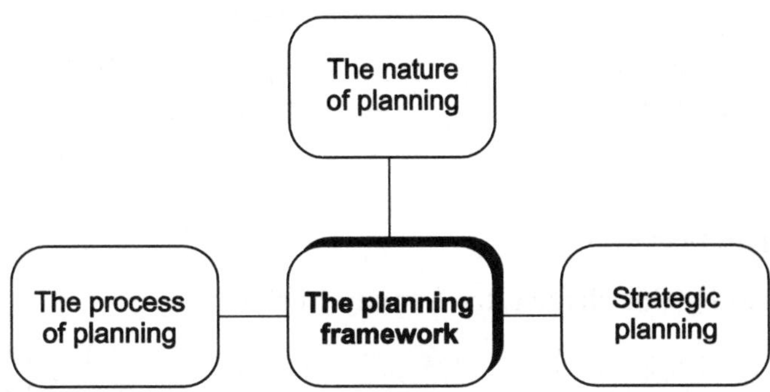

Introduction

In this chapter we look at what planning actually is, and how the different types and levels of plans in an organisation fit together as a hierarchy. We then describe the **process** of planning, looking at the **planning cycle** and the steps to take in the planning process. Finally we look at **strategic planning,** which is concerned with the future direction of the organisation.

This chapter outlines the framework of this book by describing the **rational model** approach to business strategy management. We also outline the criticisms of the model (some alternatives to it are described later in Chapter 7).

Your objectives

In this chapter you will learn about the following.

(a) The concept of planning, the reasons for its importance and the functions it can fulfil within an organisation

(b) The hierarchy of plans and the role of each type of plan in the overall planning process

(c) The strategic planning cycle, architecture and the steps in a typical planning exercise

(d) The nature of, and processes involved in, strategic planning

1 THE NATURE OF PLANNING

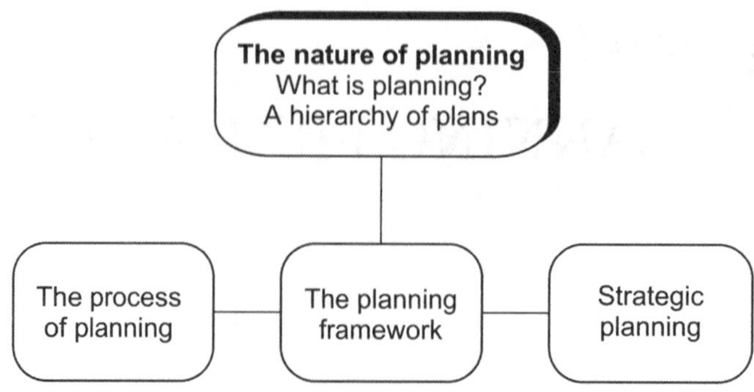

1.1 What is planning?

To prepare yourself for this chapter, try Activity 1 below.

Activity 1 **(30 minutes)**

In the 1970s as TV sets and video recorders became increasingly reliable, and people began buying instead of renting, electrical goods rental companies foresaw a decline in their income. New developments would fill some of the gap as people rented expensive wide-screen sets and NICAM stereo recorders; interactive CD might also bring new business if enough software came on the market.

The companies researched what their customers wanted and what could attract new consumers to the renting business. They looked at their existing portfolio of products and examined new areas to diversify into so as to reduce their dependence on the TV market. They reviewed their resources of shops, staff and skills and found out where inadequacies existed. The competing rental and hire purchase companies were assessed too.

Then they planned for the introduction of new products and their marketing launches: new products were phased in, staff were trained and after-sales services were set up. The results were evaluated and the lessons learned were applied to the next launch.

Take a walk down your High Street and find out what the companies are renting today, and examine their terms. You will find that they offer their core products of TV and video and their variants, as well as computers and a whole range of domestic items such as washing machines.

Make a list of the key elements in the plans that the rental companies made for coping with change. Then write a short description of what might have happened to a rental company that failed to plan for change.

Definition

Planning is the process of deciding what should be done, how and when it should be done and who should do it.

If we answer the questions 'Where are we now?' And 'Where do we want to be?', the gap between them is what needs to be done. This is known as the planning gap (Figure 6.1).

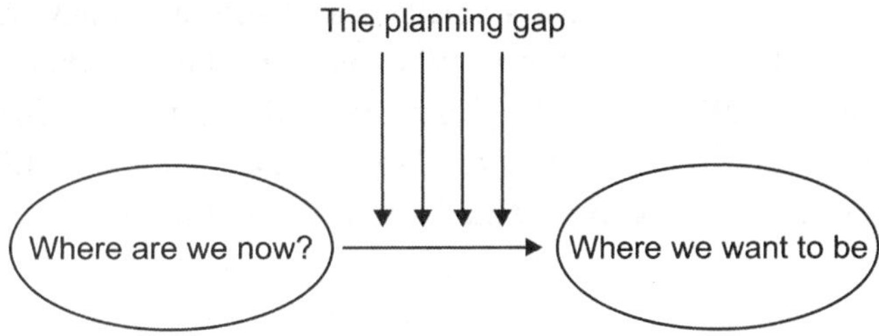

Figure 6.1: The planning gap

Planning involves working out how what needs to be done can be done in the most **efficient** manner with the **resources** available.

Definitions

> **Planning** is the process of deciding which objectives need to be achieved and of preparing how to meet them.
>
> **Objectives** are the anticipated end result of activity. They are the things that you hope to achieve.
>
> **Efficiency** refers to how well resources are utilised.

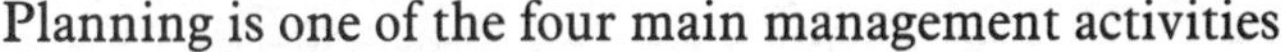

Planning is one of the four main management activities.

- Planning
- Organising
- Motivating
- Controlling

Obviously planning must precede all the other management activities because if it is not done properly, the others will probably fail.

There are many reasons **why planning is important**.

(a) It **focuses attention on objectives** by uniting the organisation and its activities.

(b) It **removes uncertainty** by providing a framework of activities that can be placed in a context.

(c) It facilitates **control** by supplying targets for performance.

(d) It leads to **economical operations** by emphasising **efficiency** and **consistency**.

We now move on to discuss the various types of plan that fit together to form a hierarchy.

1.2 A hierarchy of plans

Within any organisation many plans will be made. Some will relate to the whole organisation, others will relate to just a small area of activity. They will vary in **scope** and in the **periods of time** they cover. What is important is that **all the plans fit together** to form an overall view of the planning needs for the organisation. So, before going on to examine the different types of plan in more detail we will first look at the way in which plans form a **hierarchy**. This is shown in Figure 6.2.

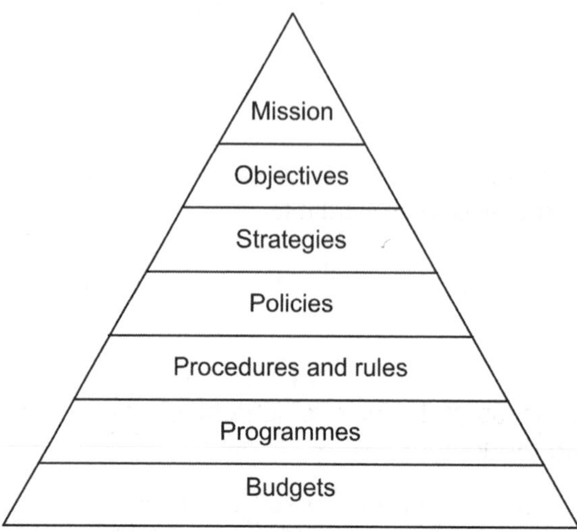

Figure 6.2: The planning hierarchy

Definitions

- **Mission** describes the organisation's basic function in society, in terms of the products and services it produces for its clients.
- **Strategies** are courses of action, including those that specify resources required, to achieve an overall objective.
- **Policies** are general statements that guide thinking and action.
- **Procedures** are customary methods of action.
- **Rules** are specific statements of what may or may not be done.
- **Programmes** are collections of activities that need to be carried out to achieve desired outcome.
- **Budgets** are statements of expected results expressed in financial terms.

In this hierarchy, the most important level is the **mission**. This identifies the purpose of the organisation and it can be broken down into many types and levels of **objectives**. These objectives specify the things that the organisation wants to achieve.

Once the objectives have been agreed, **strategies** need to be designed. These describe the broad actions that must take place so that the objectives can be achieved. **Policies, procedures** and **rules** help to shape the nature of these actions, whereas **programmes** are the detailed activities needed to carry out the actions.

EXAMPLE

A government's objective of reducing road traffic accidents might be achieved in a number of ways, such as stricter policing, lower speed limits, raising driving test standards, targeting drink drivers etc.

Underlying all these types of plan are **budgets**. These are plans that provide information about the extent of the resources available.

Activity 2 **(10 minutes)**

Think about what you would expect to happen in an organisation that does not have overall objectives and the strategies to fulfil them.

Write down two or three of the consequences you would foresee.

We now need to examine how planning works in practice, and so we are going to look at the process of planning.

2 THE PROCESS OF PLANNING

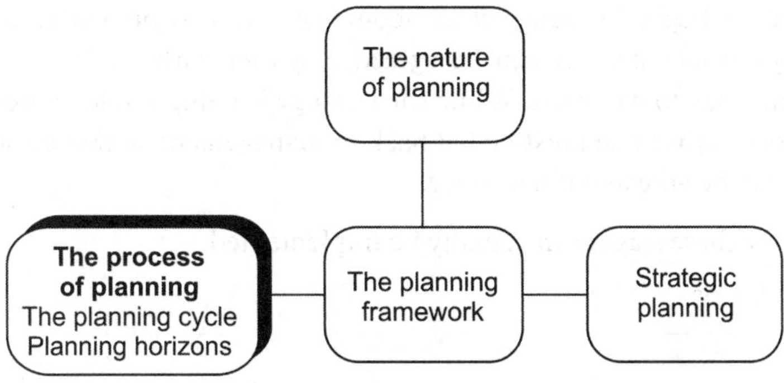

2.1 The planning cycle

As Figure 6.3 illustrates, all the main stages of planning can be incorporated into a simple 'planning cycle'.

Figure 6.3: The planning cycle

To ensure that plans have the best chance of success, questions must be asked at each stage of the planning cycle.

Establish objectives	What do we want to achieve?
Plan the strategy	How can we achieve our objectives?
Decide tactics	What has to be done in order to make the strategy a success?
Implement the strategy	How best can the strategy be implemented?
Review progress	How successful have we been in terms of implementing the strategy and achieving our objectives?

It is important to begin by being clear about what has to be achieved. Once this is known, an appropriate strategy can be agreed, together with tactics for implementing that strategy on a day to day basis. While the strategy is being implemented, information as to its success or otherwise must be fed back to management so that either the plans or the objectives can be adjusted if necessary.

Let's look at how these stages can actually be implemented.

EXAMPLE: LAUNCHING A MAGAZINE

What activities will be required at each stage of the planning cycle for the launch of a magazine? These are likely stages.

(a) **Objective**. To launch a new national magazine successfully, the initial sales for which will be high and will then stabilise at a minimum of 25,000 copies during the first three years of production.

(b) **Strategy**. This will need to address the nature of the marketplace and the potential scope for a new magazine. Thought must be given to magazines currently on the market and any gaps in the market, as well as to the various types of customer and sales outlets that exist.

A knowledge of such factors facilitates ideas as to what type of magazine might appeal and the place it might fill in the market. One key decision that must be made is whether to create a new market or to compete with existing magazines for their

market share. Strategy must also cover production levels, marketing, distribution systems and overall costings and sales targets.

(c) **Tactics**. Once an overall strategy has been established, tactics are drawn up. These specify in detail how the strategy will be put into action. Tactics will cover the ways in which the magazine is designed, promoted to advertisers, produced, printed and marketed. Of particular importance to a new magazine is marketing and the way in which initial interest is built up (promotion methods, free offers, cheap introductory prices and so on).

(d) **Implementation**. The next part of the cycle deals with the activities that are needed to successfully implement the strategy and tactics. For a magazine launch this will involve the co-ordination of the different departments such as design, writing, production, sales and so on. For a launch it is essential that the timing of activities is correct. Production must be ready to satisfy initial sales and promotion must begin well in advance of the launch to ensure enough sales.

(e) **Review**. As the preparations for the launch continue, continuous comparisons must be made between progress to date and the estimates made at the planning stage. This ensures that the timetable is kept to and that all aspects of the work are completed ready for the launch. Finances must also be monitored carefully for any overspending.

Activity 3 **(30 minutes)**

A student union has decided to support a local charity by fund-raising on a Rag Day to be held in the town. Key events include a fancy dress relay race with teams sponsored by local businesses, a disco, 'Rag Raids' of collectors on local shopping centres and a raffle with prizes donated by businesses and celebrities.

Either as an individual or in a small team, write a short report to the Union Charity Rag Committee setting out the stages of the planning cycle for one of these events and making clear the issues relevant to each stage.

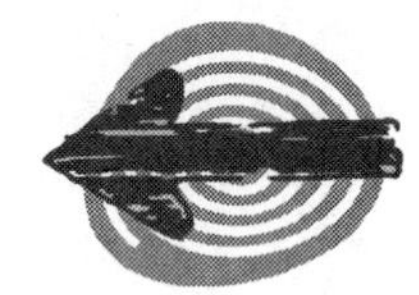

So far we have looked at the various stages in the drawing up and implementation of a plan. We now need to consider the time scales involved.

2.2 Planning horizons

Planning should cover both the **long-** and **short-term**.

Definition

A **planning period** or 'horizon' is the length of time between making a planning decision and implementing that decision. For example, a decision to move to new premises might have a time horizon of many years, whereas a production or sale schedule might be implemented within a few days or weeks.

Plans covering various time periods will be made within an organisation. The longer the planning horizon, the more senior within the organisation the planner is likely to be.

(a) **Long-term plans** indicate a significant commitment to a certain course of action.

(b) **Short-term plans** might conflict with long-term objectives, so planning must always attempt to reconcile the needs of both the long-and short-terms.

For example, if an organisation has only limited funds, it might be tempting in the short term to spend all of this on maintaining current profit levels. But if spending on **capital investment** or **research and development** is ignored in the long term, this will eventually affect profitability.

Definition

Profitability is the prospect of a particular course of action generating profits for the organisation.

In the short-term, an organisation might consider **profitability as its major objective**. In the longer-term, however, other considerations (such as employee welfare, company image, standards of service, reputation and so on) take on added importance.

Plans should not be viewed as rigid. The future is always uncertain and plans may need to be changed due to unforeseen circumstances. Some people would argue that while short planning periods are necessary because of the need for **flexibility** in planning, the preparation of long-term plans is a waste of time because they will inevitably change.

A compromise must therefore be found between the **need for flexibility** and the **need for commitment** to decisions already taken. The best compromise may involve **reviewing plans** regularly and adjusting them as necessary.

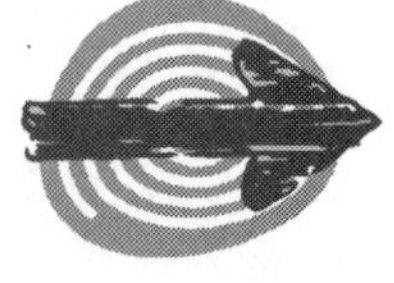

Having looked at the planning process in general, we now turn to strategic planning, which is concerned with the long-term strategy for the whole organisation.

3 STRATEGIC PLANNING

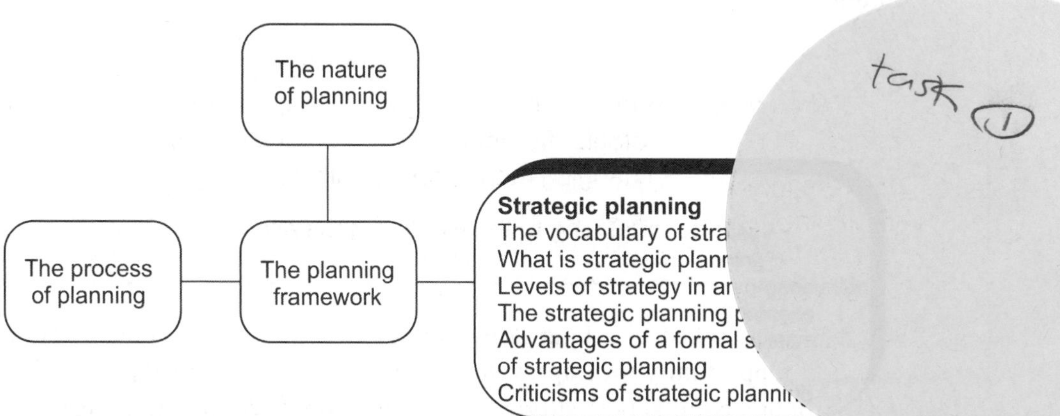

3.1 The vocabulary of strategy

Johnson and Scholes (2002) list the **key elements of strategy terminology** as follo .

TERM	DEFINITION
Mission	Overriding purpose in line with the values or expectations of stakeholders
Vision or strategic intent	Desired future state: the aspiration of the organisation
Goal	General statement of aim or purpose
Objective	Quantification or more precise statement of the goal
Core competencies	Resources, processes or skills which provide distinctive competitive advantage
Strategies	Long-term direction
Strategic architecture	Combination of resources, processes and competencies to put strategy into effect
Control	The monitoring of action steps to: • Assess effectiveness of strategies and actions • Modify strategies and/or actions as necessary

We looked at core competencies and strategic architecture in the context of resources in Chapter 3.

3.2 What is strategic planning?

Strategic planning is often referred to as **corporate planning** because it deals with the whole organisation.

Definitions

- **Strategic planning** is the managerial process of developing and maintaining a strategic fit between the organisation's objectives and resources and its changing market opportunities.
- **Corporate** means relating to the whole organisation.

If planning is not linked to a long-term strategy it is likely to become a routine task rather than an opportunity for improvement. Organisations attempting to get by with a routine approach are unlikely to survive in the increasingly competitive world that faces them.

Strategic plans are used to define the direction of all other plans and so they must be:

- Long-term
- Comprehensive
- Based upon a clear mission or purpose for the organisation
- Developed and controlled by top management

Although strategies are set by senior management, they must be based upon the delivery of results by the rest of the organisation.

EXAMPLE:

Military situation

'Strategy' was a term originally used by the military, and this origin gives us a good idea of how a strategy should be drawn up. In a war situation the senior military commanders must define exactly what their objectives are (to capture an area of land, to destroy an army and so on). To achieve these objectives they must decide on:

(a) The resources, such as troops and materials that will be needed (resource requirements)

(b) The strength of the enemy forces (the strength of the competition)

(c) The actions the enemy are likely to take (competitor moves)

(d) How best to achieve the objectives (strategy)

(e) When to attack (timetable for action)

(f) What to do if plans do not go as expected (contingency plans)

From this simple example, we can easily see the factors that the military commanders need to take account of so as to stand a good chance of victory. The terms in brackets show the corresponding factors that an **organisation** must consider when setting a competitive business strategy.

Another important consideration in strategic planning is the hierarchy of plans and objectives. While the senior military figures design the **strategy**, the commanders in the field will have **tactical plans and objectives**. Although these field commanders must be able to change the tactical plans according to the circumstances that arise, they must always bear in mind the overall strategy, which they will not be able to alter. Likewise, departmental managers in an organisation will set and implement tactical plans.

Staff even lower down the ladder of command will be involved with **operational plans and objectives** that deal with the day-to-day issues such as supply, support, communications and so on.

Definitions

- **Tactics** determine the most efficient deployment of resources to execute an agreed strategy.
- **Operations** are the routine activities that convert the resource inputs into relevant activities.

Tactical and operational plans and objectives are often closely related since they are normally short term and removed from the overall strategy of which they form a part. Tactical plans are sometimes referred to as **functional plans** because they deal with the activities of the functions of an organisation.

Figure 6.4 shows how planning and decisions are related to the levels of an organisation's hierarchy.

Figure 6.4: The organisation hierarchy, planning and decision-making

3.3 Levels of strategy in an organisation

Any level of the organisation can have objectives and devise strategies to achieve them. The strategic management process is multi-layered.

As we have already hinted at, there are three levels of strategy: **corporate, business** and **functional/operational**.

Corporate strategies

Definition

> **Corporate strategy** is concerned with what types of business the organisation is in. It 'denotes the most general level of strategy in an organisation'.
> *(Johnson and Scholes)*

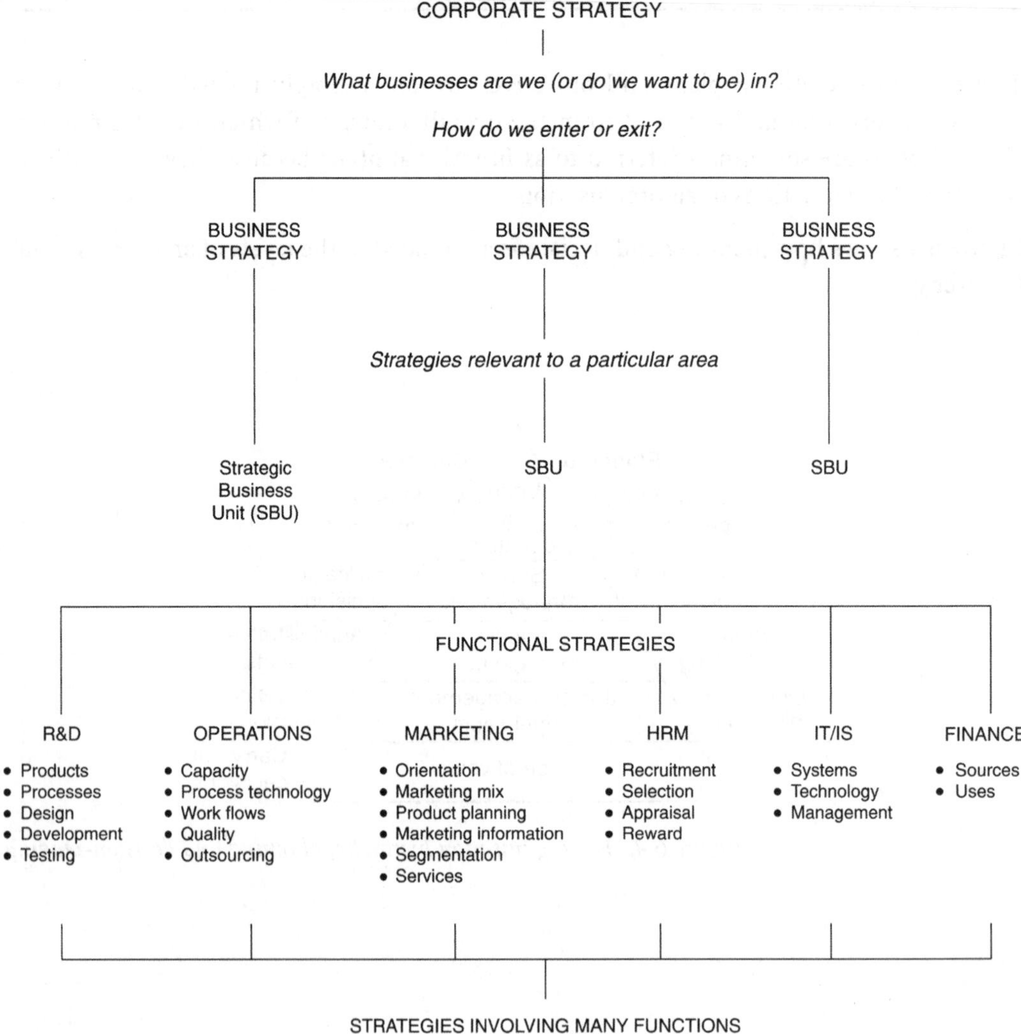

Figure 6.5: Levels of strategy

Characteristics of corporate strategic decisions

Characteristic	Comment
Scope of activities	Products and markets. Corporate strategy might involve diversifying into a new line of business or closing a business down. It might mean global expansion or contraction.
Environment	The organisation counters threats and exploits opportunities in the environment (customers, clients, competitors).
Capability	The organisation matches its activities to its resources: ie it does what it is able to do.
Resources	Strategy involves choices about allocating or obtaining resources now and in future.
Operations	Corporate strategies always affect operations.
Values	The value systems of people in power influence them to understand the world in a certain way.
Direction	Corporate strategy has a long-term impact.
Complex	Corporate strategy involves uncertainty about the future, integrating the operations of the organisation and change.

Business strategy

Definition

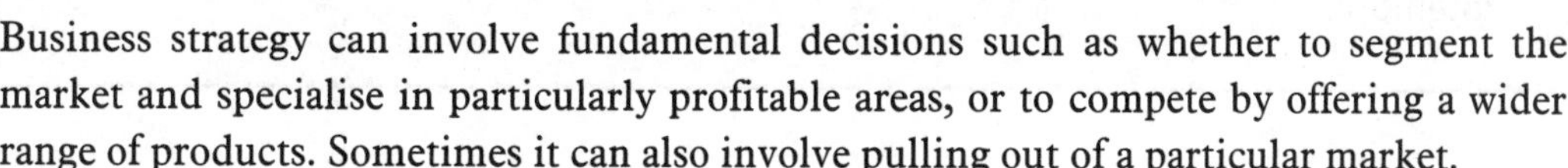
Business strategy: how an organisation approaches a particular product market area.

Business strategy can involve fundamental decisions such as whether to segment the market and specialise in particularly profitable areas, or to compete by offering a wider range of products. Sometimes it can also involve pulling out of a particular market.

EXAMPLE

Mercedes-Benz wished to expand its product range to include four wheel drive vehicles and smaller cars, culminating in the merger with Chrysler.

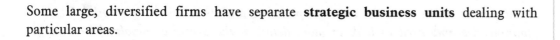

Some large, diversified firms have separate **strategic business units** dealing with particular areas.

Functional/operational strategies

Functional/operational strategies deal with **specialised areas of activity**.

Functional area	Comment
Marketing	Devising products and services, pricing, promoting and distributing them, in order to satisfy customer needs at a profit. Marketing and corporate strategies are interrelated.
Production	Factory location, manufacturing techniques, outsourcing
Finance	Ensuring that the firm has enough financial resources to fund its strategies by identifying sources of finance and using them effectively
Human resources management	Secure personnel of the right skills in the right quantity at the right time, and to ensure that they have the right skills and values to promote the firm's overall goals
Information systems	A firm's information systems are becoming increasingly important, as an item of expenditure, as administrative support and as a tool for competitive strength.
R&D	New products and techniques

Activity 4 **(15 minutes)**

Ganymede Ltd is a company selling widgets. The finance director says: 'We plan to issue more shares to raise money for new plant capacity – we don't want loan finance – which will enable us to compete better in the vital and growing widget markets of Latin America. After all, we've promised the shareholders 5% profit growth this year, and trading is tough.'

Identify the *corporate*, *business* and *functional* strategies in the above statement.

FOR DISCUSSION

Consider how relevant the military example is to business planning.

What might be the advantages and disadvantages of adopting military-style planning techniques?

Having outlined the nature of strategic planning and its relationship to other levels of planning, we now need to look in more detail at the processes involved in strategic planning. These are crucial to designing a successful strategy for an organisation.

3.4 The strategic planning process

Definitions

- **Strategic analysis** is an assessment of an organisation and its current and projected circumstances.
- **Strategic options** are the suitable strategies for developing the organisation, from which choices have to be made.

Clearly, the strategic planning process is not simple. The process will vary according to the **type and size** of organisation, the organisation's **current activities** and its ideal future **direction**.

Figure 6.6 shows an outline of the **rational** strategic planning process. It has three distinct stages, as follows.

(a) **Strategic analysis** in which a thorough assessment of the organisation is undertaken, covering its objectives, its resources and capabilities, its external influences and its future potential.

(b) **Strategic choice,** in which the strategic options that exist are considered and the most appropriate one selected.

(c) **Strategic implementation,** in which the selected strategy is developed and put into action.

***We explore the stages of the rational model on the following pages, and indicate in the table (which follows the diagram) the key planning techniques associated with each one. This helps you to pull together the issues relating to strategy and how they can be split between strategic* analysis *and strategic* choice.**

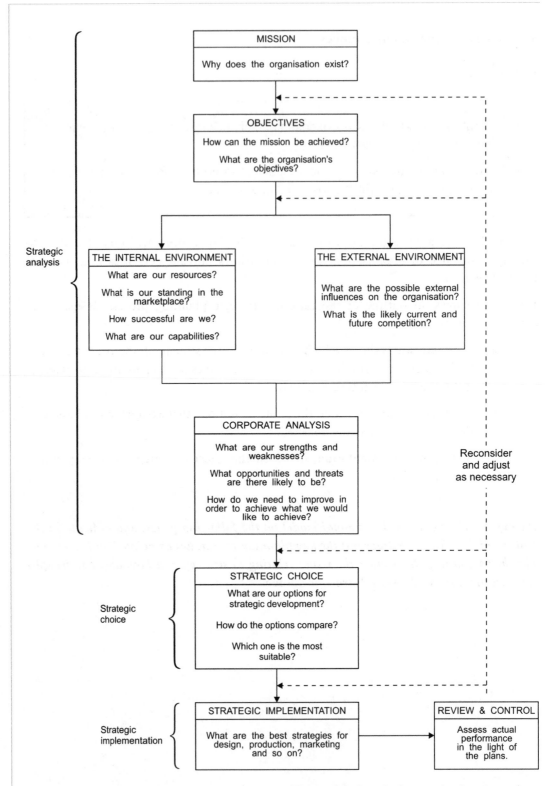

Figure 6.6: A typical strategic planning process

Strategic analysis

	Stage	Comment	Key tools, models, techniques
Step 1	Mission and/or vision	Mission denotes values, the business's rationale for existing; vision refers to where the organisation intends to be in a few years' time	• Mission statement
Step 2	Goals	Interpret the mission to different stakeholders	• Stakeholder analysis
Step 3	Objectives	Quantified embodiments of mission	• Measures such as profitability, time scale, deadlines
Step 4	Environmental analysis	Identify opportunities and threats	• PEST analysis • *Porter's* five force analysis and competitive advantage of nations • Scenario building
Step 5	Position audit or situation analysis	Identify strengths and weaknesses Firm's **current** resources, products, customers, systems, structure, results, efficiency, effectiveness	• Resource audit • Distinctive competence • Value chain • Product life cycle • Boston (BCG) matrix • Directional policy matrix • Marketing audit • Market share (PIMS)
Step 6	Corporate appraisal	Combines Steps 4 and 5	• SWOT analysis charts
Step 7	Gap analysis	Compares outcomes of Step 6 with Step 3	• Gap analysis

Strategic choice

Stage	Comment	Key tools, models, techniques
Strategic options generation	Come up with new ideas • How to compete (competitive advantage) • Where to compete • Method of growth	• Value chain analysis • Scenario building • *Porter's* generic strategic choices • *Ansoff's* growth vector • Acquisition vs organic growth
Strategic options evaluation	Normally, each strategy has to be evaluated on the basis of • Acceptability • Suitability • Feasibility • Environmental fit	• Stakeholder analysis • Risk analysis • Financial measures

NOTES

Implementation

Stage	Comment	Key tools, models, techniques
Resource planning	Deploying the resources to achieve the strategy	• Critical success factors • Outsourcing
Operations plans		• Activity schedules • Budgets • Project management
Organisation structure and culture	Designing the organisation to implement the strategy	• Centralisation vs decentralisation
Change	Implement changes	
Functional strategies	HRM	• Personnel planning • Appraisal schemes
	Production	• Quality management
	Marketing	• Marketing information systems • Marketing mix • Segmentation • Product life cycle

Review and control

Throughout the implementation stage it is important that progress made is constantly reviewed. Regular review allows progress to be controlled and, if necessary, changes to be made.

Review involves treating the strategic planning process as a planning cycle and returning to the appropriate earlier stage if necessary.

(a) If the **implementation** is not going according to plan, the implementation processes should be reconsidered.

(b) If the **strategic choice** is no longer appropriate, the options could be reconsidered.

The strategic planning process works when it is developed carefully over come considerable time, and when people within the organisation are consulted and informed about the process. This provides a 'sense of ownership', which will lead to greater commitment and understanding when the time comes to implement the strategy.

Planning techniques

From the table above, the Edexcel Guidelines specifically mention the following.

(a) The **BCG** Growth Share Matrix (see Chapter 3)

(b) **SPACE (Strategic Position and Action Evaluation)**

This analyses the position of a company and suggests a strategy on the basis of

(i) Financial strength
(ii) Environmental stability
(iii) Industry strength
(iv) Competitive advantage

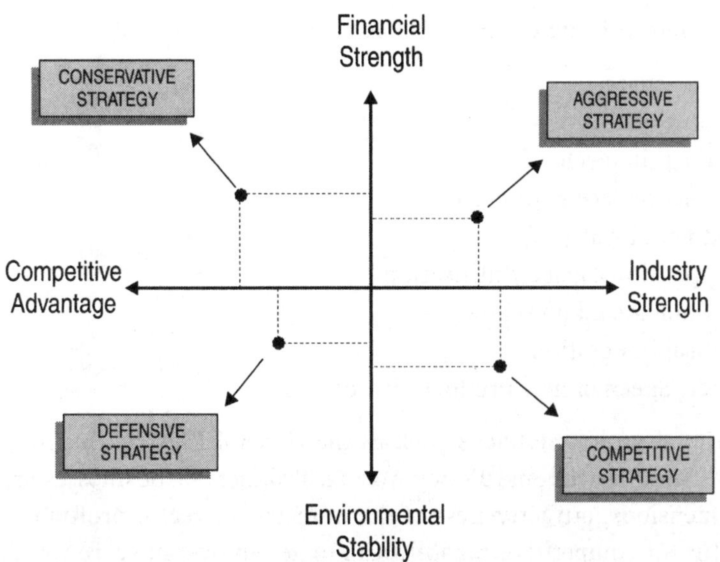

Figure 6.7: Space analysis (Source: Koplyay, T. and Paquin, J.-P., 2002)

Factors determining each of the key issues are then determined.

Factors determining environmental stability

- Technological changes
- Rate of inflation
- Demand variability
- Price range of competing products
- Barriers to entry into market
- Competitive pressure/rivalry
- Price elasticity of demand
- Pressure from substitute products

Factors determining financial strength

- Return on investment
- Leverage
- Liquidity
- Capital required vs available
- Cash-flow
- Ease of exit from market
- Risk involved in business
- Inventory turnover
- Economies of scale and experience

Factors determining industry strength

- Growth potential
- Profit potential
- Financial stability
- Technological know-how
- Resource utilisation
- Capital intensity
- Ease of entry into market
- Productivity, capacity utilisation
- Other: Manufacturer's bargaining power

Factors determining competitive advantage

- Market share
- Product quality
- Product life-cycle
- Product replacement cycle
- Customer loyalty
- Competition capacity utilisation
- Technological know-how
- Vertical integration
- Other: Speed of new product introductions

(c) **Directional policy matrices** such as the General Electric Business Screen (GEBS) and the Shell Directional Policy Matrix. Products or businesses are plotted against two dimensions: attractiveness of the industry (or sector profitability) and business strengths (or competitive capabilities), to get an overall score which can then make the difference between further investment or withdrawal.

This can be shown on a diagram. **General Electric's Business Screen** compares the following.

(a) The **strength of attraction** that the product has in general for customers (for whatever reasons).

(b) The **competitive position** of products compared with rival products in the market.

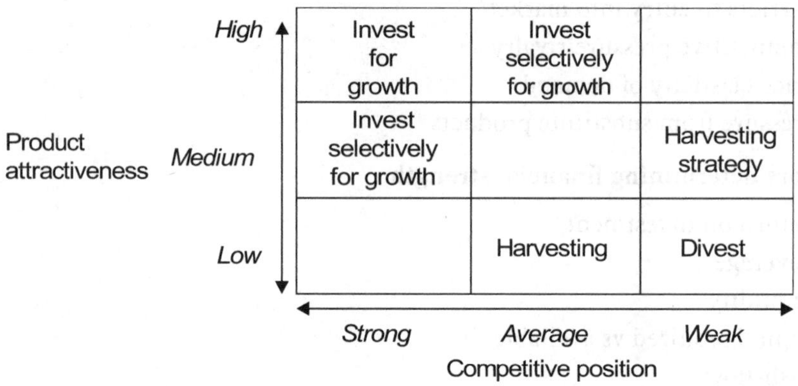

Figure 6.8: General Electric's Business Screen

In the matrix above 'invest for growth' is self-explanatory. 'Harvest' means that the firm should invest no more, but earn what profits it can before quitting.

- **PIMS** (Profit Impact of Market Share). This indicates a positive relationship between market share and profitability. Companies with high market share tend to have high profits, so high market share is often an objective laid down at the planning stage.

Activity 5 **(20 minutes)**

Swan Cruises was formed in 20X1 by a group of four friends who each owned cabin cruisers and used redundancy payments to purchase another four. From their own boating activities and contacts they concluded that there was a good opportunity in the market for family cruising holidays on the canal system. They produced rough budgets and drew up an advertising plan. Because they wanted to get started quickly to catch the spring season, the partners did not give time to strategic planning.

After their publicity leaflets and advertising in the press brought them a good number of bookings, they began to run into problems.

(a) The waterways authority demanded more safety measures and insurance premiums were more than budgeted

(b) Customers found the cruisers too small for family parties to live in for a week

(c) Customers regularly got into difficulties with running the boats and at the locks and the partners had to spend much time teaching and helping customers

(d) There were a lot of complaints and demands for refunds

(e) Three of the boats were damaged by novice sailors

(f) The waterways authority threatened to withdraw the licence because of speeding by young customers

Write a short memorandum to the partners setting out how they would benefit from using strategic planning.

EXAMPLE: A LOCAL RECYCLING BUSINESS

The key points in the strategic planning process of a local recycling business which aims to promote recycling of various items might include the following.

(a) The **mission** of the organisation is to protect the local environment by promoting and carrying out a range of initiatives to conserve natural resources and eliminate unnecessary waste.

(b) The main **objectives** of the organisation

   (i) To undertake a campaign of promotion and education to encourage conservation

   (ii) To assist local businesses to improve their environmental impact

   (iii) To provide collection points for items that can be recycled

   (iv) To provide advice and consultancy services on all aspects of conservation

(c) The **internal environment**

   (i) An established project that undertakes practical conservation work through a government-funded training scheme

   (ii) A spacious operating depot provided at nominal rent by the local council

   (iii) A good public image and a strong body of local support

   (iv) Proven management potential

(d) Effects of the **external environment**

   (i) Political changes might erode support from both central and local government

   (ii) Economic changes are increasingly influencing the desire of both businesses and individuals to be more economical with resources

   (iii) Social influences continue to make it more fashionable to support conservation

   (iv) Technological changes mean that machinery for recycling is getting cheaper and more efficient to use

   (v) Other recycling and conservation initiatives are starting to appear

(e) The **strategic analysis**

   (i) As an established and respected environmental organisation, there is already a strong base on which to build a business

   (ii) There is at present a weakness in experience of commercial and competitive operations

   (iii) There are many developing areas of environmental conservation that present opportunities for involvement

   (iv) Grants are available at present for environmental work, but these might not continue indefinitely

   (v) The business world offers good scope for consultancy, grant aid and high-level promotion

(f) The **strategic options**

(i) To introduce an advisory and consultancy service targeted at businesses

(ii) To establish a collection and recycling service for materials including paper and aluminium cans

(iii) To undertake a long-term promotional campaign of environmental awareness

Of these options the promotional campaign is the easiest to establish as financial support is readily available. It would also provide a good base for other developments. The advisory and consultancy business would take some time to establish yet cost little to promote. Grants currently available could help to support the establishment of this promising initiative. The recycling service would take considerable planning and capital investment would have to be raised.

In conclusion, both the promotion and the consultancy service (which can bring in income to help establish the recycling business later on) should begin immediately. Other ideas should also be explored for future potential.

(g) The strategic implementation will involve drawing up plans for fundraising, publicity, marketing and networking to build support.

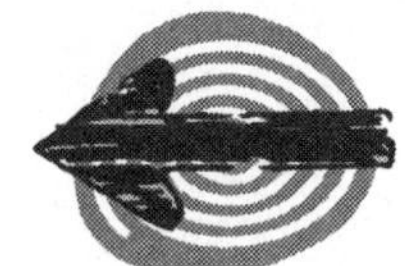

This example is not meant to be comprehensive, but it does illustrate the sort of issues that are encountered in strategic planning. Remember that the essence of strategic planning is that it relates to the organisation, its aspirations and its circumstances, and these are all factors that are constantly changing. Successful strategic planning is an ongoing process.

FOR DISCUSSION

You have just taken over responsibility for a clothes shop in a small town. The shop is not performing particularly well due to lack of direction and dynamism, and you feel that it could be developed and expanded. There is no current plan for future development. How would you go about establishing a strategic plan for the shop?

Strategic planning relies heavily on a comprehensive assessment of the organisation's planning environment. We conclude this chapter by looking at some of the advantages and criticisms of strategic planning.

3.5 Advantages of a formal system of strategic planning

Advantages	Comment
Identifies risks	Strategic planning helps in managing these risks.
Forces managers to think	Strategic planning can encourage creativity and initiative by tapping the ideas of the management team. Planning carries from the **top** and **down** to more junior staff.
Forces decision-making	Companies cannot remain static – they have to cope with changes in the environment. A strategic plan draws attention to the need to change and adapt, not just to 'stand still' and survive.
Better control	Management control can be better exercised if targets are explicit.
Enforces consistency at all levels	Long-term, medium-term and short-term objectives, plans and controls can be made consistent with one another. Otherwise, strategies can be rendered ineffective by budgeting systems and performance measures which have no strategic content.
Public knowledge	Drucker has argued that an entrepreneur who builds a long-lasting business has 'a theory of the business' which informs his or her business decisions. In large organisations, that theory of the business has to become public knowledge, as decisions cannot be taken by one person.
Time horizon	Some plans are needed for the long-term.
Co-ordinates	Activities of different business functions need to be directed towards a common goal.
Clarifies objectives	Managers are forced to define what they want to achieve.
Allocates responsibility	A plan shows people where they fit in.

3.6 Criticisms of strategic planning

Despite the benefits of strategic planning, many people are critical of the concept for a number of reasons.

(a) Strategic plans often fail due to **outside influences** such as changes in the economic environment, competitor actions and/or technological change.

(b) The strategic planning process often ignores the **political** environment of organisations and the **conflicts** between different power groups.

(c) Strategic planners often miss important signals in **operational level** information. This can make the strategy impractical.

(d) The people who design the strategy are not generally **responsible** for its implementation.

(e) Senior managers are not all-knowing , and there are obviously **limits** to the extent which they can control the behaviour of an organisation.

(f) Strategic plans tend to be too **rigid**, restricting an organisation's ability to be **innovative** when opportunities arise.

(g) Some industries (such as fashion) simply cannot **predict** long-term developments, but must respond to **changes in market demand** and the opportunities that these present.

(h) Strategic planning, if done thoroughly, is always a **costly and time-consuming exercise**, and the benefits are not immediately visible.

Although the idea that planning is the only means by which strategies can be made is flawed, planning does have many uses.

- It can force people to think
- It can publicise strategic decisions
- It can help direct activities in some cases
- It can focus debate

Activity 6 **(20 minutes)**

Using the example of a local recycling business just discussed, look again at these criticisms of strategic planning and state briefly how each of them might apply to this case. Consider a local recycling scheme to see if factors such as lack of operational control or residents' opposition to having a bottle bank sited locally might have an effect.

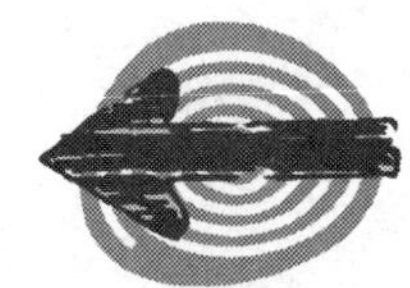

We look at other models of strategic planning in Chapter 7.

Chapter roundup

- Planning helps to bridge the gap between where we are and where we want to be.
- Planning is one of the main management activities, and should be carried out before all other management activities.
- Planning involves taking account of a hierarchy of plans, all of which are related to each other and which cover both the long- and short-term.
- Planning is a cyclical process that must be done thoroughly and in stages.
- Strategic planning is a process of developing the organisation's objectives in the light of threats, opportunities and resources available.
- The strategic planning process involves a detailed understanding of the organisation and the external environment in which it operates.
- Once a strategic option has been chosen, a detailed strategy must be drawn up to show how this option can be successfully implemented.
- Strategy is a course of action, specifying the resources required, to achieve an objective. There are many levels of strategy in an organisation.
  - Corporate: the general direction of the whole organisation
  - Business: how the organisation or its SBUs tackle particular markets.
  - Operational/functional: specific strategies for different departments of the business.
- According to the rational model, strategy is about the achievement of goals and objectives.
  - Mission, goals and objectives. An organisation's mission answers the question 'what business are we in?' Goals and objectives determine what the business should achieve if it is to satisfy its mission.
  - Analysis of the environment of the organisation and its internal position
  - Generation of alternative options to satisfy objectives
  - Choice of preferred option, based on rational and objective criteria of evaluation
- The rational model implies that strategies are best generated from the top down.
- The rational model might work in stable environments. There are practical and theoretical problems in asserting that a planning process is the only or best way of generating strategy.

Quick quiz

1 What is the purpose of planning?

2 Planning is one of the four main types of management activity. What are the other three?

3 Why is planning so important?

4 What does the hierarchy of plans consist of?

5 What is an objective?

6 What are the differences between policies, procedures and rules?

7 What is a programme?

8 What is a budget?

9 What are the components of the planning cycle?

10 What are the main steps in planning?

11 What is a planning horizon?

12 How does strategic planning differ from routine planning?

13 What are the three main components of the strategic planning process?

14 List the advantages of planning.

Answers to quick quiz

1 To decide which objectives need to be achieved and how to meet them.

2 Organising, motivating and controlling.

3 Because it focuses attention on objectives by uniting the organisation and its activities; it removes uncertainty; it facilitates control by supply targets for performance; and it leads to economical operations by emphasising efficiency and consistency.

4 Mission, strategies, policies, procedures, rules, programmes and budgets.

5 Something that the organisation wants to achieve.

6 Policies are general statements that guide thinking and action. Procedures are customary methods of action. Rules are specific statements of what may or may not be done.

7 A collection of activities that need to be carried out to achieve a desired outcome.

8 A statement of expected results expressed in financial terms.

9 Establishing objectives, planning the strategy, deciding tactics, implementing the strategy, reviewing progress.

10 Define the mission, set the objectives, assess the internal environment, assess the external environment, carry out corporate analysis, identify the strategic options, compare these options and select the most suitable strategic option; design strategies; specify tactics, operations and standards; set budgets.

11 The length of time between making a planning decision and implementing that decision.

NOTES

12 Strategic planning is the managerial process of developing and maintaining a strategic fit between the organisation's objectives and resources and its changing market opportunities. Planning that is not linked to a long-term strategy is likely to be a routine task of carrying out programmes.

13 Strategic analysis, strategic choice and strategic implementation

14 Identification of risk
Forces thought and decision-making
Better control
Enforces consistency
Promotes public knowledge
Enables timeliness
Encourages co-ordination
Clarifies objectives
Allocates responsibility

Answers to activities

1 Your list might have included:

- Forecasting the future to identify the planning gap
- Appraisal of the firm's resources
- Researching the environment and the market
- Objective setting
- Planning strategies to achieve the objectives
- Implementing the strategies
- Evaluating the results and amending the strategies

A company that failed to plan for the future, would be likely to fade away as consumers switched to buying TV sets, video recorders and new products, as events proved.

2 The probable outcome in this type of organisation is that all planning – and indeed all other activities – would be done in isolation by separate parts of the organisation. People working in these different parts would make their own decisions based upon their idea of where the organisation was going and how it expected to get there. Although a good communications system might alleviate some of the problems, in reality the organisation would probably suffer from indecision, confusion and a series of disjointed, counterproductive efforts.

3 Your report should have covered each of the stages.

(a) **Establish objectives** – how many teams, how much sponsorship (and in what forms?), fund-raising targets, and so on;

(b) **Plan the strategy** – what organisations to approach, how and by whom, what publicity and advertising;

(c) **Decide tactics** – specific actions by whom and to what timetable;

(d) **Implement the strategy** – detailed arrangements for each event, team briefings, and so on;

(e) **Review progress** – periodic, reporting back and adjustment of the effort, so that progress is maintained according to the quantified plan.

A final overall review should be used in planning for the next year.

4 The corporate objective is profit growth. The corporate strategy is the decision that this will be achieved by entering new markets, rather than producing new products. The business strategy suggests that those markets include Latin America. The operational or functional strategy involves the decision to invest in new plant (the production function) which is to be financed by shares rather than loans (the finance function).

5 Swan Cruises would have benefited from strategic planning, since this process would have ensured that the partners had the right resources to serve the target market. The stages to be covered are as follows.

(a) **Strategic analysis**. Setting out a clear mission statement, objectives, and an assessment of the organisation's resources and capabilities would show if Swan had the potential to achieve its objectives. Assessment of the external environment might predict changes in the economy and in competition likely to affect this ability to achieve objectives. (This can be summarised in a 'SWOT' analysis, which we will come to later.)

(b) **Strategic choice**. This would involve identifying the strategic options and selecting the most suitable. Given their resources and abilities this process many have decided them on a different objective, like day trips, or have made them choose different boats to buy. This would also be related to choice of tactics and operations and their budget.

(c) **Review and control**. These would be essential throughout the planning and implementation of the project so that they know if they are achieving targets and working within budget limits.

6 Your list might have included examples like those shown below.

(a) Strategic plans often fail due to outside influences such as changes in the economic environment, competitor actions and/or technological change. At first newspaper recycling paid quite well, then there was a glut of newsprint as Scandinavian and Canadian planting projects reached harvest stage, and then recycled paper was not worth collecting. Now there is a shortage of newsprint again as newspapers have become bigger. Changes in government investment allowances can affect the viability of a project.

(b) The strategic planning process often ignores the 'political' environment of organisations and the conflicts between different power groups. A change of control in the council could affect its priorities, or pressure could bring about changes in resource allocation.

(c) Strategic planners often miss important signals in operational-level information. This can make the strategy impractical. There could be resistance because workers lose traditional perks, like selling scrap.

(d) The people who design the strategy are not generally responsible for its implementation. Planning is often not based on reality. One collection scheme failed because dustcarts with a trailer attached could not negotiate narrow streets with parked cars, another because residents and businesses would not separate materials.

(e) Senior managers are not all-knowing, and there are obviously limits to the extent to which they can control the behaviour of an organisation. The move to competitive tendering for collection services could mean that time pressure for clearing a round result in staff having to skimp on procedures.

(f) Strategic plans tend to be too rigid, restricting an organisation's ability to be innovative when opportunities arise. New opportunities for recycling could be missed because the plan dealt with only certain materials or types of customer for advice.

(g) Some industries (such as fashion) simply cannot predict long-term developments, but must respond to changes in market demand and the opportunities which these present. This is unlikely to apply in recycling, but government policy can change quite suddenly and this could affect demand, especially for consultancy.

(h) Strategic planning, if done thoroughly, is always a costly and time-consuming exercise, and the benefits are not immediately visible. It does not fit well into the one year planning and budget cycle of a local authority.

Chapter 7 :
DIFFERENT APPROACHES TO STRATEGIC PLANNING

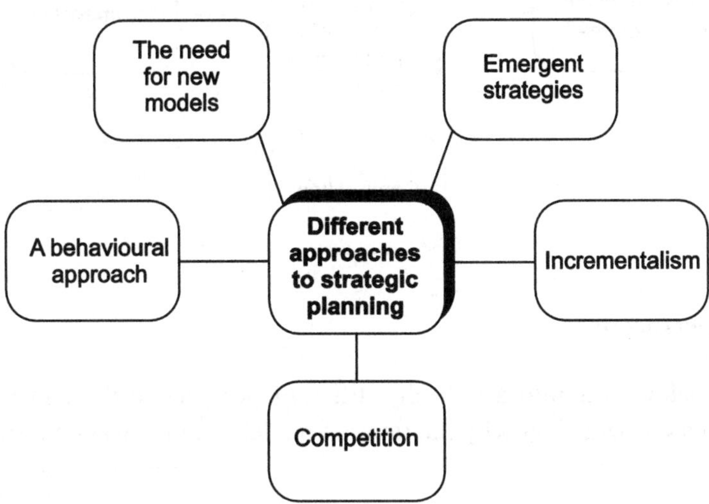

Introduction

This chapter contains some alternative approaches to the rational model. The **incrementalist model** suggests that small scale adjustments are preferred to wholesale reviews.

Both the incrementalists and *Johnson and Scholes* (2002) recognise the political and **behavioural context.** *Mintzberg's* **emergent strategies** model suggests that some strategies develop by accident, and strategic management involves shaping or **crafting** these developments from the **bottom-up.** *Porter* describes strategy in **competitive** terms.

Your objectives

In this chapter you will learn about the following.

(a) Incremental and emergent approaches to strategy and the benefits and limitations of each

(b) The impact of competition on strategic choices

1 THE NEED FOR NEW MODELS

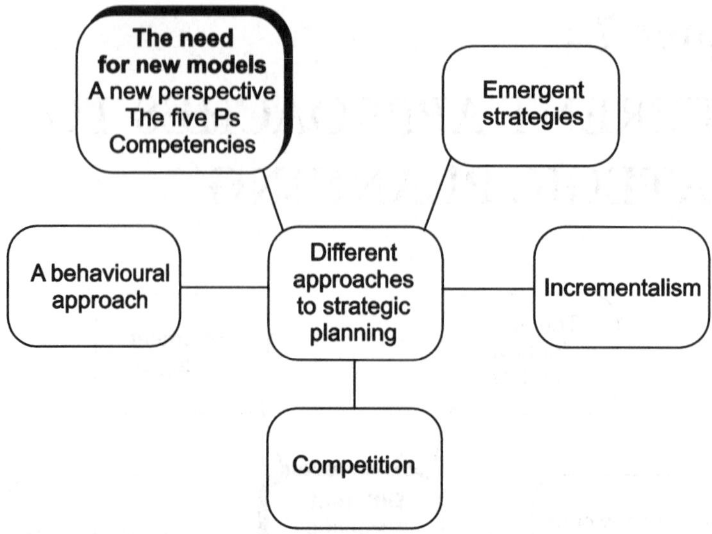

1.1 A new perspective

The example below puts into a radically different perspective the issues raised in the previous chapters. It will show why the rational model cannot always be trusted.

EXAMPLE:

Honda

Honda is now one of the leading manufacturers of motorbikes. The company is credited with identifying and targeting an untapped market for small 50cc bikes in the US, which enabled it to expand, trounce European competition and severely damage indigenous US bike manufacturers. By 1965, Honda had 63% of the US market. But this occurred by accident. On entering the US market, Honda's planned strategy was to compete with the larger European and US bikes of 250ccs and over. These bikes had a defined market, and were sold through dedicated motorbike dealerships. Disaster struck when Honda's larger machines developed faults – they had not been designed for the hard wear and tear imposed by US motorcyclists. Honda had to recall the larger machines.

Honda had made little effort to sell its small 50 cc motorbikes – its staff rode them on errands around Los Angeles. Sports goods shops and ordinary bicycle and department stores had expressed an interest, but Honda did not want to confuse its image in its 'target' market of men who bought the larger bikes.

The faults in Honda's larger machines meant that reluctantly, Honda had no alternative but to sell the small 50cc bikes just to raise money. They proved very popular with people who would never have bought motorbikes before. Eventually the company adopted this new market with enthusiasm with the slogan: 'You meet the nicest people on a Honda.'

The strategy had emerged, against managers' conscious intentions, but they eventually responded to the new situation.

1.2 The five Ps

Mintzberg's (2000) overview of the work of many writers on strategy suggests five ways in which the term strategy is used. A strategy can be a plan, ploy pattern, position or perspective. They are not mutually exclusive.

'P'	Comment
Plan	A 'consciously intended course of action'.
Ploy	A manoeuvre in a competitive game. For example, a firm might add unnecessary plant capacity. The strategy is not to produce the goods but to **discourage a competitor** from entering the market.
Pattern	Emergent strategies fit into this definition.
Position	**Environmental fit** and relationships with other organisations. A position might be a distinctive niche, whereby the firm makes distinctive products or services or exploits a **distinct competence**.
Perspective	A unique way of looking at the world, of interpreting information from it, judging its opportunities and choices and acting. Different strategic perspectives might respond to the same environmental stimulus in different ways.

Activity 1 **(10 mins)**

Here are some issues of strategy. Which of *Mintzberg's* categories (plan, position, ploy, perspective, pattern) do you think they fit into?

(a) The general manager of the Beardsley Hospital prepares a strategy. To minimise the time doctors spend walking from place to place she has rearranged the hospital so that services are clustered around patients. She has the resources so that this change will be phased in over three years, first Ophthalmology, second Oncology, third Paediatrics, and so on.

(b) Two market traders sell fruit and vegetables. One decides to specialise in exotic fruits, as he feels there are enough well-off and/or experimentally minded people in his area to make it worth his while.

1.3 Competencies

Definition

The **distinctive competence** of an organisation is what it does well, uniquely, or better than its rivals. For example, for a relatively undifferentiated product like cement, the ability of a maker to run a truck fleet more effectively than its competitors will give it competitive strengths (if, for example, it can satisfy orders quickly).

Strategic opportunities must be related to the firm's resources. A strategic approach involves identifying a firm's **competencies**. Members of organisations develop judgements about what they think the company can do well – **its core of competence**. These competencies may come about in a variety of ways.

- **Experience** in making and marketing a product or service
- The talents and potential of **individuals** in the organisation
- The **quality of co-ordination**

2 EMERGENT STRATEGIES

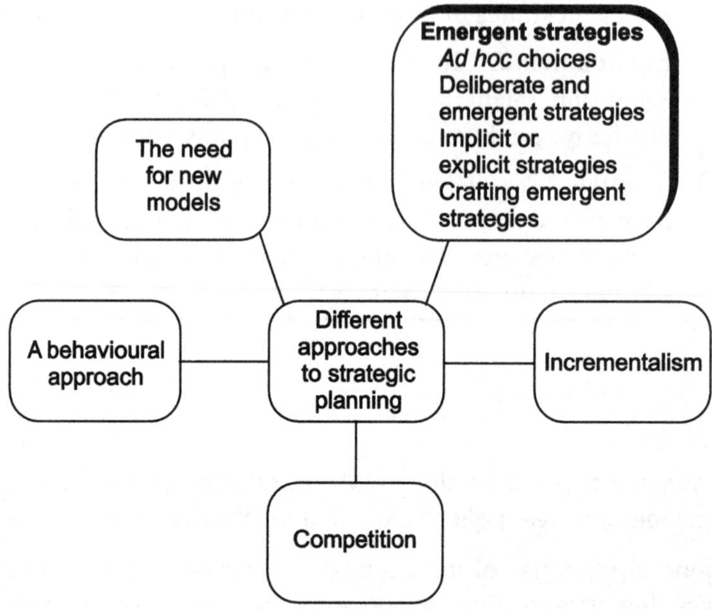

2.1 *Ad hoc* choices

In the Honda case example at the beginning of this chapter, we mentioned that the planned strategy of selling large motorbikes had to give way to a strategy which had emerged by accident, almost. *Mintzberg* (2000) develops this theme further.

Definition

> **Emergent strategies** do not arise out of conscious strategic planning, but from a number of *ad hoc* choices, perhaps made **lower down the hierarchy**. They may not initially be recognised as being of strategic importance. Emergent strategies develop out of patterns of behaviour, in contrast to planned strategies or senior management decisions which are **imposed from above**.

An activity will make the point clearer.

Activity 2 **(20 minutes)**

Aldebaran Ltd is a public relations agency founded by an entrepreneur, Estella Grande, who has employed various talented individuals from other agencies to set up in business. Estella Grande wants Aldebaran Ltd to become the largest public relations agency in North London. Management consultants, in a planning document, have suggested growth by acquisition. In other words, Aldebaran should buy up the other public relations agencies in the area. These would be retained as semi-independent business units, as the Aldebaran Ltd group could benefit from the goodwill of the newly acquired agencies. When Estella presents these ideas to the Board there is general consensus with one significant exception. Livia Strange, the marketing director, is horrified. 'How am I going to sell this to my staff? Ever since we've been in business, we've won business by undercutting and slagging off the competition. My team have a whole culture based on it. I give them champagne if they pinch a high value client. Why acquire these new businesses – why not stick to pinching their clients instead?'

What is the source of the conflict?

2.2 Deliberate and emergent strategies

The diagram below should help explain the point.

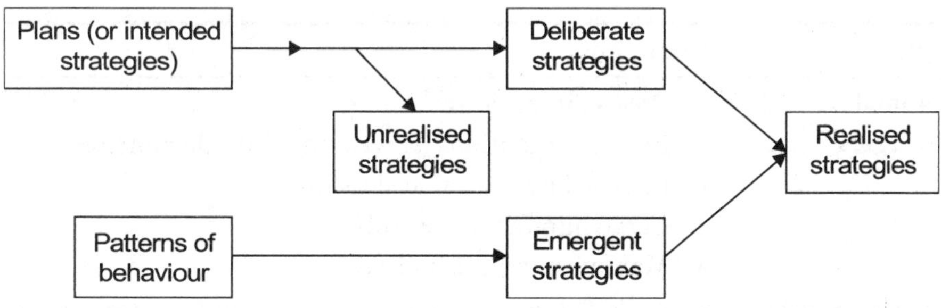

Figure 7.1: Genesis of strategies
Adapted from Mintzberg (2000)

(a) **Intended strategies** are plans. Those plans or aspects of plans which are actually realised are called **deliberate strategies**.

(b) **Emergent strategies** are those which develop out of patterns of behaviour.

The task of **strategic management** is to control and shape these emergent strategies as they develop.

EXAMPLE: BPP

BPP began life as a training company. Lecturers had to prepare course material. This was offered for sale in a bookshop in the BPP building. Owing to the demand, BPP began offering its material to other colleges, in the UK and worldwide. BPP Learning Media, which began as a small offshoot of BPP's training activities, is now a leading publisher in the market for targeted study material for the examinations of many professional bodies. It is unlikely that this development was anticipated when the course material was first prepared.

No realised strategy will be wholly deliberate or wholly emergent. The line between deliberate and emergent elements within each strategy will be in part influenced by organisation structure and culture.

2.3 Implicit or explicit strategies

Entrepreneurs often have a **theory of the business**, which they may or may not document.

- Implicit strategies may exist only in the chief executive's mind
- Explicit strategies are properly documented

Some plans are more explicit than others.

With these in mind, *Mintzberg* (2000) identified eight styles of strategic management.

Style	Comment
Planned strategies	• Precise intentions • Explicit intentions (ie written down, documented) • Imposed by central leadership • Large number of controls • Maximises predictability
Entrepreneurial strategies	• Intended strategy derives from the vision of strong leadership • Not always explicit
Ideological strategies	• Intended strategy is the collective vision of the organisation's members • Control is through shared values • These strategies involve changing the environment
Umbrella strategies	• Strategic targets ('ends') are defined and deliberate • How they are achieved ('means') is emergent
Process strategies	• Processes are formal (eg hiring) and deliberate • Content of strategies (what is done) is emergent
Disconnected strategies	• Members of subunits 'do their own thing' • Strategies are emergent for the whole organisation, deliberate for subunits
Consensus strategies	• Groups in the organisation converge on common patterns of activity
Imposed strategies	• Strategy is imposed by the environment (eg a strong customer) – which pre-empts the organisation's own choice

2.4 Crafting emergent strategies

Managers cannot simply let emerging strategies take over. Why?

(a) **Direction.** The emergent strategy may be **inappropriate** for the long-term direction of the organisation and may have to be corrected.

(b) **Resources**. It may have future implications for **resource use** elsewhere: in most organisations, different parts of the business compete for resources.

(c) Managers might wish to build on the strategy by **actively devoting more resources** to it.

Mintzberg (2000) uses the metaphor of **crafting strategy** to help understand the idea. Strategies are shaped as they develop, with managers giving help and guidance, devoting more resources to some, exploiting new opportunities and **responding** to developments. For example, Honda's management reacted to the emergent strategy, eventually, and shaped its development.

Separating 'thinking' and 'doing' has the following result.

(a) A **purely deliberate strategy prevents learning**. For example it is hard with deliberate strategies to 'learn from mistakes', or stumble by accident into strategic growth.

(b) A **purely emergent strategy defies control.** It may in fact be a bad strategy!

Deliberate strategies introduce strategic change as a sort of quantum leap in some organisations. In this case, a firm undergoes only a few strategic changes in a short period but these are very dramatic.

The strategist must be able to **recognise** patterns and to manage the process by which emergent strategies are created. In other words, the strategist must be able to **find strategies** as well as **invent them**.

How to craft strategy

Mintzberg (2000) lists these activities in crafting strategy.

Activity	Comment
Manage stability	• Most of the time, managers should be implementing the strategies, not planning them. • Obsessions with change are dysfunctional. Knowing when to change is more important. • Formal planning is the detailed working out of the agreed strategy.
Detect discontinuity	• Environments do not change regularly, nor are they always turbulent, though managers should be on the lookout for changes. Some small environmental changes are more significant for the long term than others, though guessing which these are is a problem.
Know the business	• An intimate feel for the business has to include an awareness and understanding of operations.
Manage patterns	• Detect emerging patterns and to help them take shape. Some emergent strategies must be uprooted, others nurtured.
Reconciling change and continuity	• 'Crafting strategy ... requires a natural synthesis of the future, present and past.'

Activity 3 **(15 minutes)**

Britannia Hospital has just appointed a new director, Florian Vole, imported from the private sector, where he had run 'Hanky House' a niche retail operation specialising in handkerchiefs and fashion accessories. The recession put the business into receivership, but Mr Vole was sought out to inject his private sector expertise into running a public sector institution. He calls a meeting of the hospital's senior managerial, medical and nursing staffs. 'What the public sector has been missing too long is vision, and when you're eyeball-to-eyeball with change, it's vision that you need, not planning documents and statistics. We need to be nimble and quick to adapt to our customer's ever changing needs. That is our strategy!'

What do you think of Florian Vole's approach?

3 A BEHAVIOURAL APPROACH

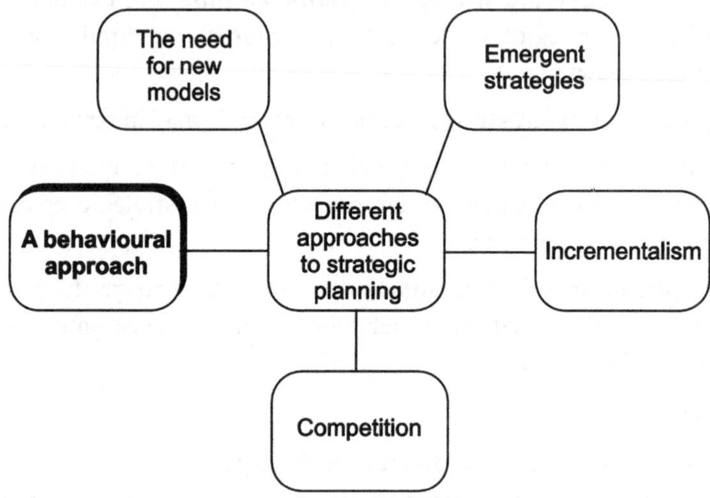

Johnson and Scholes (2002) state that 'strategy needs to be understood as an outcome of the social, political and cultural processes of management in organisations'. They describe the following phases in the strategic decision-making process.

Step 1 **Problem awareness**

(a) Internal results, customer responses or environmental changes can make individuals aware of a problem.

(b) A trigger alerts the formal information system to the problem, so that organisational activity takes over from the individual's consideration of the problem.

Step 2 **Problem diagnosis**. Managers try to analyse and get to the root of the problem.

Step 3 **Solution development**. Solutions begin with a vague idea, which is further refined and explored by internal discussion.

(a) Memory search: solutions which worked in the past

(b) Passive search: wait for a solution to suggest itself

From the possible solutions, the best fit to the problem is selected and developed.

Step 4 **Solution selection**

(a) **Eliminate unacceptable plans.** This screening process involves bargaining, diplomacy and judgement rather than formal evaluation according to the business case.

(b) **Endorsements.** Many strategic decisions originate from management subsystems, which senior managers authorise. Junior managers might filter strategic information, or ignore certain options, to protect themselves.

FOR DISCUSSION

A criticism of the rational model is that it ignores the fact that strategists are human beings, and strategy formation reflects the internal politics of the organisation.

4 INCREMENTALISM

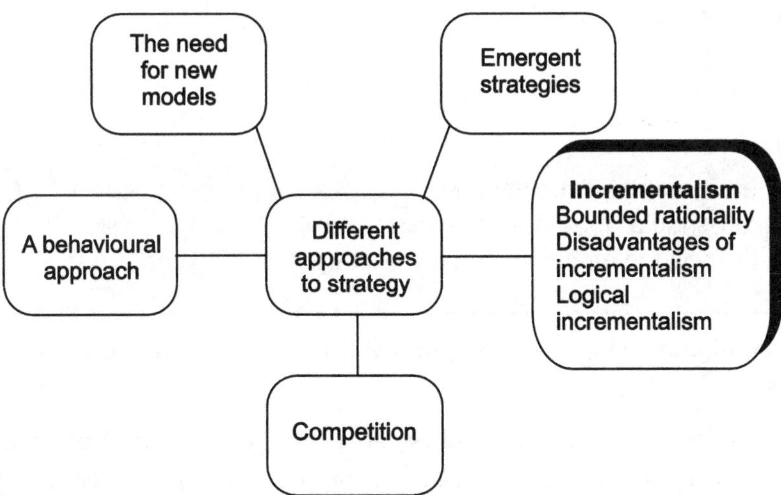

4.1 Bounded rationality

In practice, managers are limited by time, by the information they have and by their own skills, habits and reflexes.

- Strategic managers do **not** evaluate all the possible options open to them in a given situation, but choose from a small number of possibilities.
- Strategy making necessitates compromises with interested groups through political bargaining. This is called **partisan mutual adjustment**.
- The manager **does not optimise** (ie get the best possible solution).
- Instead **the manager satisfices.** The manager carries on searching until he or she finds an option which appears tolerably satisfactory, and adopts it, even though it may be less than perfect. This approach Herbert Simon characterised as **bounded rationality**.

NOTES

Definition

Incrementalism involves small scale extensions of past practices.

- It avoids major errors.
- It is more likely to be acceptable, because consultation, compromise and accommodation are built into the process

4.2 Disadvantages of incrementalism

- Incrementalism does not work where radical new approaches are needed, and it has a built-in **conservative** bias. Forward planning does have a role.
- Incrementalism ignores the influence of **corporate culture**, which filters out unacceptable choices.
- It might only apply to a **stable** environment.

4.3 Logical incrementalism

Definition

Logical incrementalism: managers have a vague notion as to where the organisation should go, but strategies should be tested in small steps, simply because there is too much uncertainty about actual outcomes.

Strategy is best described as a **learning process**. Logical incrementalism has the best of both worlds.

- The broad outlines of a strategy are developed by an in-depth review
- There is still practical scope for day-to-day incremental decision making

5 COMPETITION

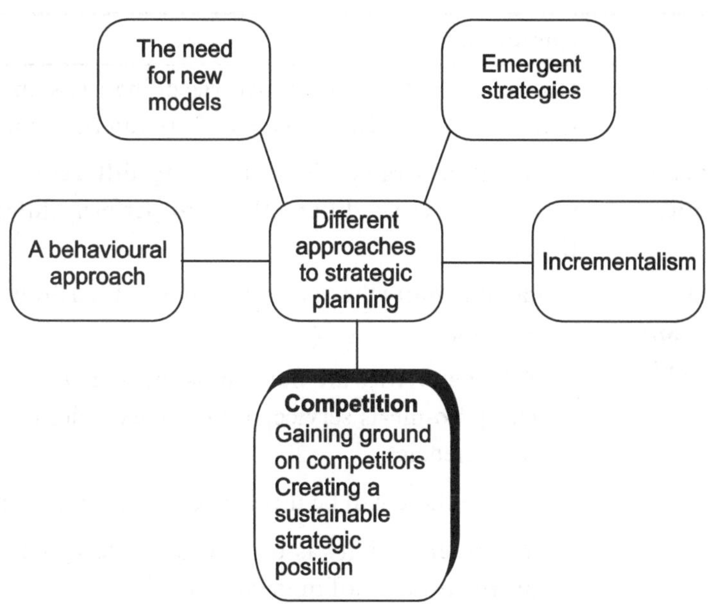

5.1 Gaining ground on competitors

Most businesses face competitors. According to *Ohmae* (1982), what counts is performance in **relative terms.** 'A good business strategy' is 'one by which a firm can gain significant ground on its competitors at an acceptable cost'.

Method	Comment
Re-adjust current resources	Identify the key factors for success (or distinctive competence) and concentrate resources on these activities.
Relative superiority	A relative advantage can still be achieved by exploiting the competitors' actual or potential weaknesses.
Challenge assumptions	Challenge the accepted assumptions of doing business in a particular market (eg telephone and Internet banking challenges the need for branch networks in banks).
Degrees of freedom	Finding new ways of exploit markets (eg by segmentation, product/service differentiation etc).

In all cases, direct competition on the competitors' own turf is avoided. Successful strategy is the interplay of **three Cs**: **customers, competitors** and the **corporation.** *Ohmae* (1982) calls this the **strategic triangle.**

Michael Porter (1996) defines strategy in similar competitive terms.

Definition

Competitive strategy is 'the taking of offensive or defensive actions to create a defendable position within an industry ... and ... a superior return on investment'. (*Porter*, 1996)

NOTES

5.2 Creating a sustainable strategic position

Task	Comment
Operational effectiveness	Operational effectiveness involves doing the **same** things better than other firms. Improvements here can be imitated.
Strategy rests on unique activities	Competitive strategy is about being **different** ... choosing to perform activities differently or to perform different activities than rivals.'
A sustainable strategic position requires trade-offs	Trade-offs limit what a company does. Trade-offs occur in three ways. • When activities are not compatible (eg an airline can offer a cheap no-meals service, or offer meals; doing both results in inefficiencies). • Where there will be inconsistencies in image and reputation. • Where an activity is over or underdesigned for its use (eg overqualified staff in menial positions).
Strategy is about combining activities	This is hard to imitate.
Strategy is about choices, not blindly imitating competitors	Many firms operate inefficiently, and so can benefit by improving operational effectiveness.

Chapter roundup

- Strategy is often seen to arise from a pattern of senior management decisions, and must always be related to available resources and competences.
- *Mintzberg* suggests that 'strategy' is used to mean plan, a ploy, a pattern, a position and a perspective.
- *Johnson and Scholes* suggest an approach which follows a similar outline to the rational model, but which accounts for the 'political' and cultural influences on managers.
- The rational approach also fails to identify emergent strategies, or allow for them, according to *Mintzberg*. Operations level can be a source of strategic change. Emergent strategies arise out of patterns of behaviour. They are not the result of the conscious intentions of senior managers. They have to be shaped or crafted. Realised strategies include intended and emergent strategies.
- Approaches to strategic management differ in the extent to which they are deliberate or emergent, and the extent to which they are explicit or implicit.
- *Porter* and *Ohmae* see business strategy in competitive terms. Competitive advantage is always relative to competitors.
- Many businesses, concentrating on improving operational effectiveness, have lost sight of the fact that strategy is unique. It involves making trade-offs, choices and combining activities.
- Managers are not able to take all factors into account. Bounded rationality forces them to satisfice not optimise.
- Incrementalism involves small scale adjustments to current policies, as they are less risky.

Quick quiz

1 What is a distinctive competence?

2 Distinguish between deliberate strategies and emergent strategies.

3 How does *Mintzberg* suggest strategy is crafted?

4 According to *Johnson and Scholes*, what happens in 'problem diagnosis'?

5 What is meant by optimising and satisficing?

6 What are the problems with incrementalism?

7 What is logical incrementalism?

8 What are the three sides of the strategic triangle?

Answers to quick quiz

1 What the organisation does well, uniquely or better than its rivals.

2 Deliberate strategies are actually realised and arise out of plans (or intended strategies). Emergent strategies arise out of *ad hoc* choices, and patterns of behaviour, perhaps lower down the hierarchy.

3 *Mintzberg* sees the following stages in crafting strategy:

   Manage stability

   Detect discontinuity

   Know the business

   Manage patterns

   Reconciling charge and continuity

4 Problems are analysed to try and understand their cause.

5 Optimising is getting the best possible solution. Satisficing is getting a solution which is satisfactory, rather than perfect.

6 Essentially conservative ignores corporate culture and might only apply to a stable environment.

7 Logical incrementalism combines both rational and incremental approaches in that managers have an idea where they are going (because strategy has been developed in outline), but there is still scope to adapt incrementally for future uncertainties.

8 Customers, competitors and the corporation.

Answers to activities

1 (a) This is probably strategy as plan. A document is being prepared by senior management.

   (b) This is strategy as position. The market trader specialising in exotic fruit is trying to carve himself a niche.

2 Livia Strange's department has generated its own pattern of competitive behaviour. It is an emergent strategy. It conflicts directly with the planned strategy proposed by the consultants. This little case history also makes the additional point that strategies are not only about numbers, targets and grand plans, but about the organisational cultures influencing a person's behaviour.

3 Mr Vole hasn't quite made the transition from the fashion industry, where desire for silk handkerchiefs is relatively fickle, to an institution like Britannia Hospital. Here planning is necessary. Resources must be obtained to cope with future needs. Customer needs are likely to be fairly basic (ie security, comfort, medical attention, stimulation). However, in the actual delivery of care and services, Florian Vole has a point: experimentation with new care techniques might improve the hospital's service to its patients.

Part C

Strategy Evaluation and Selection

Chapter 8 :
STRATEGY EVALUATION

Introduction

This chapter aims to show how a systematic and rational approach to evaluating company strategic options can be achieved.

Your objectives

In this chapter you will learn about the following.

(a) The concepts behind strategy evaluation

(b) Examples of evaluation techniques

(c) The importance of risk assessment in strategy evaluation

1 EVALUATION

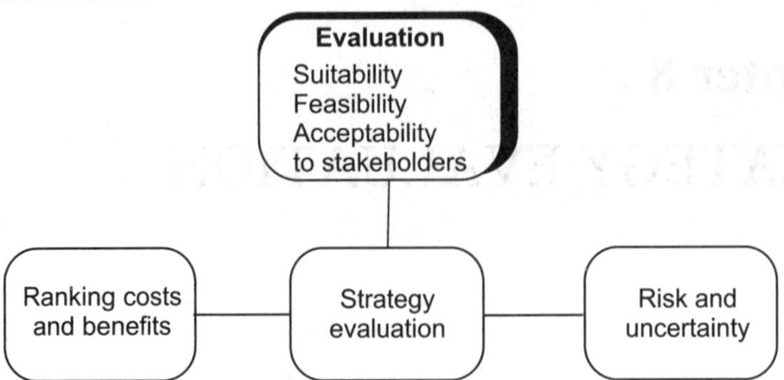

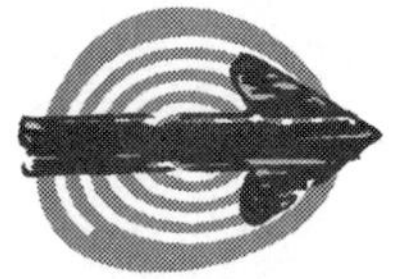

According to the rational model, individual strategies have to be evaluated, according to a number of criteria, before a strategy or a mixture of strategies is chosen. As noted in the syllabus, these three criteria are suitability (appropriateness), feasibility and acceptability (or desirability).

1.1 Suitability

Suitability relates to the **strategic logic** of the strategy. The strategy should fit the situation of the firm. It should satisfy a range of requirements.

- **Exploit** company strengths and distinctive **competencies**
- Rectify company **weaknesses**
- **Neutralise** or deflect environmental **threats**
- Help the firm to seize **opportunities**
- **Satisfy the goals** of organisation
- **Fill the gap** identified by gap analysis
- Generate/maintain **competitive advantage**
- Involve an acceptable level of **risk**
- Suit the **politics** and corporate **culture**

1.2 Feasibility

Feasibility asks whether the strategy can in fact be implemented. This depends on the capacities of the organisation.

Activity 1 **(20 minutes)**

Think of some examples of the organisational capacities to be evaluated when considering a strategy.

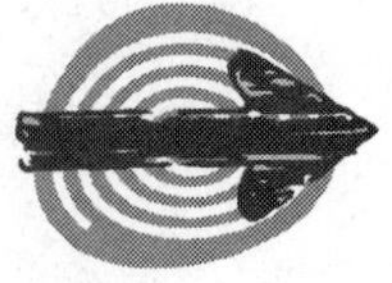

Strategies which do not make use of the existing competences, and which therefore call for new competencies to be acquired, might not be feasible since gaining competencies takes time and can be costly.

1.3 Acceptability to stakeholders

The acceptability of a strategy relates to people's expectations of it. It is here that **stakeholder analysis** can be brought in.

(a) **Financial considerations.** Strategies will be evaluated by considering how far they contribute to meeting the dominant objective of increasing shareholder wealth.

   (i) Return on investment
   (ii) Cash flow
   (iii) Profits
   (iv) Price/Earnings
   (v) Growth
   (vi) Market capitalisation
   (vii) EPS

(b) **Customers** may object to a strategy if it means reducing service, but on the other hand they may have no choice.

(c) **Banks** are interested in the implications for cash resources, debt levels and so on.

(d) **Government.** A strategy involving a takeover may be prohibited under competition legislation.

(e) **The public.** The environmental impact may cause key stakeholders to protest – out of town superstores are now frowned upon by national and local government.

(f) **Risk.** Different shareholders have different attitudes to risk. A strategy which changed the risk/return profile, for whatever reason, may not be acceptable.

2 RANKING COSTS AND BENEFITS

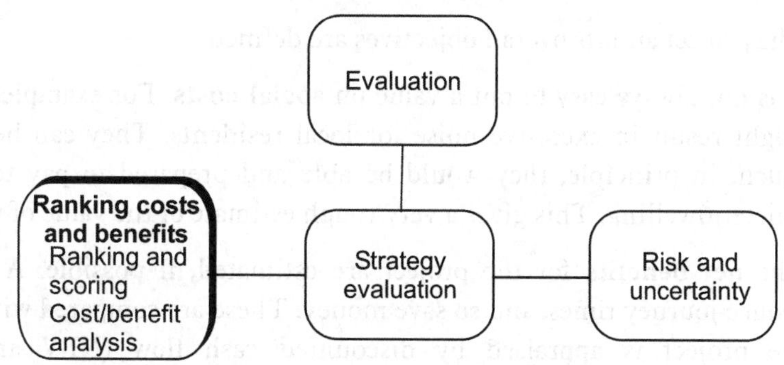

FOR DISCUSSION

A strategy can be assessed on how it achieves the organisation's objectives, but some **objectives may conflict** and the choice may not be clear cut. Try to think of some examples.

NOTES

2.1 Ranking and scoring

Ranking and scoring methods are best illustrated by means of a simple example. The **objectives are weighted** in relative **importance** (eg minimising competitive threats may be more important than other objectives). We assume for the example below that the strategic options cannot be realistically combined.

Objectives **Strategic option**	*Growth in profit by over 10%*	*Reduce dependence on suppliers*	*Minimise competitive threats*	*Score*	*Rank*
Objective weighting	4	3	5		
Do nothing	X	X	X	–	–
Cut costs by subcontracting	✓	X	X	4	3rd
Expand product range	✓	X	✓	9	1st
Offer discounts to customers for fixed term contract	X	X	✓	5	2nd

In the above example, expanding the product range would be chosen as the firm believes it will enhance profits and minimise competitive threats.

In many cases, the strategies may not be mutually exclusive, or it might be possible to implement all the strategic options.

2.2 Cost/benefit analysis

Cost/benefit analysis (CBA) is a strategy evaluation technique often used in the public sector, where many of the costs and benefits of a project are **intangible** and where market forces do not capture all costs and benefits.

(a) The project and its overall objectives are defined.

(b) It is not always easy to put a value on **social costs**. For example, a new road might result in excessive noise for local residents. They can be asked how much, in principle, they would be able and prepared to pay to move to a quieter dwelling. This gives a very rough estimate of the value of tranquillity.

(c) The **net benefits** for the project are estimated, if possible. A road might reduce journey times, and so save money. These are compared with costs, and the project is appraised by discounted cash flow (NPV and IRR) or cost/benefit ratios.

Private sector companies might be interested in CBA for the following reasons.

(a) CBA can be applied **internally** (eg assessing an information systems project).

(b) **It can help them negotiate with public sector officials.** For example, large building projects require permission from the local authority. Local government officials sometimes insist on certain social benefits to be included in a project, so that some of the potential nuisance costs can be covered.

3 RISK AND UNCERTAINTY

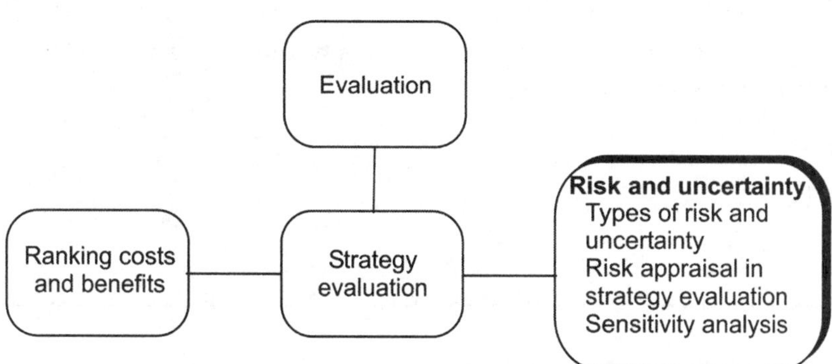

Strategies, by definition, deal with future events: the future cannot be predicted. We can make a distinction between **risk** and **uncertainty,** but often the terms are used **interchangeably**.

Definitions

- **Risk** is sometimes used to describe situations where outcomes are not known, but their probabilities can be estimated. (This is the underlying principle behind insurance.)
- **Uncertainty** is present when the outcome cannot be predicted or assigned probabilities. (Many insurance policies exclude 'war damage, riots and civil commotion'.)

3.1 Types of risk and uncertainty

Risk	Comment
Physical risk	Earthquakes, fire, flooding, and equipment breakdown. In the long-term, climatic changes: global warming, drought (relevant to water firms).
Economic risk	Assumptions about the economic environment might turn out to be wrong. Not even the government forecasts are perfect.
Financial risk	This term has a specific technical meaning: **the risk to shareholders caused by debt finance**. The risk exists because the debt finance providers have first call on the company's profits. The need to pay interest might prevent capital growth or the payment of dividends, particularly when trading is difficult. The converse is that when business is buoyant, interest payments are easily covered and shareholders receive the benefit of the remaining profits.
Business risk	Lowering of entry barriers (eg new technology); changes in customer/supplier industries leading to changed relative power; new competitors and factors internal to the firm (eg its culture or technical systems); management misunderstanding of core competences; volatile cash flows; uncertain returns; changed investor perceptions increasing the required rate of return.
Political risk	Nationalisation, sanctions, civil war, political instability, can all have an impact on the business.

Activity 2 **(15 minutes)**

A firm might require that all investments make a return of, say, 5%. How might the following measures be adjusted for risk?

(a) Return

(b) Payback

(c) Finance

3.2 Risk appraisal in strategy evaluation

Planners try to **quantify the risk**, so as to compare the estimated riskiness of different strategies.

(a) **Rule of thumb** methods might express a range of values from worst possible result to best possible result with a best estimate lying between these two extremes.

(b) **Basic probability theory** expresses the likelihood of a forecast result occurring. This would evaluate the data given by informing the decision-maker that there is, for example, a 50% probability that the best estimate will be achieved, a 25% chance that the worst result will occur and a 25% chance that the best possible result will occur. This evaluation of risk might help the executive to decide between alternative strategies, each with its own risk profile.

3.3 Sensitivity analysis

Ansoff suggests that **sensitivity analysis** should be used in measuring risk. This involves:

- Identifying each variable factor in the calculation
- Assessing the effect on the result if the variable was amended by x% up or down.

This will highlight those variables which are most likely to have a significant effect on the final result. This helps managers identify which strategies are the riskiest, as certain environmental variables might lead to great volatility in returns.

Sensitivity analysis involves asking 'what if?' questions, and so it can be used for strategic planning. By changing the value of different variables in the model, a number of different **scenarios** for the future will be produced.

EXAMPLE

Wage increases can be altered to 10% from 5%; demand for a product can be reduced from 100,000 to 80,000, the introduction of new processing equipment can be deferred by six months, on the revised assumption that there will be delays, and so on. Sensitivity analysis can be formalised by identifying key variables in the model and then changing the value of each, perhaps in progressive steps.

For example, wage costs might be increased in steps by 5%, 7½%, 10%, 12½% and 15% and the effect on profits and cash- flows under each of these five wage cost assumptions can be tested.

In this way, a full picture would emerge of how the achievement of planning targets would be affected by different values for each key variable. **Once the most critical variables have been established,** management then can:

(a) **Apply the most stringent controls** to the most critical variables.

(b) **Alter the plans** so that the most critical variables are no longer as critical. For example, if a car manufacturing company's marketing management are planning to stop producing an old model of car and switch production resources to an entirely new model, sensitivity analysis might show that its profitability will be critically dependent on the speed with which the new model gains acceptance in the market.

(c) Choose a lower-risk plan. For example, if a London-based company has the choice of expanding its operations into either the rest of the UK or into France and the Low Countries, it might find that Continental operations would offer prospects of bigger profits, but the risk of failure might be bigger too and so it might opt to expand in the UK instead.

Chapter roundup

- Strategies are evaluated according to their suitability to the firm's situation, their feasibility in terms of resources and competences and their acceptability to key stakeholder groups (eg shareholders).
- Management can use a number of techniques to assess a firm's current situation, to suggest plans for the future, and to evaluate the viability of different strategic options. None of these techniques should be considered as anything other than 'tools to think with'. All aim to clarify strategic decision making by simplifying it.
- Much strategy evaluation is involved with reducing the risk of a particular course of action, or assessing what that risk is. Risk is classified as business, financial, economic, political and physical.
- Ranking and scoring methods enable the strategist to give weights to certain objectives, and to score a strategy or set of strategies accordingly.
- Risk can sometimes be quantified, using probability theory. The standard deviation of a number of outcomes is a measure of risk.
- Sensitivity analysis is a way of analysing the degree to which a strategy is vulnerable to changes in certain variables.

Quick quiz

1 What three criteria are used to evaluate strategies?

2 Why do organisations use ranking and scoring methods?

3 List five types of risk and uncertainty.

4 What is sensitivity analysis?

Answers to quick quiz

1 Suitability
Feasibility
Acceptability

2 Ranking and scoring methods enable business to compare strategies which support some objectives and not others, by weighting objectives according to their relative importance.

3 Physical
Economic
Financial
Business
Political

4 Sensitivity analysis involves identifying all variables in a decision, and assessing the effect on the result if these variables are amended. A number of different anticipated scenarios can be produced.

Answers to activities

1
- Enough **money**
- The **ability** to deliver the goods/services specified in the strategy
- The ability to deal with the likely **responses that competitors** will make
- Access to **technology, materials and resources**
- Enough **time** to implement the strategy

2
(a) **Return**. The target return could be raised to compensate for the risk.

(b) **Payback**. To protect cash-flows, it might be made a condition of all new investment projects that the project should pay back within a certain period of time.

(c) **Finance**. It might be determined that the investment should be financed under strict conditions (eg only from profits).

Chapter 9 :
STRATEGY SELECTION

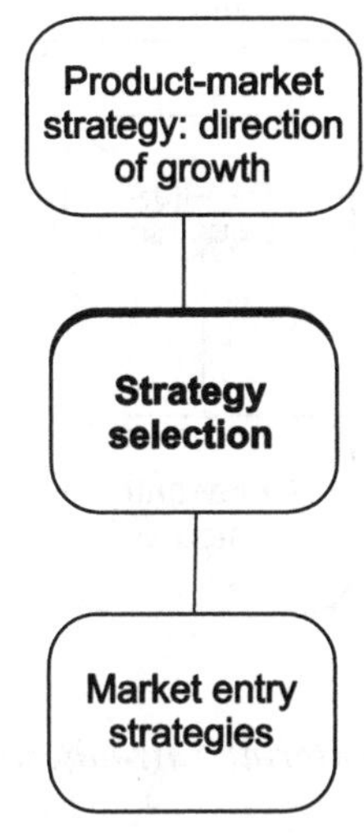

Introduction

Once strategic options have been evaluated, then a choice needs to be made. This chapter builds on the outline of strategic positioning begun in Chapter 5, and goes into more detail on *Ansoff's* model – **where** you compete, and also the **method** of growth.

Your objectives

In this chapter you will learn more about the following.

(a) The *Ansoff* matrix of product-market strategies

(b) Methods of growth, and the issues to consider when selecting a strategy

1 PRODUCT-MARKET STRATEGY: DIRECTION OF GROWTH

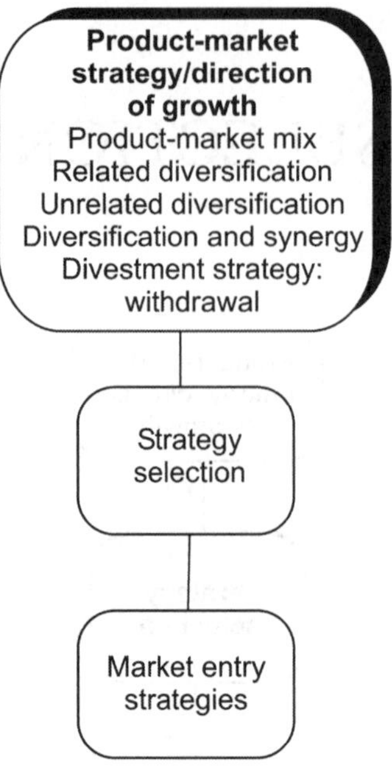

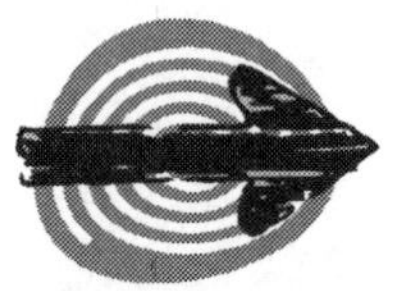

In this section we elaborate on material introduced in Chapter 5 in the context of strategic positioning.

Definition

Product-market mix is a short-hand term for the products/services a firm sells (or a service which a public sector organisation provides) and the markets it sells them to.

1.1 Product-market mix

Ansoff (1987) drew up a **growth vector matrix**, describing a combination of a firm's activities in current and new markets, with **existing** and **new** products.

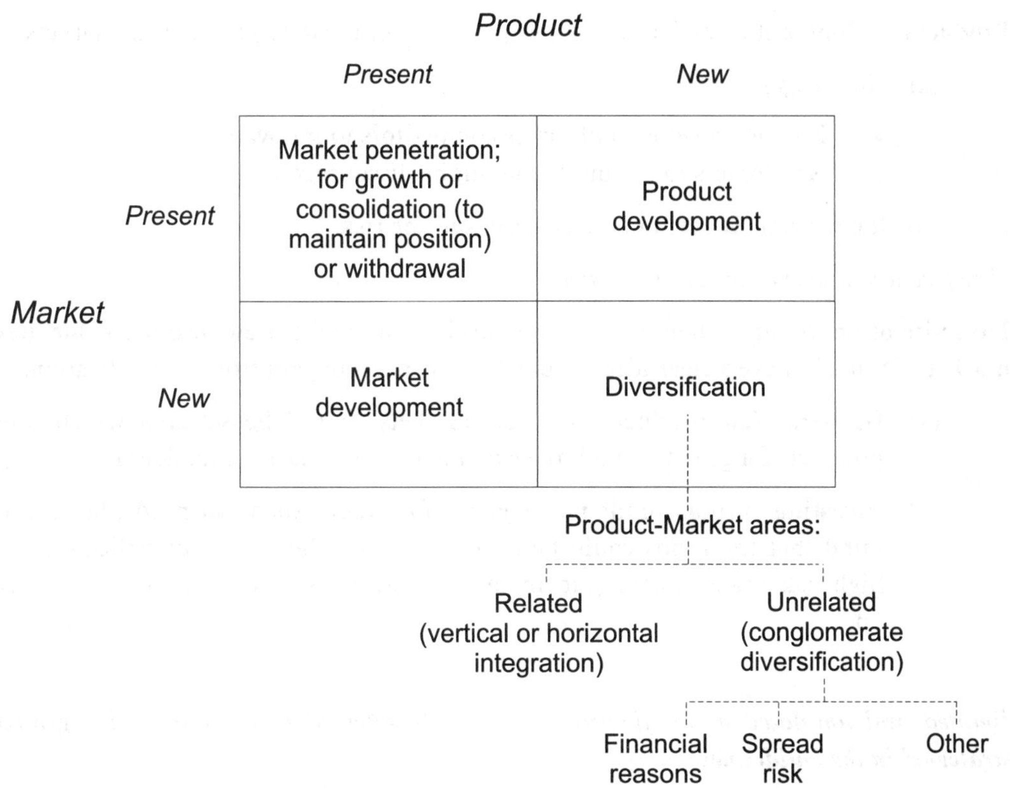

Figure 9.1: Ansoff's matrix

Current products and current markets: market penetration

The firm has four objectives.

(a) **Maintain or increase its share** of current markets with current products, eg through competitive pricing, advertising, sales promotion

(b) Secure dominance of growth markets

(c) Restructure a mature market by driving out competitors

(d) Increase usage by existing customers (eg airmiles, loyalty cards)

Present products and new markets: market development

Market development is the process by which the firm seeks new markets for its current products. There are many possible approaches. Here are some examples.

(a) **New geographical areas** and export markets (eg a radio station building a new transmitter to reach a new audience).

(b) **Different package sizes** for food and other domestic items so that both those who buy in bulk and those who buy in small quantities are catered for.

(c) **New distribution channels** to attract new customers (eg organic food sold in supermarkets, not just specialist shops)

(d) **Differential pricing policies** to attract different types of customer and create **new market segments**. For example, travel companies have developed a market for cheap long-stay winter breaks in warmer countries for retired couples.

New products and present markets: product development

Product development is the launch of new products (**innovation**) to existing markets.

(a) *Advantages*

- Product development forces competitors to innovate
- Newcomers to the market might be discouraged

(b) The *drawbacks* include the expense and the risk.

New products: new markets (diversification)

Diversification occurs when a company decides to make **new products for new markets.** It should have a clear idea about what it expects to gain from diversification.

(a) **Growth.** New products and new markets should be selected which offer prospects for growth which the existing product-market mix does not.

(b) **Investing surplus** funds not required for other expansion needs, bearing in mind that the funds could be returned to shareholders. Diversification is a high risk strategy, having many of the characteristics of a new business start-up.

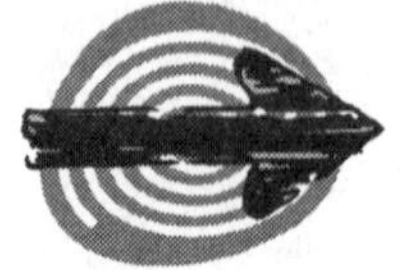

Related and unrelated diversification are directly referred to as 'substantive growth strategies' in the Guidelines.

1.2 Related diversification

Definition

> **Related diversification** is 'development beyond the present product market, but still within the broad confines of the industry ... [it] ... therefore builds on the assets or activities which the firm has developed' (*Johnson and Scholes*, 2002). It takes the form of vertical or horizontal integration.

Horizontal integration is the development into activities which are competitive with or directly **complementary** to a company's present activities.

Vertical integration occurs when a company becomes its own supplier or distributor. For example, **backward integration** would occur where a milk processing business acquires its own dairy farms rather than buying raw milk from independent farmers. If a manufacturer of synthetic yarn began to produce shirts from the yarn instead of selling it to other shirt manufacturers, that would be **forward integration.**

Advantages of vertical integration

- A **secure supply of components** or **materials,** hence lower supplier bargaining power
- **Stronger relationships** with the final consumer of the product
- A share of the **profits** at all stages of the value chain
- More effective pursuit of a **differentiation strategy**
- Creation of barriers **to entry**

Disadvantages of vertical integration

(a) **Overconcentration.** A company places 'more eggs in the same end-market basket' (*Ansoff*, 1987). Such a policy is fairly inflexible, more sensitive to instabilities and increases the firm's dependence on a particular aspect of economic demand.

(b) The firm **fails to benefit from any economies of scale or technical advances** in the industry into which it has diversified. This is why, in the publishing industry, most printing is subcontracted to specialist printing firms, who can work machinery to capacity by doing work for many firms.

1.3 Unrelated diversification

Definition

Unrelated or **conglomerate diversification** is development beyond the present industry into products/ markets which, at face value, may bear no close relation to the present product/market.

Conglomerate diversification is now very unfashionable. However, it has been a key strategy for companies in Asia, particularly South Korea.

Advantages of conglomerate diversification

(a) **Risk-spreading.** Entering new products into new markets offers protection against the failure of current products and markets.

(b) **High profit opportunities**. An improvement of the **overall profitability and flexibility** of the firm through acquisition in industries which have better economic characteristics than those of the acquiring firms.

(c) **Escape** from the present business

(d) **Better access to capital** markets

(e) **No other way to grow**

(f) **Use surplus cash**

(g) **Exploit under-utilised resources**

(h) **Obtain cash,** or other financial advantages (such as accumulated tax losses)

(i) **Use a company's image and reputation** in one market to develop into another where corporate image and reputation could be vital ingredients for success

Disadvantages of conglomerate diversification

(a) The **dilution of shareholders' earnings**

(b) **Lack of a common identity and purpose**. A conglomerate will only be successful if it has a high quality of management and financial ability at central headquarters, where the diverse operations are brought together.

(c) **Failure in one of the businesses** will drag down the rest, as it will eat up resources.

(d) **Lack of management experience.** Japanese steel companies have diversified into areas completely unrelated to steel such as personal computers, with limited success.

Activity 1 **(20 minutes)**

Diversification may be achieved by internal growth or through pursuing a policy of acquisition and mergers. Whether the diversification is related or unrelated to the organisation's existing business activities, it is a high-risk strategy for closing the planning gap because it takes the organisation into the development of new products and markets simultaneously.

What are the potential advantages of diversification to a company in pursuing the strategic management of markets?

Explain the statement that diversification is a high-risk approach.

EXAMPLE

The farming sector is particularly open to unrelated diversification as farmers attempt to generate revenue as a means of coping with increasingly pressurised prices and powerful customers. By 2009, The Royal Bank of Scotland predicts that over 25% of turnover generated by farms will come from non-farming activities. Currently around 40% of farms have expanded or diversified with tourism and on–farm activities being cited as the most popular options. These categories include holiday accommodation, outdoor pursuits, rare–breeds visitor centres and children's educational and play activities.

Adapted from Farmers Weekly Interactive 'Diversification to account for a quarter of farm income by 2009' as at: www.fwi.co.uk 11.1.07

1.4 Diversification and synergy

Definition

Synergy occurs when the combined results produce a better rate of return than would be achieved by the same resources used independently. Synergy is used to justify diversification.

Combined results produce a better rate of return than would be achieved by the same resources used independently. Synergy is used to justify diversification.

Obtaining synergy

(a) **Marketing synergy:** use of common marketing facilities such as distribution channels, sales staff and administration, and warehousing.

(b) **Operating synergy:** arises from the better use of operational facilities and personnel, bulk purchasing and a greater spread of fixed costs whereby the firm's competence can be transferred to making new products. For example, although there is very little in common between sausages and ice cream, both depend on a competence of refrigeration.

(c) **Investment synergy:** The wider use of a common investment in fixed assets, working capital or research, such as the joint use of plant, common raw material stocks and transfer of research and development from one product to another

(d) **Management synergy:** the advantage to be gained where management skills concerning current operations are easily transferred to new operations because of the similarity of problems in the two industries.

FOR DISCUSSION

At one time Tesco was reported to have put in a bid for the garden centre chain Dobbies. In your opinion, based on your knowledge of Tesco, would you regard this as related or unrelated diversification?

Activity 2 **(20 minutes)**

A large organisation in road transport operates nationwide in general haulage. This field has become very competitive and with the recent down-turn in trade has become only marginally profitable. It has been suggested that the strategic structure of the company should be widened to include other aspects of physical distribution so that the maximum synergy would be obtained.

Suggest two activities which might fit into the suggested new strategic structure. Explain how each of these activities could be incorporated into the existing structure. State the advantages and disadvantages of such diversification.

1.5 Divestment strategy: withdrawal

Most strategies are designed to **promote growth**, but management should consider what **rate of growth** they want, whether they want to see any growth at all (a possible '**do nothing**' strategy), or whether there should be **contraction** of business.

It might be the right decision to cease producing a product and/or to pull out of a market completely. This is a hard decision for managers to take if they have invested time and money or if the decision involves redundancies.

Definition

Divestment means selling off a part of a firm's operations, or pulling out of certain product-market areas.

Exit barriers make this difficult.

(a) Cost barriers include redundancy costs and the difficulty of selling assets.

(b) Managers might fail to grasp the idea of decision-relevant costs ('we've spent all this money, so we must go on').

(c) Political barriers include government attitudes. Defence is an example.

(d) Marketing considerations may delay withdrawal. A product might be a loss-leader for others, or might contribute to the company's reputation for its breadth of coverage.

(e) Psychology. Managers hate to admit failure, and there might be a desire to avoid embarrassment.

(f) People might wrongly assume that carrying on is a low risk strategy.

Reasons for exit

(a) The **company's business** may be in buying firms, selling their assets and improving their performance, and then selling them at a profit.

(b) **Resource limitations** mean that less profitable businesses have to be reduced or abandoned. A business might be sold to a competitor, or occasionally to management (as a buy-out).

(c) A company may be forced to quit, because of **insolvency**.

EXAMPLE

It was anticipated in 2007 that the motor industry would witness many divestments in the next few years as manufacturers are expected to slim down and specialise in their most profitable marques. In almost every other industry consolidation appears to be the common trend, however since the problematic pairing of Mercedes and Chrysler, mergers are out of favour. Ford is likely to divest itself of Jaguar, Land Rover and Volvo in order to concentrate on its high volume US business. This move follows the sale of Aston Martin in March 2007. Total losses made in 1996 by the whole Ford Group equalled $12.6bn. It is anticipated that 350,000 fewer cars will be sold in 2007 than the previous year, annual sales have not been that low since 1998.

Sources:
www.autoindustrynews.co.uk 'Ford confirms Jaguar and Land Rover sales, 12.6.07
Reed, J. (2007) 'Open road lies beyond the traffic jam' Financial Times, 11.9.07
'Ford US sales plummet by 14%' The Times, 6.9.07

Definition

> **Liquidation** is the term given to the termination of a business operation by using its assts to discharge its liabilities.

(d) **Change of competitive strategy**, or **rationalisation** of the business as a result of strategic appraisal.

(e) **Decline in attractiveness of the market**

(f) **Funds can earn more elsewhere**

(g) **Reduction in expenditure** in order to become financially stable – a process known as **retrenchment**.

(h) As part of a **turnaround strategy:** a fresh orientation with a changed set of objectives in the hope of reviving a company's fortunes.

The next section examines how a firm might grow in size to take advantage of market opportunities.

2 MARKET ENTRY STRATEGIES

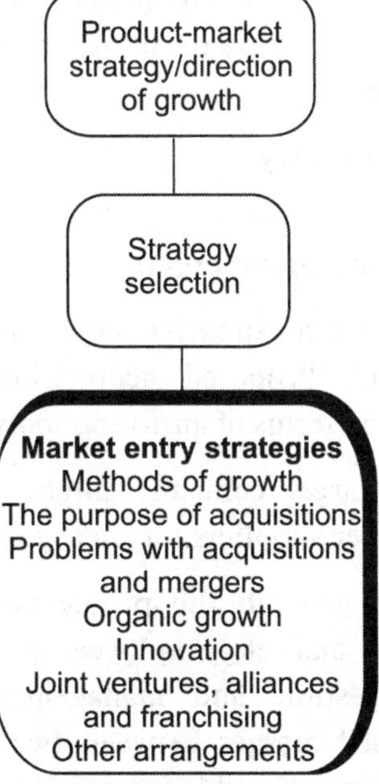

2.1 Methods of growth

- **Building up new businesses** from scratch and developing them
- **Acquiring** already existing businesses from their current owners
- **Merger** of two or more separate businesses
- Spreading the costs and risks by **joint ventures** or other forms of **co-operation**

NOTES

2.2 The purpose of acquisitions

(a) **Marketing advantages**

- Buy in a new product range
- Buy a market presence (especially true if acquiring a company overseas)
- Unify sales departments or rationalise distribution and advertising
- Eliminate competition or protect an existing market

(b) **Production advantages**

- Gain a higher utilisation of production facilities
- 'Buy in' technology and skills
- Obtain greater production capacity
- Safeguard future supplies of raw materials
- Improve purchasing by buying in bulk

(c) **Finance and management**

- Buy a high quality management team, which exists in the acquired company
- Obtain cash resources where the acquired company is very liquid
- Gain undervalued assets or surplus assets that can be sold off
- Obtain tax advantages (eg purchase of a tax loss company)

(d) **Risk-spreading**

(e) **Independence**. A company threatened by a take-over might take over another company, just to make itself bigger and so a more expensive target for the predator company.

(f) **Overcome barriers to entry**

2.3 Problems with acquisitions and mergers

(a) **Cost**. They might be too expensive, especially if resisted by the directors of the target company. Proposed acquisitions might be referred to the government under the terms of anti-monopoly legislation.

(b) **Customers** of the target company might resent a sudden takeover and consider going to other suppliers for their goods.

(c) **Incompatibility**. In general, the problems of assimilating new products, customers, suppliers, markets, employees and different systems of operating might create 'indigestion' and management overload in the acquiring company. A proposed merger between two UK financial institutions was called off because of incompatible information systems.

(d) **Incomplete information**. The acquisitions market for companies is rarely efficient. The existing management always knows more than the potential purchaser.

(e) **Driven by the personal goals** of the acquiring company's managers

(f) **Corporate financiers and banks** have a stake in the acquisitions process as they can charge fees for advice.

(g) **Poor success record of acquisitions.** Takeovers benefit the shareholders of the acquired company often more than the acquirer. According to the Economist Intelligence Unit, there is a consensus that fewer than half of all acquisitions are successful.

(h) **Firms rarely take into account non-financial factors**. A survey by London Business School examining 40 acquisitions (in the UK and USA) revealed some major flaws.

  (i) All acquirers conducted financial audits, but only 37% conducted anything approaching a management audit: despite detailed audits of equipment, property, finances etc, few bothered with people.

  (ii) Some major problems of implementation relate to **human resources and personnel issues** such as morale, performance assessment and culture. Especially in service industries and 'knowledge-based' or creative businesses, many of the firm's assets are effectively the staff. If key managers or personnel leave, the business will suffer.

2.4 Organic growth

Definition

> **Organic growth** (sometimes referred to as internal development) is the primary method of growth for many organisations, for a number of reasons. Organic growth is achieved through the development of internal resources.

Reasons for pursuing organic growth

(a) **Learning.** The process of developing a new product gives the firm the best understanding of the market and the product.

(b) **Innovation.** It might be the only sensible way to pursue genuine technological innovations, and exploit them. (Compact disc technology was developed by Philips and Sony, who earn royalties from other manufacturers licensed to use it.)

(c) There is **no suitable target for acquisition.**

(d) Organic growth can be **planned more meticulously** and offers little disruption.

(e) It is often **more convenient** for managers, as organic growth can be financed easily from the company's current cash flows, without having to raise extra money.

(f) The **same style of management and corporate culture** can be maintained.

(g) **Hidden or unforeseen losses are less likely** with organic growth than with acquisitions.

(h) **Economies of scale** can be achieved from more **efficient use of central head office** functions such as finance, purchasing, personnel, management services etc.

Problems with organic growth

(a) **Time** – sometimes it takes a long time to climb a **learning curve**.

(b) **Barriers to entry** (eg distribution networks) are harder to overcome

(c) The firm will have to **acquire the resources independently.**

(d) Organic growth may be **too slow for the dynamics of the market.**

Organic growth is probably ideal for market penetration, and suitable for product or market development, but it might be a problem with extensive projects.

2.5 Innovation

If we assume that existing products have a finite life, a strategy of organic growth must include plans for **innovation.**

- It provides the organisation with a **distinctive competence**
- It maintains the organisation's **competitive advantage** and market share

EXAMPLE

Managers responsible for product development may be assigned the strategic objective of finding eight or so successful new products at regular intervals during the next ten years so as to achieve given sales and profit targets over that period of time.

Key questions to ask will include the following.

- Who are our customers?
- What do they want now?
- What will they want next year?
- Why should they come to us rather than one of our rivals?
- How do we generate, capture and develop ideas?
- How should we set about identifying and meeting business opportunities?

Innovation strategies can be grouped into three broad categories.

(a) **Attack or leader strategies**. An organisation can try to be the first one to exploit an innovation, by marketing a new product. The new product might be aimed initially at a particular niche market, and if this is successful, other niche markets can subsequently be 'attacked' and exploited one by one.

(b) **Defensive or follower strategies**. An organisation might have to respond to innovation by a competitor, either by introducing the same innovation itself, or protecting itself by taking measures to maintain customer loyalty, for example.

(c) **Counter-attack strategies**. An organisation might respond to a competitor's innovation by taking measures to 'go one better', and to innovate itself. This might take the form of 'leap-frogging' – ie developing an even more technologically-advanced product than its rival. Leap-frogging has been a feature of competition in the computer manufacturing industry.

Successful innovation depends on the following.

(a) Responding to or anticipating **customer and market needs**

(b) Having people within the organisation who are innovators in **outlook**, and have sufficient **authority** to innovate

(c) Having a culture, leadership and organisation structure that **encourages innovation**

EXAMPLE

Organic growth by innovation is not always the guarantee of success. *The Economist* reported a research study into successful innovations.

(a) Pioneers often fail to conjure up a mass market. The first video recorder was developed in 1956 by Ampex – they sold for $50,000. The firm made no attempt to expand the market. Sony, JVC and Matsushita spent 20 years turning it into a mass market product.

(b) Another reason is financial strength. Coca-Cola's Fruitopia brand was positioned against firms such as Snapple which had pioneered the market in non-cola 'alternative beverages'.

Innovative companies are not necessarily the most successful. Success is based upon other factors such as distribution capability, technical expertise and marketing skills.

2.6 Joint ventures, alliances and franchising

Short of mergers and takeovers, there are other ways by which companies can co-operate.

(a) **Consortia**: organisations co-operate on specific business areas such as purchasing or research.

(b) **Joint ventures**: two firms (or more) join forces for manufacturing, financial and marketing purposes and each has a share in both the equity and the management of the business.

(i) **Share costs**. As the capital outlay is shared, joint ventures are especially attractive to smaller or risk-averse firms, or where very expensive new technologies are being researched and developed (such as the civil aerospace industry).

(ii) **Cut risk**. A joint venture can reduce the risk of government intervention if a local firm is involved (eg Club Mediterranée pays much attention to this factor).

(iii) Participating enterprises **benefit from all sources of profit.**

(iv) **Close control** over marketing and other operations.

(v) Overseas joint ventures provide **local knowledge, quickly**.

(vi) **Synergies**. One firm's production expertise can be supplemented by the other's marketing and distribution facility.

(vii) **Learning.** Alliances can also be a 'learning' exercise in which each partner tries to learn as much as possible from the other.

(viii) **Technology**. New technology offers many uncertainties and many opportunities. Such alliances provide funds for expensive research projects, spreading risk.

(ix) **The alliance itself can generate innovations**

(x) The alliance can involve **'testing' the firm's core competence** in different conditions, which can suggest ways to improve it

Disadvantages of joint ventures

(a) **Conflicts of interest** between the different parties.

(b) **Disagreements** may arise over profit shares, amounts invested, the management of the joint venture, and the marketing strategy.

(c) One partner may wish to **withdraw** from the arrangement.

2.7 Other arrangements

A **licensing agreement** is a commercial contract whereby the licenser gives something of value to the licensee in exchange for certain performances and payments.

(a) The licenser may provide rights to produce a patented product or to use a patented process or trademark as well as advice and assistance on marketing and technical issues.

(b) The licenser receives a **royalty**.

Subcontracting is also a type of alliance. Co-operative arrangements also feature in supply chain management, JIT and quality programmes.

Franchising is a method of expanding the business on less capital than would otherwise be possible. For suitable businesses, it is an **alternative business strategy to raising extra capital** for growth. Franchisers include Budget Rent-a-car, Dyno-rod, Express Dairy, Holiday Inn, Kall-Kwik Printing, KFC, Prontaprint, Sketchley Cleaners, Body Shop and even McDonald's. The franchiser and franchisee each provide different inputs to the business.

(a) The **franchiser**

(i) Name, and any goodwill associated with it

(ii) Systems and business methods

(iii) Support services, such as advertising, training and help with site decoration

(b) The **franchisee**

(i) Capital, personal involvement and local market knowledge

(ii) Payment to the franchiser for rights and for support services

(iii) Responsibility for the day-to-day running, and the ultimate profitability of the franchise.

Disadvantages of franchising

(a) The **search for competent candidates** is both costly and time consuming where the franchiser requires many outlets.

(b) **Control** over franchisees.

Chapter roundup

- Product-market strategies involve determining which products should be sold in which markets, by market penetration, market development, product development and diversification. Diversification is assumed to be risky, especially conglomerate diversification, which is entirely unrelated to current products and markets.
- The method of growth can vary.
  - Companies can grow organically, building up their own products and developing their own market.
  - They may choose to acquire these ready-made by buying other companies. Acquisitions are risky because of the incompatibility of different companies.
  - Many firms grow by other means, such as joint ventures or franchising.

Quick quiz

1 What are the disadvantages of vertical integration?

2 What are the disadvantages of conglomerate diversification?

3 Why might firms contemplate making acquisitions?

4 Describe joint ventures.

Answers to quick quiz

1 Overconcentration (putting too many eggs in one basket) and inflexibility. Also means that there is less chance of benefiting from economies of scale or technical advances.

2 Dilution of shareholder earnings, lack of a common purpose, one failure drags down the rest, lack of management experience.

3 Marketing and production advantages, finance and management benefits, risk-spreading, independence and overcoming barriers to entry.

NOTES

4 Two firms or more join forces for manufacturing, financial and marketing purposes. Each shares in the equity and management of the business. (See Section 2.6.)

Answers to activities

1 (a) Diversification involves moving to new markets, with new or different product offerings.

The advantages of diversification appear when the firm's existing product market areas are unattractive for whatever reason.

(i) Related diversification is where the new products and markets bear some similarity with existing product offerings. A possible example might be Sony's decision to enter the market for computer games, competing with Nintendo and Sega.

The example of Sony and computer games might be called horizontal diversification.

(1) Competitive advantage. CD technology is becoming the format for many new multimedia products, and developing expertise in this area may be essential for Sony to retain its competitive advantage.

(2) Competitive leadership. Moving into computer games may be an essential strategy. When markets and technology change, diversification may be essential in order to harness these developments for the company's benefits.

(ii) Unrelated or conglomerate diversification is the entry of completely dissimilar product market areas, either organically, or more commonly, by acquisition. An example of unsuccessful diversification is provided again by Sony, which purchased a Hollywood film studio. The rationale was that Sony produced hardware (eg video recorders) and there would be marketing advantages in producing 'software' (films) as well. These advantages have failed to materialise. Running a film production business requires a wholly different set of management skills to running a manufacturing business.

(iii) Other reasons for diversification

(1) **Vertical integration.** A firm might expand by buying a supplier or a distributor, to garner more of the wealth in the supply chain, or to secure supplies. In many cases, it is not true diversification, if the final consumer stays the same. A problem is that the acquired business cannot benefit from **economies of scale** in the industry as a whole, and that different management expertise may be required.

(2) **Spreading risk** across several businesses, and possible synergies in which different businesses can contribute to each other.

(b) For the business as a whole, diversification would appear to be a higher risk strategy than the others.

(1) **Uncertainty.** The diversifier is maximising the degree of uncertainty which it faces.

(2) **Learning.** The diversifier will need to climb a learning curve, in both production and marketing terms. (Devising and marketing computer games to teenagers requires different marketing and product development skills to those needed to sell hi-fis or televisions.)

(3) **Turbulence.** Diversifying increases the degrees of environmental turbulence to which the businesses are subject.

(4) **Competitor behaviour.** The diversifier may be a new entrant, and competitors may respond by building higher barriers to entry or other spoiling tactics.

(5) **Management problems.** Many diversified businesses are run at arms length from each other, but there may be problems in corporate culture. This was reported when UK clearing banks purchased stock-broking firms where management styles and systems were very different.

(6) Related diversification may appear safer, but vertically integrated businesses still depend on the same end market, and will be investing more resources in servicing it.

Although diversification is unfashionable at the moment, there are arguments in its favour.

(1) In practice, it may be **less risky** than the other options.

(2) Diversification may be a **competitive tactic**, if potential competitors are attacked on their own turf.

(3) The risk inherent in diversification might be reduced if there is **synergy**.

2 The first step in a suggested solution is to think of how a company operating nationwide in general road haulage might diversify, with some synergistic benefits. Perhaps you thought of the following.

(a) To move from nationwide to international haulage, the company might be able to use its existing contacts with customers to develop an international trade. Existing administration and depot facilities in the UK could be used. Drivers should be available who are willing to work abroad, and the scope for making reasonable profits should exist. However, international road haulage might involve the company in the purchase of new vehicles (eg road haulage in Europe often involves the carriage of containerised products on large purpose-built vehicles). Since international haulage takes longer, vehicles will be tied up in jobs for several days, and a substantial investment might be required to develop the business. In addition, in the event of breakdowns, a network of overseas garage service arrangements will have to be created. It might take some time before business builds up sufficiently to become profitable.

(b) Moving from general haulage to speciality types of haulage, perhaps haulage of large items of plant and machinery, or computer equipment. The same broad considerations apply to speciality types of haulage. Existing depot facilities could be used and existing customer contacts might be developed. However, expertise in specialist work will have to be brought in as well as developed within the company and special vehicles might need to be bought. Business might take some time to build up and if the initial investment is high, there could be substantial early losses.

Part D

Strategy Implementation

Chapter 10 : COMMUNICATION

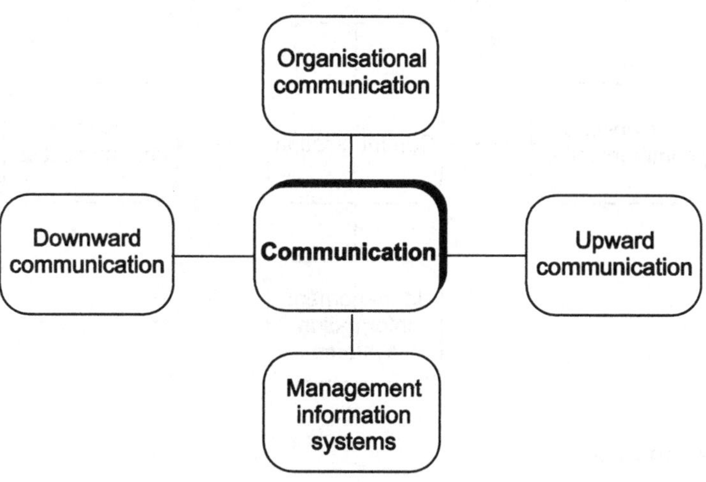

Introduction

One of the keys to successful strategy implementation is that of communication throughout the organisation. This should help to ensure that objectives are clear.

Communication in the context of managing tasks raises wider organisational issues. It is about how a manager communicates goals and instructions about strategy implementation to his or her team; how the information required for tasks and decisions can be gathered and shared; how the team can feed back information on performance for the purposes of control, and so on.

In this chapter we will be looking at the implementation of strategy in the context of communications by examining the purpose, direction and mechanisms of organisational communication.

Your objectives

In this chapter you will learn about the following.

(a) The importance of information and communications in the effective management of activities

(b) The purposes and media of downward and upward communication in organisations

(c) Basic managerial communication tasks

(d) The purposes and design of different types of Management Information System

1 ORGANISATIONAL COMMUNICATION

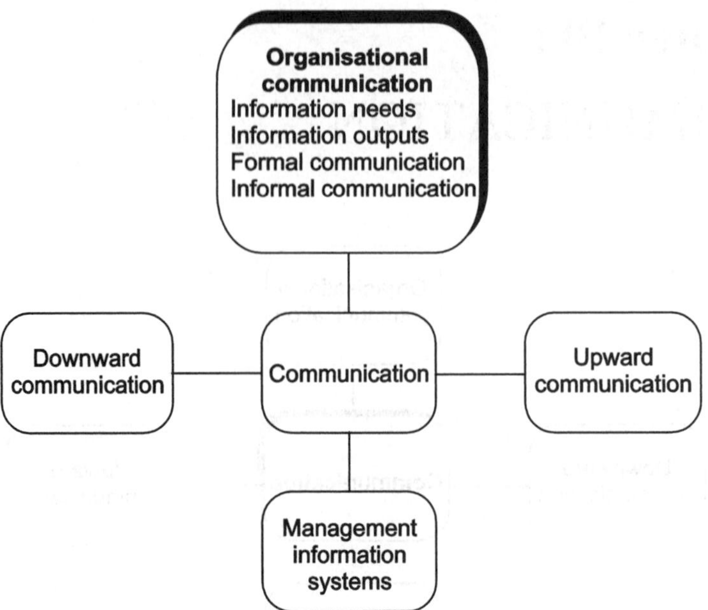

1.1 Information needs

Information-gathering, processing and dissemination are the vital functions of any organisation. Information about customer requirements gives the organisation purpose and objectives. Information about objectives enables managers to direct and co-ordinate the activities of others. **Information is the basis of strategic planning and decision-making.** Feedback information is necessary for control.

We suggest some further examples of management uses of information in the table on the following page.

Information needs of employees

Employees require information from the organisation for a variety of purposes.

(a) **In order to perform their tasks effectively and efficiently**. They need to know about work schedules, resource availability, how to use tools and machinery efficiently and safely, what procedures have been laid down and so on. This kind of information may be provided through briefings, schedules, job descriptions, procedures manuals, or specific memos, notices or meetings.

(b) **For motivation, learning and development**. Employees need to know what is required from them: performance criteria and standards, targets, budgets, rules and expectations. They need feedback on how their performance measures up to the criteria on which they are judged: without it, they cannot be motivated or enabled to correct sub-standard performance, or to take satisfaction in good performance.

(c) **For job satisfaction.** Employees may feel more trusted if information is freely given about areas relevant to their work. If the information helps them to see how their work relates to that of others, and how it contributes to the organisation, it gives their work additional meaning and satisfaction.

Management function	Some of the purposes of information	Type and sources of information
Planning	• To establish objectives, or end goals towards which all plans must contribute • To establish strategies for achieving objectives and policies, procedures, rules, budgets etc to guide day to day decision-making towards fulfilment of strategies	• Attitudes/expectations of owners, customers and other stakeholders • Information from the environment on foreseeable opportunities and threats, past events indicating trends and future probabilities • Information from within the organisation on identifiable strengths and weaknesses. • Creative thinking within the organisation, on opportunities and solutions to problems
Control	• To indicate whether and how far a plan has been carried out, whether and how far it has been successful in achieving its objective • To suggest the adjustment of performance, or the plan itself, to correct any deviation	• Feedback from results of plan • Feedback from subordinates charged with carrying out plan on how it went • Information from the environment about changes, requiring adjustment of plans • Information from within the organisation: suggestions for improvements, identification of problems
Decision-making/ problem-solving	• To identify and analyse a problem or opportunity • To appraise available resources • To compare alternative solutions and select optimum solution	• Internal and external information of a wide variety, relevant to situation • Investigation of internal resources and potential external sources • Information on likely outcomes of a number of different solutions
Co-ordinating	• To guide planning, so as to avoid duplication of effort – or gaps in effort – between individuals, teams or functions	• Overall objectives of the department/organisation • Feedback on results of overall activity • Plans, deadlines etc of other teams and departments • Reports on co-ordination problems
Organising	• To indicate how tasks relate to each other, and who should do what	• Information about task requirements, methods and resources required • Information on staff skills, abilities, motivation • Information on needs of employees to work in particular conditions, methods, teams etc
Commanding	• To indicate employees' needs and wants, so that they can be offered appropriate motivators • To ensure that all rights of employees are being fulfilled • To supply the information required for outside agencies and internal systems: manpower planning, employee appraisal and reward, training etc	• Information about employees' needs, wants and expectations • External information about employment rights: legal and customary • Internal information about individual employees and the workforce as a whole

Figure 10.1: Employee information needs

1.2 Information outputs by the organisation

Communication by the organisation to the outside world is far wider than advertising, promotion and press releases. Some organisations (banks, consultancies, research organisations, travel agencies and suchlike) are in effect offering and/or selling information itself as their main product or service.

Activity 1 **(15 minutes)**

See if you can think of some of the matters about which an organisation may need to give out information (other than information requested by customers as part of the organisation's service) and to whom they would need to give it.

Good business information will be suited to its purpose and to its audience. As you can see from your solution to Activity 1 (or ours), this covers a huge variety, and requires a great deal of flexibility from the business communicator.

Since information is the lifeblood of the organisation, the process of communication cannot just be left to chance or individual discretion. Information, like other resources, must be co-ordinated. The organisation's subsystems therefore include a formal communication system.

1.3 Formal communication

The formal structure of an organisation implies a formal structure or system for communication.

(a) The **delegation of authority** down the chain of command implies communication from superior to subordinate in the form of instructions, orders, job-related information, encouragement, incentive and so on.

(b) **Accountability** back up the line of command implies communication from subordinate to superior, accounting for the use of delegated authority, reporting results, appealing to the superior with problems or decisions which are not within the area of the subordinate's delegated authority and so on.

(c) **Co-ordination** links individuals, teams and departments in co-operative systems of working. These links are reflected by the horizontal lines at each 'tier' of the organisation chart: they imply the sharing of information by different units in order to harmonise their efforts, and to fulfil the requirements of their joint superiors (at the next level up).

You can see why people talk about the direction of information flow: downwards, upwards and horizontally/sideways. We will be discussing vertical communication in more detail below.

Communication routes

You have probably come across the phrase 'going through channels'. Because of the need for co-ordination and control, and to preserve the formal organisation structure, the normal channel of communication will follow the line of command: superiors will deal only with their own immediate subordinates, and vice versa. Communication diagonally – with someone both at a different level of the hierarchy and in a different section or department – is generally discouraged: individuals are expected to pass the message vertically and horizontally through appropriate linking individuals. See Figure 10.1.

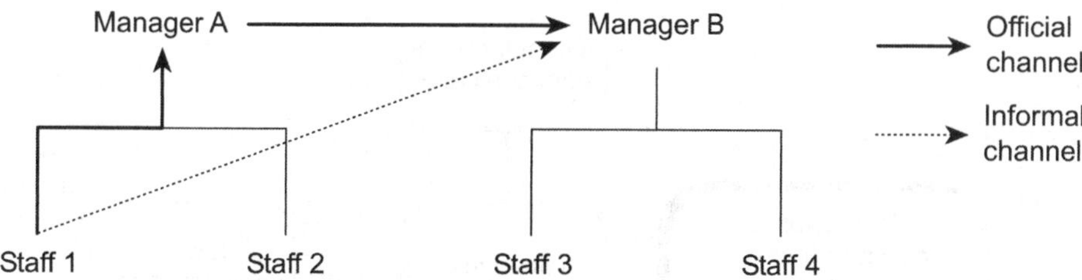

Figure 10.2: Formal and informal communication routes

In a matter of particular urgency the formal channels may be by-passed by simply leaving out the linking individuals. For example, the managing director might wish to declare an important decision directly to all staff. This route should be used only in emergencies, however, since regularly ignoring one link in the communication chain (usually middle-level managers) can cause resentment: 'Why am I always the last one to know?'

It has to be accepted that in some circumstances, 'going through channels' will be time-consuming and frustrating. The use of empowered teams in organisations is a radical way of cutting out the levels and channels through which information has to pass.

Formal communication will usually fulfil the need to know, but the organisation may not necessarily satisfy the 'want' to know. This will result in the informal network, which will sometimes spread irregular and unreliable information.

1.4 Informal communication

The **formal** system of communication in an organisation is always supplemented by an **informal** one: casual talks in the canteen, at the pub, on the way home and so on.

The **grapevine,** the network for rumours and gossip, works very fast – 'word gets around' often before the formal structure has conveyed news. The problem is that it tends to distort information on organisational issues, through rumour and speculation – especially on sensitive issues like pay, redundancy or change.

Formal communication systems do, however, need the support of a good – accurate – informal system. This might be encouraged by:

(a) Setting up official communications to feed information into the informal system, eg house journals or briefings

(b) Encouraging and offering opportunities for 'networking'. A network is a collection of people, usually with a shared interest, who tend to keep in touch to exchange informal information.

Activity 2 **(10 minutes)**

How might you, as a manager, use the grapevine to help you manage your team?

2 DOWNWARD COMMUNICATION

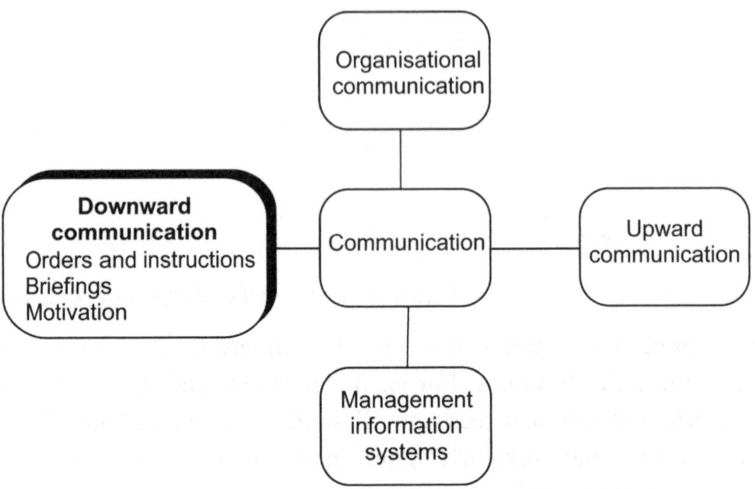

2.1 Orders and instructions

The most basic form of downward communication is giving subordinates orders and instructions to get work done: the management function of **commanding**. This can be done using a number of communication media.

An organisation manual or handbook

An organisation manual is often used to draw together information about the structure and products of the organisation, conditions of employment and so on. In a bureaucratic organisation, where work is routine in nature, it may also be used to give guidance or instruction on:

(a) Rules and regulations
(b) Standards and procedures for health and safety, grievance, discipline
(c) Procedures and standards for routine tasks

Oral communication

Oral communication can be achieved face-to-face or remotely, by telephone. The advantage of oral communication for giving orders and instructions is that it allows immediate feedback to be sought and given: the team member(s) can ask for clarification of points which are not clear, or for more information, and can signal clearly to the manager that the orders have been understood and accepted. The advantage of using the telephone is that it cuts down on the time and physical movement required for a face-to-face exchange (the manager going to the team member or *vice versa*).

However, face-to-face communication allows:

(a) More people to be reached in one go, for example in a team meeting

(b) Even clearer feedback, since both parties can also use non-verbal signals (perplexed expression or confident nod of the head) to reinforce their messages

(c) Greater responsiveness to personal factors, and greater persuasiveness, which may be important if the task is difficult, unpleasant or somehow sensitive.

With continued advances in technology, it is now possible to use conference facilities and videophones, enabling contact with more than one person at a time.

Written direct communication

If you want to give an instruction to your bank manager, say, what method would you use? You might telephone initially, but you would probably want, or be asked, to put your instructions in writing. Written communication has major advantages in business, as it provides concrete evidence and confirmation of the message. Details cannot be forgotten – or misremembered – as easily as with a spoken message; nor is understanding subject to the interpretation of tone of voice, or mishearing. Instructions, especially if they are lengthy or complicated, may be best provided in writing: alternatively, team members should be encouraged to take notes themselves, in any oral briefing.

A memorandum is an often-used format for internal written communication in organisations. A standard memo format is as follows.

Organisation's name (optional)
'MEMORANDUM' heading

'To:' (recipient's name or designation) 'Reference:' (for filing)
'From:' (author's name or designation) 'Date:' (in full)
'Subject:' (main theme of message)
The message of the memorandum is set out simply in good English and spaced paragraphs.
'Copies to:' (recipient(s) of copies) 'Signed:' (optional)
'Enc:' (= enclosure: to indicate accompanying material) author signs/initials

Here is an example of an order (which you will see is put courteously as a request) in memorandum form.

MEMORANDUM

To: Administrative Staff, SE region Ref: JW/nn SE 22
From: I M Bossere, Office Manager Date: 4th January 20XX
Subject: Staff meeting, January 20XX

The Managing Director intends to hold an informal general meeting with administrative staff at some point during January, to discuss any matters that may be of concern.

Tentative dates for the meeting are Wednesday 23rd or Friday 25th: it will in either case be held in Meeting Room 3 at 6.00pm. Refreshments will be provided by the canteen afterwards, should staff wish to stay.

Please let me know as soon as possible (no later than Wednesday 16th):

1. which date you would find most convenient;
2. whether you are likely to stay for refreshments;
3. any topics which you would like to see on the agenda for the meeting.

Copies to: Managing Director. IMB

Activity 3 **(30 minutes)**

Write a memo to Mr Bossere, answering the above invitation and request for information. Use the company's 'house style' for memos.

The content of orders and instructions

Orders and instructions will vary widely, from 'Take that package down to the post room, please' to the plan for a complete work process or project.

The main point about orders and instructions is that they should be clear and sufficient for the recipient to be able to proceed to fulfil the instructions to your satisfaction.

Complete and detailed instructions for a complex task may include the following elements.

(a) Desired outcomes or results, including:
   (i) The standard to which they should be achieved
   (ii) The criteria on which successful performance will be judged
   (iii) The time-scale within which the task or project must be completed
   (iv) Resources available financial targets and budgets set, payments agreed and so on

(b) **Definition of all relevant terms,** to minimise misunderstanding.

(c) **A breakdown of the task or project into logical components,** and their:
   (i) Context
   (ii) Requirements
   (iii) Resource budgets (if any)
   (iv) Methods (if required)
   (v) Relevant background

(d) **Information required** to understand and carry out the task.

FOR DISCUSSION

How helpful are the following common phrases, when it comes to giving clear, sufficient orders and instructions?

- 'As soon as possible' (or even 'ASAP')
- 'Whenever it's convenient'
- 'Use your own judgement'
- 'Let's see how far we get'
- 'Either type will do'

The term 'briefing' (or 'brief') is often used for the giving of instructions: the content of such a briefing will be as described above. However, you might prefer to distinguish briefings as being more concerned with stage (d) above: the giving of information necessary to do the job.

2.2 Briefings

Briefings on specific tasks or topics will be much like the giving of instructions, as outlined above. However, briefings can also be used as a wider communication medium, as part of the empowerment of work teams. An organisation, or individual manager, may wish to have a scheme of regular short meetings in order to communicate and explain, on an on-going basis, such issues as:

(a) Organisational policy and any changes to it
(b) Plans
(c) Progress in comparison to plan
(d) Results: 'good news swapping' from around the organisation

As in any form of communication, the important considerations will be:

- **The purpose of the communication**
  - What information is necessary and helpful?
  - What information is relevant and what is irrelevant?
  - What will the information be used for – and can it be provided in a way that it will make it easier to use (diagrams, say, or tables of data)?
- **The needs and abilities of the audience**
  - What information is relevant to the audience's needs – or can be made to seem relevant to them?
  - How much information will they be able to take in at one go?
  - What words and styles of communication will they be able to understand easily?
  - Will the audience be receptive to the message, or might there be reasons why they will be resistant to it (in which case how can this resistance be overcome – perhaps, by persuasion)?

Team briefings can be seen as a way of motivating employees by communicating more freely with them the kind of information that used to be held only at the top of the hierarchy. We will look briefly at other types of downward communication used in this way.

2.3 Motivation

You should be aware that downward communication is not just about directly 'getting things done'. It is also about maintaining the **ability** and **willingness** of team members to carry out your orders and instructions.

(a) **Positive and negative reinforcement**. Downward communication plays a role in motivation in the form of:

  (i) Praise for good work or effort

  (ii) Encouragement

  (iii) Discipline: expression of dissatisfaction with poor performance, re-emphasising required standards and so on

  (iv) Constructive criticism

(b) **Culture**. Leaders communicate the organisation's values and beliefs to their teams.

(c) **Performance feedback**. Team leaders should constantly provide feedback to members on:

(i) How they are doing in their tasks and in the team

(ii) How results are progressing in comparison to the plans and standards set for them.

Feedback is essential both for **motivation** and for **learning and development** – for the adjustment of performance to bring it (where necessary) back in line with the original plan.

3 UPWARD COMMUNICATION

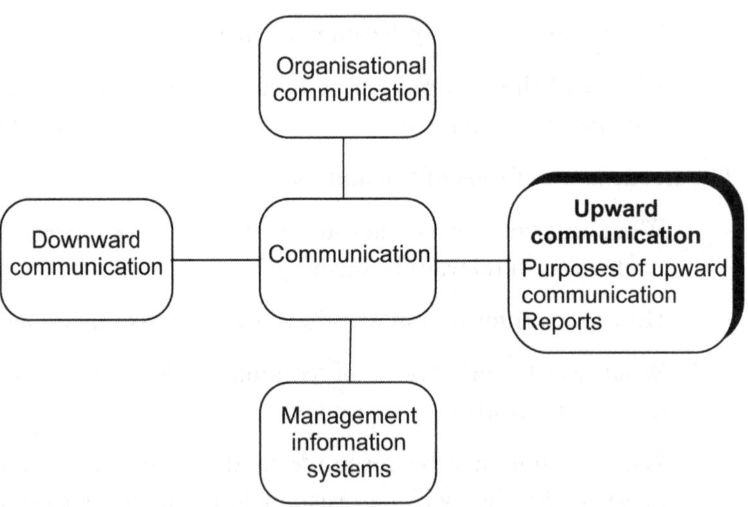

3.1 Purposes of upward communication

The main purposes of upward communication are as follows.

To give feedback on performance

Subordinates report to superiors in the organisation hierarchy: if you have been given orders or delegated authority to make a decision or perform a task, you are accountable for the results of that decision or task to your superior. Managers may not be as close to the nitty gritty of daily work as their team members, so they require the team to report on how things are going, progress and problems.

A useful principle to bear in mind here is **management by exception**. If a manager has made a detailed plan, (s)he does not need regular reports about things going according to plan: (s)he already knows what to expect in that case. However, if performance deviates from plan, the manager needs to know, in order to take control action to put things right. 'Reporting by exception' means that only deviations from the plan or norm need be reported.

To give information

Managers monitor information which is relevant to the task and team, and which may affect decisions made even higher up the organisation. Information provided by team members includes performance feedback, but may also cover other matters. A manager may, for example, require information for a meeting or report, which subordinates possess or have access to; a team member may have closer knowledge of the production technology involved in her work; a subordinate may be given the task of researching a new product, technology or idea to give the manager a summary or digest of the information that will be relevant.

To give suggestions

Being in possession of practical knowledge and information about the work, team members may be in a position to offer helpful insights for problem-solving or new methods of working, which managers may not have thought of. This is one of the important principles behind the **empowerment** of teams.

FOR DISCUSSION

Can you see ways in which your course, for example, could be improved?

(a) What enables you to have an insight into the problem or opportunity, that your course designers/leaders may not have?

(b) What holds you back (if anything) from suggesting the improvements to your course designers/leaders? What would encourage you to do so?

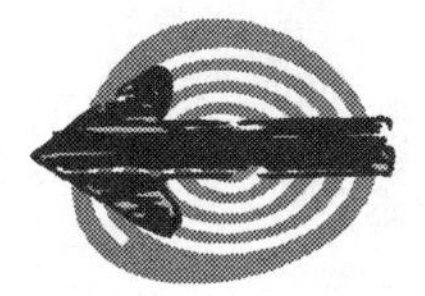

Like downward communication, upward communication can be done face-to-face, on the telephone, or in writing. We will look briefly at one particular format, which is much used in business: the written report.

3.2 Reports

Planning a report

Unless you have an extremely orderly mind, compiling a report takes planning.

If you know who the user is, what information (s)he wants and why, and if you are aware of any requirements of size and time, you will have a good framework for planning the structure and content of your report. Ask yourself the following questions.

(a) What information do I need to provide? What is relevant to the user's requirements?

(b) What is the information for: explanation? description? recommendation? instruction?

(c) Do I need to follow a line of reasoning? If so, what is the most logical way in which data can be organised, to make my reasoning clear? (For/against? Advantage/disadvantage? Chronological order?)

NOTES

(d) Do I need to include my own personal views? What form should these take: recommendations or suggestions? interpretation? opinion?

(e) What can I do to make the report easier to read? (Headers, numbered points, spacing, non-technical vocabulary, diagrams, clear and precise language and so on.)

Jot down a skeleton of the headings and sub-headings you have decided to use (with notes of any particular points that occur to you as you go along) and you will be ready to write. The formal headings of standard business reports (discussed below) may be useful to help you to organise your thoughts – but may not be necessary or even advisable, if they simply act as a constraint on what you actually want to say, and how you want to shape your argument.

Report structure and style

When a formal request is made by a superior for a report to be prepared, such as in a formally worded memorandum or letter, the format and style of the report will obviously have to be formal as well: it will be highly organised in structure and layout, and impersonal in tone.

An informal request for a report – 'Can you jot down a few ideas for me about...?' or 'Let me know what happens, will you?' – will result in an informal report, in which the structure will be less rigid, and the style slightly more personal (depending on the relationship between the writer and user).

The following are standard structures for formal and informal reports.

SHORT FORMAL REPORT

TITLE

At the top of every report (or on a title page, for lengthy ones) should be the title of the report (its subject), who has prepared it, for whom it is intended, the date of completion, and the status of the report ('Confidential' or 'Urgent').

(i) TERMS OF REFERENCE

Here is laid out the scope and purpose of the report: what is to be investigated, what kind of information is required, whether recommendations are to be made etc. (This section may more simply be called 'Introduction', and may include the details set above under 'Title'. The title itself would then give only the subject of the report.)

(ii) PROCEDURE or METHOD

This outlines the steps taken to make an investigation, collect data, put events in motion etc. Telephone calls or visits made, documents or computer files consulted, computations or analyses made etc. should be briefly described, with the names of other people involved.

(iii) FINDINGS

In this section the information itself is set out, with appropriate headings and sub-headings, if the report covers more than one topic.

(iv) CONCLUSIONS

This section allows for a summary of main findings (if the report is complex and lengthy). For a simpler report it may include action taken or decisions reached (if any) as a result of the investigation, or an expression of the overall 'message' of the report.

(v) RECOMMENDATIONS

Here, if asked to do so in the terms of reference, the writer of the report may suggest the solution to the problem investigated so that the recipient will be able to make a decision if necessary.

(vi) APPENDICES

When additional information is required which does not appear in the body of the report, it should be provided as an appendix, and should be referred to in the main text of the report.

SHORT INFORMAL REPORT

Title

Again, the subject title, 'to', 'from', 'date' and 'reference' (if necessary) should be provided, perhaps in the same style as memorandum headings.

1 *Background or Introduction or Situation*

This sets the context of the report. Include anything that will help the reader to understand the rest of the report: the reason why it was requested, the current situation, and any other background information on people and things that will be mentioned in the following detailed section.

2 *Findings or Analysis of the situation or Information*

Here is set out the detailed information gathered, narrative of events or other substance of the report as required by the user. This section may or may not require subheadings: concise prose paragraphs may be sufficient.

3 *Action or Solution or Conclusion or Recommendations*

The main thrust of the findings may be summarised in this section and conclusions drawn, together with a note of the outcome of events, or action required, or recommendations as to how a problem might be solved.

4 MANAGEMENT INFORMATION SYSTEMS

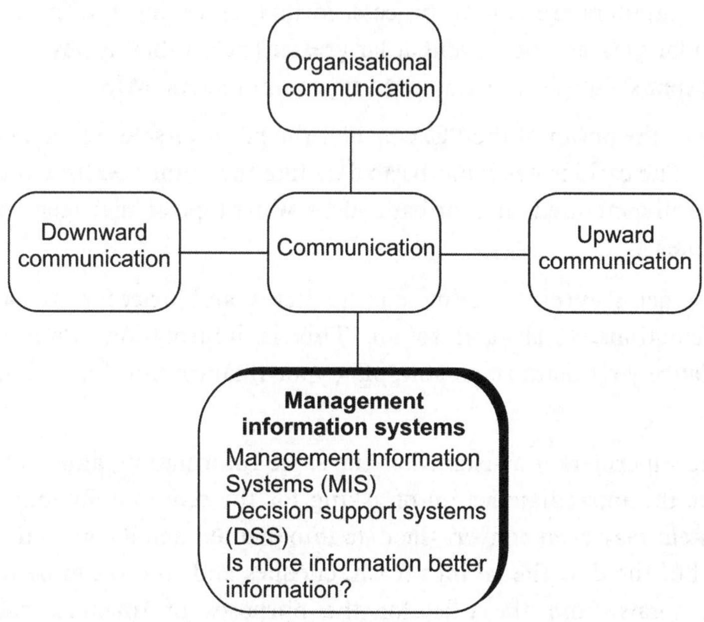

4.1 Management Information Systems (MIS)

We discussed in Section 1 of this chapter some of the many types of information managers require to make decisions. It should be fairly obvious that if the information gathering process is not carefully planned:

(a) Managers may 'miss' important items of information, while being overloaded with less relevant items

(b) Managers may receive information too late – or too early – for it to be helpful in making a given decision

(c) The right information, at the right time, may go to the wrong managers

(d) Managers may receive data in an unfriendly format, so that its underlying value is not easily seen.

Definitions

Data are the raw materials of information: facts and figures in an unprocessed state.

Information is data which have been processed (selected, sorted, analysed, formatted) so as to:

- have meaning for the person who receives it
- be suitable for a particular purpose.

A **Management Information System (MIS)** is a system designed to collect data from all available sources and to convert it into information relevant to managers at all levels, for the purposes of planning and control of the activities for which they are responsible.

Nowadays, Management Information Systems (MIS) are almost inevitably seen as computerised systems. Despite this, even small businesses which are not entirely computer dependent showed being able to map exactly where their key information can be obtained. Computers are able to process, format, store and retrieve certain types of information in far greater volume and at far greater speeds than is possible with manual, paper-based systems – but it does not mean no computers, no MIS.

As an example of the power of the PC, consider the point-of-sale system at a supermarket checkout desk. The cashier has input basic data like the items you have bought and their prices (perhaps all contained on their bar codes). What type of 'management information' is made available?

(a) You get a receipt, listing all the items and prices, with subtotals, VAT calculations, totals and so on. This is information which will help you balance your bank statement, plan your finances and future purchases and so on.

(b) The supermarket assistant has the same information, allowing him or her to take the immediate action of asking for the required amount of money: the system may even convert the data into printed details on your cheque. At the end of the day, the takings (cash, cheques and so on) can be reconciled with the totals from the tills, for the purposes of financial control. Details, including VAT totals, will be entered in the accounts.

(c) The supermarket's managers may need different types of information from the system. A computerised point-of-sale system may be able to process the simple sales data gathered over time, to gather important date such as:

   (i) What stock needs to be replenished on the shelves as a result of sales; what stock needs to be replenished in the storerooms or warehouses, as a result of waning supplies and fast usage rates; (this is called stock or inventory control)

   (ii) Which product lines are selling well, and which badly; earnings (and therefore profit margins) of particular product lines

(iii) Buying patterns of customers: which are the busiest days, or times of day; which products people tend to buy in multiples or large quantities; whether people buy a high proportion of goods on special offer and so on

(iv) Whether customers pay most by cash, cheque or debit card

Activity 4 **(20 minutes)**

What kind of strategic decisions might be based on the information given in (c)? Give an example relating to each of (c) (i) – (iv) above.

You may have noticed that an MIS can process data to provide information for all levels of decision-making and planning.

Operational level MIS

Operational decisions are essentially every-day, small-scale and largely routine. They are sometimes called programmed decisions, because they do not have to be made fresh each time, but are dictated by the procedures of which they are a part, and can usually be worked out by a computer: the variables are quantifiable and the rules for making the decision are clear cut.

An MIS at this level is usually used for processing transactions and updating files.

Tactical level MIS

Tactical decision-making is concerned with how the organisation goes about achieving its objectives, and particularly with its control systems.

An MIS at this level will tend to:

(a) Gather information from a wider range of sources than an operational-level MIS, taking into account information from the external environment as well as the organisation's own processes

(b) Filter out much of the detail, which may not be required at this level: in other words, make more use of reporting by exception

(c) Investigate, analyse and process data acquired at the operational level, in order to apply it to tactical decisions. So, for example, basic sales information can be formulated for use in marketing decisions, stock supply decisions, product development decisions and so on.

Three types of formal MIS are often used at the tactical level.

(a) **Control systems** monitor and report on the organisation's activities.

(b) **Database systems** store information which can be drawn upon as and when a manager needs it. The database may consist of the organisation's own files, or information from outside the organisation (like the Internet).

(c) **Decision support systems** store and process information for the analysis of problems and the testing of possible solutions.

Strategic level MIS

As you know from the earlier part of the book, strategic decisions are the long-term decisions which define the organisation's purpose and direction, goals and practices. These tend to be non-repetitive, non-routine decisions, which involve a number of variables, not all of which will be clear-cut or quantifiable (values, consumer behaviour patterns and so on). Human judgement is therefore required to a much greater extent; such decisions can rarely be programmed.

An MIS at this level tends to:

(a) Draw information from an even wider range of sources outside the organisation

(b) Include more informal information-gathering by managers

(c) Provide more subjective and less detailed information

In other words different levels of MIS can be shown as follows in Figure 10.2.

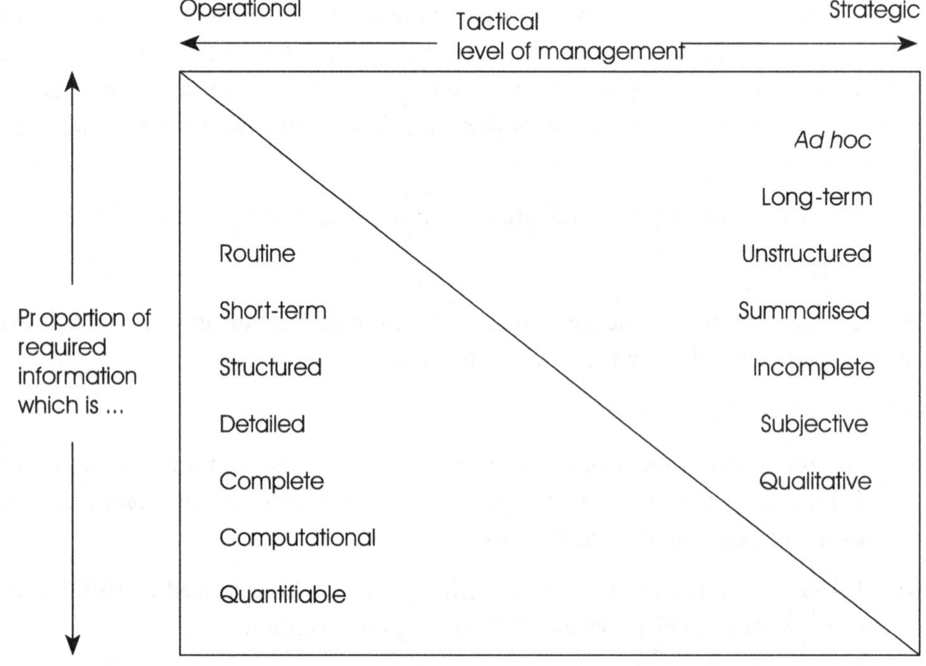

Figure 10.3: Levels of MIS

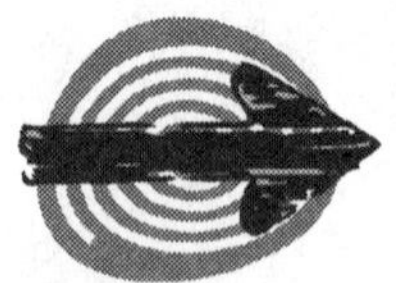

You can see that while at an operational level, the MIS may be able to make decisions which are highly structured and computational, at tactical and strategic levels this is not possible. All an MIS can do is to give managers information, and insight, into the nature and impact of their decisions.

4.2 Decision support systems (DSS)

Definition

A **decision support system** is a (usually computerised) MIS designed to produce information in such a way as to help managers make better decisions.

When management decisions are unstructured, there may be **uncertainty** about the nature of the problem, the range of possible solutions and the possible impact of each of those solutions, under a variety of potential conditions. **Decision support systems** are designed to offer highly flexible, highly interactive, information-processing capabilities, allowing such matters to be analysed.

(a) **Modelling** is the term given to the techniques which represent a real situation, by depicting the interrelationships between relevant factors in the situation in a simplified and structured way. Models can be used to increase a manager's understanding of the situation in which a decision has to be made, and to help him or her evaluate alternative decisions. In effect, models allow managers to try out decisions and see what happens – without incurring any real risks.

(b) **Sensitivity analysis** is a technique which basically asks 'What if ...?': what if a particular piece of data in a decision model were changed? A manager can see what the alternative outcome of a decision would be if different assumptions were adopted. What would be the difference in profit if a higher than planned pay rise were awarded to staff, or if market share fell by a given percentage?

(c) **Spreadsheets** are simple models which allow a manager to input a range of interrelated variables into a matrix, and to see the effect of changing one or more of them on the others. You could instantly gauge, for example, how changing the price of your raw materials would affect your cost forecasts and profit margins; how a day's slippage in the schedule for a process might affect your overall plans, and so on.

FOR DISCUSSION

Why should managers get paid so much, when it is the computer that makes all the tough decisions?

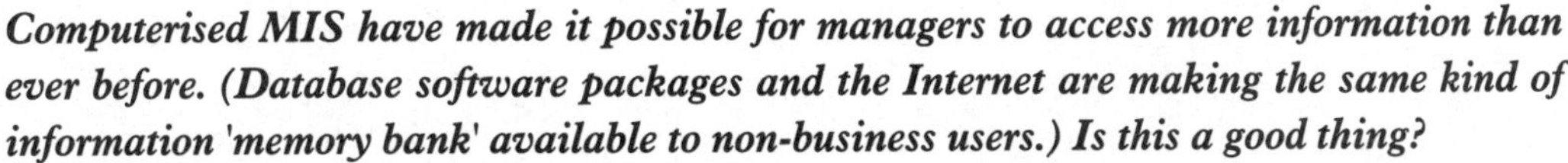

Computerised MIS have made it possible for managers to access more information than ever before. (Database software packages and the Internet are making the same kind of information 'memory bank' available to non-business users.) Is this a good thing?

4.3 Is more information better information?

Information overload

It should be clear that managers can undertake no decision-making or communicating task before first receiving appropriate information upon which to base it. However, responsibility for the outcome of decisions can make managers seek too much information, rather than too little. '**Analysis paralysis**' is a catchy term for the inertia that sets in when people attempt to get all the information they think they might need for a decision.

Most decisions are in fact based on incomplete information.

(a) All the information relevant to the decision is not **available**

(b) Beyond a certain point, the gathering of more information would not be worth the **extra time** and cost of obtaining and analysing it

(c) Beyond a certain point, the manager will be unable **effectively** to take in or take into account more information

Providers of management information need to bear in mind that information overload is counter-productive and a waste of resources. Managers (especially at the strategic level) rarely want or need to know as much detail as the people lower down the hierarchy, for whom detailed, short-term information is the staple diet of their jobs.

EXAMPLE

The marketing assistant in charge of handling customer queries will need to take in all details of customers' experience with the product, retail outlet or whatever: the marketing director, however, might require only a summary of the number and nature of complaints, or whether they were getting more or less serious/frequent, in order to devise better customer care policies, or to reward staff for improvements.

Management information should therefore be:

(a) **Summarised**, or otherwise processed in order to be easily digestible and relevant to its purpose

(b) **Provided by exception**: sparing managers routine, expected, repetitive and irrelevant information, but initiating feedback and reporting in the event of relevant new inputs of information or variance from the routine or plan.

Here is a brief checklist of ten qualities of good information.

QUALITIES OF GOOD INFORMATION

1 It should be **relevant** for its purpose.

2 It should be **complete** for its purpose.

3 It should be **sufficiently accurate** for its purpose. (Information should always be as correct as possible, however it need not always be completely accurate, in the sense that an approximation - 'about 100 labour hours' - may be all that is requested, rather than figures to the last decimal place ...)

4 It should be **clear** to the user.

5 The user should be able to have **confidence** in it. (It should appear logical, well-researched and supported and so on.)

6 It should be **communicated to the right person**. (The one who needs and can use it to do a job.)

7 There should be **no more** than the user can take in and use.

8 It should be **timely** (ie provided at the right time to be used for its intended purpose).

9 It should be communicated by appropriate media and channels.

10 It should be provided at a cost which is less than the value of its benefits to the user/ organisation.

Chapter roundup

- Information is the lifeblood of organisations, and the basis for management planning, control, co-ordinating, organising and commanding.
- Organisations have formal communication systems and channels to ensure that required information exchange takes place. There is also an informal communication system or network(s) in every organisation.
- Organisational communication can be:
  - downward (orders, instructions, briefings, motivation, appraisal etc)
  - upward (reporting, briefings, suggestions, upward appraisal etc)
  - horizontal (teambuilding, co-ordination, informal etc)
- Managers need to master basic communication formats such as memos and reports.
- Management Information Systems (MIS) collect data and convert them into information relevant to managers at all levels, to help them carry out the tasks for which they are responsible. Decision support systems (DSS) are specifically designed to help managers analyse and evaluate their decisions.

Quick quiz

1. Give four examples of (a) managers' and (b) team members' information needs.
2. What is meant by communication which is:

   (a) Upward?
   (b) Downward?
   (c) Horizontal?
3. What is the 'grapevine', and describe it?
4. What are the advantages and disadvantages of giving orders or briefings by telephone?
5. What two qualities must instructions have in order to be fulfilled satisfactorily?
6. What should be included in instructions for a complex task?
7. What might be covered in regular 'team briefings'?
8. Name the two important considerations when briefing teams.
9. Give three examples of positive reinforcement in downward communication.
10. What are the main purposes of upward communication in organisations?
11. List the headings you might use in a typical (a) formal and (b) informal report.
12. Why is there a need for a formal management information system?
13. By what other name can an 'operational decision' be called?
14. What is the difference between data and information?
15. List the ten qualities of good information.

Answers to quick quiz

1 (a) Information is needed to establish objectives, suggest adjustment of performance, appraise available resources and guide planning.

(b) Information is needed to perform tasks effectively, and for motivation, learning, development and job satisfaction.

2 (a) From subordinate to superior.

(b) From superior to subordinate.

(c) Between individuals, teams, departments on the same level of the organisation chart.

3 It is an informal network of gossip and rumours.

4 Advantages are that it cuts down on time and physical movement. Disadvantages are that there are no non-verbal signals and it is more difficult to persuade and to respond to physical factors.

5 They must be clear and sufficient.

6 Desired results, definition of all relevant terms, a breakdown of the task into logical components, all the information needed to understand and carry out the task.

7 Organisational policy and changes, plans, progress, results.

8 The purpose of communication and the needs and abilities of the audience.

9 Praise, encouragement and constructive criticism.

10 To give feedback, to inform and to make suggestions.

11 (a) Title, Terms of Reference, Procedure or Method, Findings, Conclusions, Recommendations.

(b) Title, Background or Introduction, Findings or Analysis, Action or Solution or Conclusion or Recommendations.

12 The right managers get the right information at the right time in the right format.

13 A programmed decision.

14 Data is raw material; information is data that has been appropriately processed.

15 Relevant, complete, accurate, clear, inspires confidence, communicated to the right person, appropriate volume, timely, communicated by the right means, cost effective.

Answers to activities

1 Among other information, an organisation would need to give out the following.

(i) Products/services: to customers and potential customers in the market place.

(ii) Needs and expectations (specifications, orders, requests for estimates and so on): to suppliers, potential suppliers, sub-contractors etc.

(iii) Terms and conditions of payment for products/services (eg invoices and statements): to customers.

(iv) Labour requirements, and what the organisation can offer as an employer: to potential employees in the labour pool.

(v) Financial performance and plans: to the owners (shareholders), creditors (those to whom it owes money) and other stakeholders.

(vi) Records and digests of financial transactions – reports and returns: to auditors, the tax authorities etc as required by law and regulation.

(vii) The workforce and employment practices: to agencies such as the Health and Safety Executive, Training Commission or trade unions. Also a highly regulated area.

(viii) The organisation's mission and culture: to the world in general.

2 Since the grapevine exists, and cannot be got rid of, management should learn both to accept it and to use it: to harness it towards achieving the objectives of the organisation. It is important for managers themselves to 'hook into' the grapevine, to be aware of what is going on – and what their subordinates think is going on. The grapevine may also be a useful way of 'feeding' information to staff, where the formal system would be mistrusted, or too slow.

3 You will have put in your own details in your memo answering Mr Bossere, but check that you have the same headings that he used, and that you have answered all three of his questions.

4 The supermarket might act on point-of-sale information by taking these decisions:

(i) Ordering more stock from suppliers, or increasing the standard order frequency or size.

(ii) Dropping underperforming products (or promoting them harder, with special offers etc), cutting costs on products with unacceptably low profit margins.

(iii) Encouraging shopping at 'off-peak' periods (with offers etc), designing bulk-packs of popular bulk-bought items, adjusting the terms and advertising of special offers.

(iv) Accepting more or less payment methods such as expanding range of credit cards accepted or no longer accepting cheques.

Chapter 11 : MANAGING PROJECTS

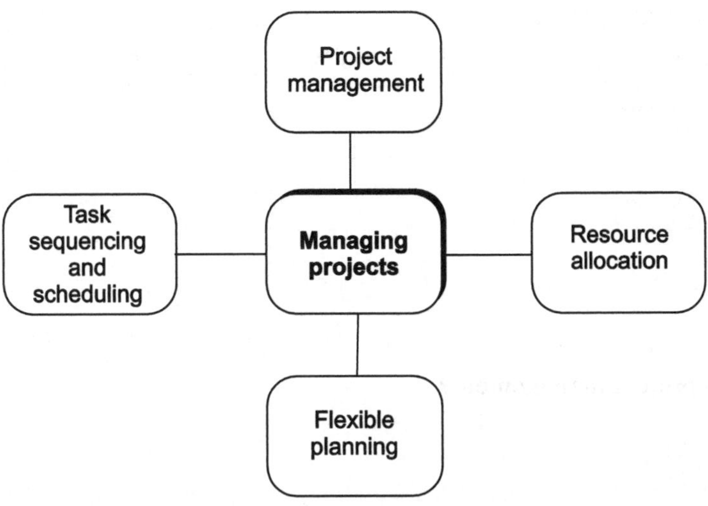

Introduction

Managers are also responsible for planning and organising the work of others, and for co-ordinating the resources and stages of a given task so that objectives (and ultimately strategy) are achieved.

In this chapter, we discuss the management of such complex tasks or projects, and look at some of the practical techniques managers use for each of these areas.

Your objectives

In this chapter you will learn about the following.

(a) The complex nature of project management, and the need for co-ordination of activities and resources

(b) Work breakdown structures and estimating job times

(c) Networks for a given activity, the critical path (using CPA) and implications for resource allocation and scheduling of time

(d) Gantt charts for scheduling and resource allocation, and interpreting data on such a chart

(e) How 'slack' can be built into the project plan, including the use of Programme Evaluation and Review Technique (PERT)

1 PROJECT MANAGEMENT

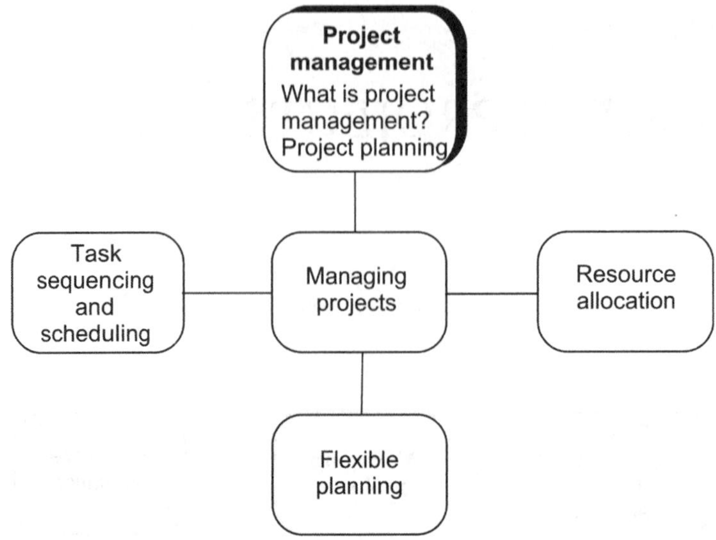

1.1 What is project management?

Definition

A **project** is an undertaking, often cutting across organisational and functional boundaries, and carried out to meet established goals within cost, schedule and quality objectives.

Project management is directed at a particular end: achieving **specific objectives** within a **specific time span**. It is not, like general management, directed at maintaining or improving continuous work activities.

Activity 1 **(20 minutes)**

See if you can think of an example of a project in each of the following areas.

(a) Building and construction

(b) Manufacturing

(c) Management

(d) Research and development

Project management therefore requires even closer attention to planning, organising and control, with regard to:

(a) **Quality** – the end result should conform to specification; in other words, the project should achieve what it was meant to do

(b) **Cost** – the project should be completed without exceeding authorised expenditure (as specified in a budget) of money and other human and material resources

(c) Time – each stage of the project's progress must conform to schedule, so that the end result is achieved when requested or required.

1.2 Project planning

A project plan aims to ensure that the project objective is achieved within the requirements of quality, cost and time. This will involve:

(a) **Breaking the project down** into manageable units of activity, and determining the sequence of, or relationships between, those units or tasks

(b) **Estimating the resources** (materials, money, time and so on) required for each unit

(c) **Sequencing and scheduling** each unit in the most appropriate way for co-ordinated performance.

We will now look at techniques and tools used for planning and organising interrelated and interdependent activities.

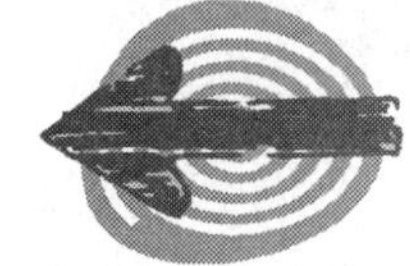

2 TASK SEQUENCING AND SCHEDULING

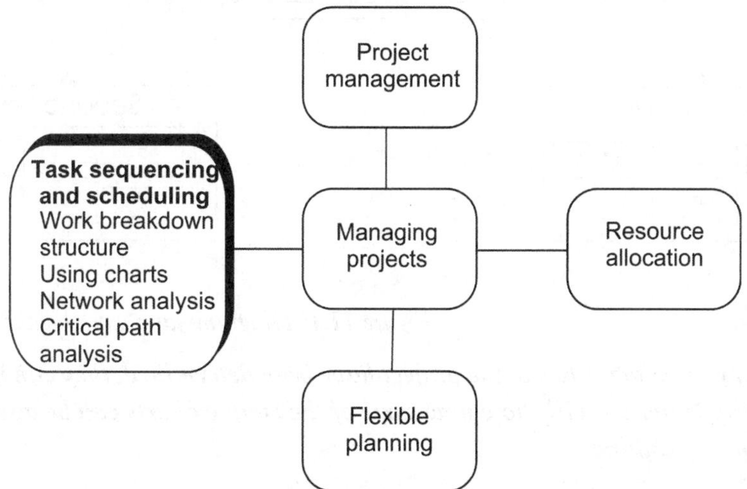

2.1 Work breakdown structure (WBS)

Breaking a project down into its component phases or stages is often the best way of:

- Discovering exactly what work must be accomplished
- Determining the resources required
- Sequencing and co-ordinating the work done.

This is called establishing a work breakdown structure (WBS) for the project.

Activity 2 **(30 minutes)**

Suppose you set yourself the project of cooking a dinner party for yourself and five friends.

(a) Define the objectives of the project: devise a three course meal menu.

(b) Estimate (roughly):

(i) the cost and
(ii) the time it will take you to prepare.

(c) Establish a work breakdown structure, in the form of a detailed list of things to do, for preparing your menu.

(d) What does your WBS tell you about your cost and time estimates?

Figure 11.1 is a simple example of a diagrammatic work breakdown structure for a house-building project. We have only broken down two of the component stages to the second level (the foundations and the wiring), but you should get the idea. The breakdown process continues until the smallest sub-unit or task is reached, for which man and machine hours can most easily be calculated and scheduled.

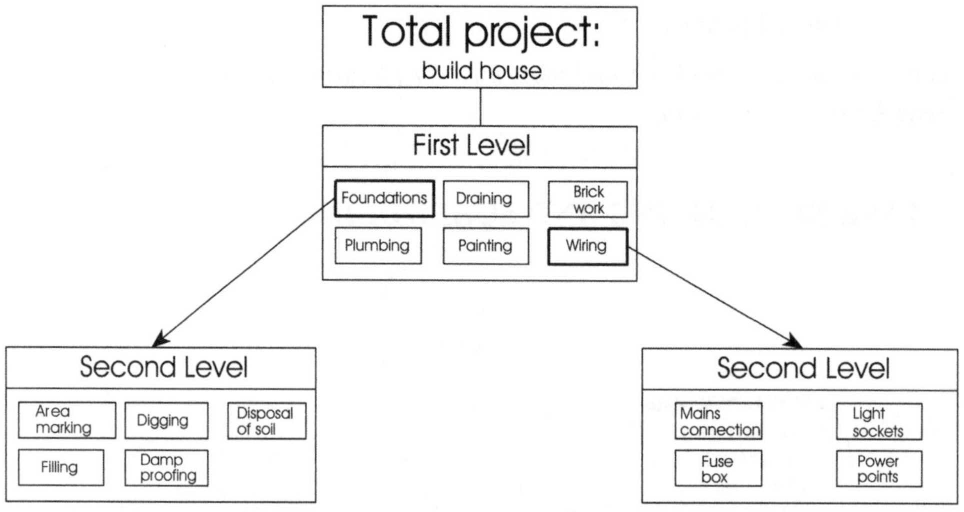

Figure 11.1: Diagrammatic work breakdown structure

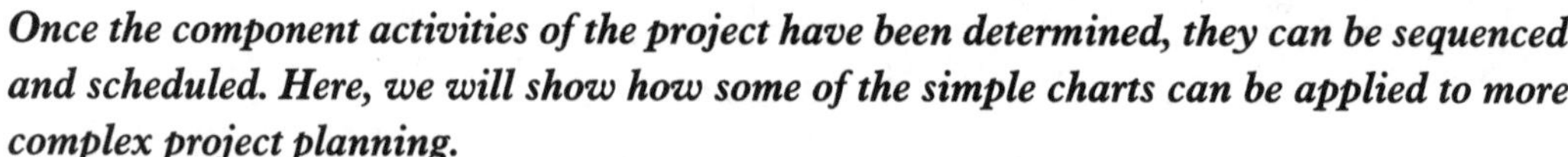

Once the component activities of the project have been determined, they can be sequenced and scheduled. Here, we will show how some of the simple charts can be applied to more complex project planning.

2.2 Using charts

Bar line charts

A simple project plan can be shown on a bar line or Gantt chart. Figure 11.2 is an example of a chart for a project to build a garage.

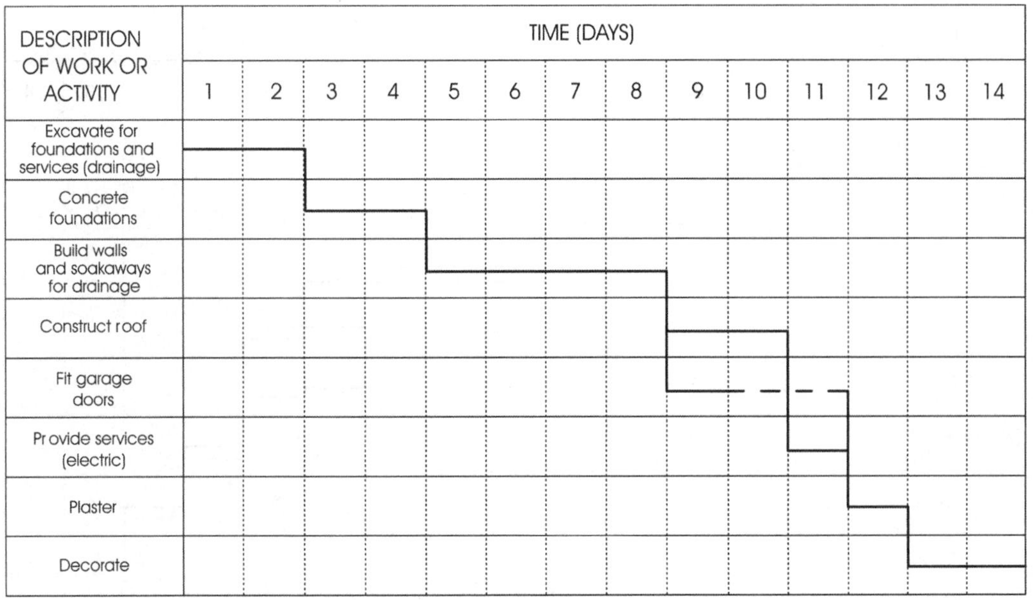

Figure 11.2: Gantt chart for building a garage

This chart shows the sequence of activities to be followed, as well as the duration of each activity. You need to excavate before you can put in foundations, before you can build walls: once you've got to that stage, you can do the roof and doors together, if you have the manpower – sheltered from the elements – you can then follow the next sequence.

Activity 3 **(15 minutes)**

How could you, very simply, turn this chart into a work schedule?

This type of chart has the advantage of being very easy to understand. It can also be used as a **progress control** chart, with the lower section of each bar being completed (eg shaded in) as the activity is completed.

Linked bar charts

In order to show more clearly where the activities are dependent on each other, you might prefer to use a linked bar chart, as in Figure 11.3.

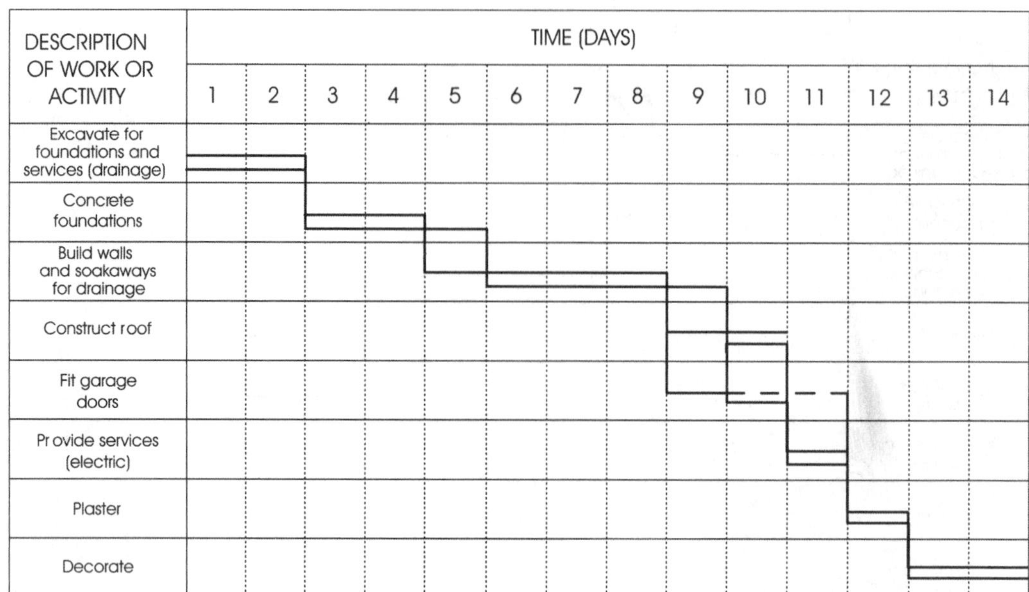

Figure 11.3: Linked bar chart

This shows the link between activities. In our example, the roofing and door-fitting can be done together, starting on day 9, but the door-fitting only takes one day, while the roofing takes two days – and needs to be finished before electrical wiring can be done, hopefully on day 11. The door-fitting therefore has a certain amount of leeway: it can be started late if necessary, since it does not hold up any other activity until the roofing and electrical installation are finished. This leeway is called **float time,** and is shown by the dotted line on the chart: the activity can be moved into the dotted area if necessary. Activities that have no float time are called **critical activities**: they must be completed on time in order to avoid a knock-on effect which will make the project as a whole run over time.

Activity 4 **(20 minutes)**

You are the site manager of the garage construction project. You have drawn up the linked bar chart above as a guide to all your on-site staff as to the order of activities and the speed of progress required to meet the customer's two-week deadline. You decide to use the chart to monitor progress. Using a different-coloured pen, you draw a line beneath the one on your plan chart to show what your team has actually accomplished.

(a) Everything takes the time it was planned to, except that on the Wednesday (day 3) the weather is too bad to work, so that concreting of the foundations actually takes three days.

(b) The door fitting takes one day, and the door-fitter is also qualified to do roofing work. His help will knock a day off the roofing schedule.

Draw the control line onto Figure 11.3. Has your project run over time?

The big advantage of such charts is that they are easily understood by all levels of staff, and without undue calculation. However they can only display a restricted amount of information, and the links between activities are fairly crude. To overcome these limitations, when planning and organising more complex projects, we use a more sophisticated technique called network analysis.

2.3 Network analysis

Network analysis is a term for project planning techniques which aim to 'map' the activities in a particular project, and the relationship between them.

(a) What tasks must be done before others can be started

(b) What tasks could be done at the same time

(c) What tasks must be completed on schedule if the completion date for the whole project is not to slip: the critical tasks.

These relationships and sequences are represented in a network diagram, which flows from left to right. The most commonly used form of network is called an **activity-on-arrow diagram**, because activities are represented by an arrowed line, which runs between one event (start or completion of the activity) and another. Events are depicted by a node, or circle.

Hence in the following example we map Activity A, which starts at a certain point (Event 1) and ends at a certain point (Event 2).

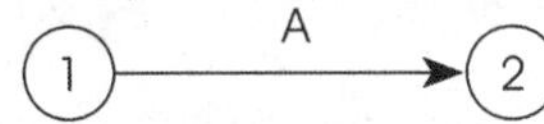

Let us tackle a more complex example. Suppose your work breakdown structure comprises six activities: we will call them Activities A–G.

(a) Activities A and B can start together.

(b) You have to have done Activity B before you can do activity C.

(c) Once activity A is completed, Activities D and E can start, at the same time.

(d) Activity F follows on from Activity D.

(e) Activity G will be completed at the same time as activity F, to end the project. However, Activities C and E must be completed before G can commence.

Activity 5 **(10 minutes)**

Do not look at the network diagram below (Figure 11.4). Read (a)–(e) above again. Working from left to right, draw the network diagram showing Activities A–G and Events 1–6.

It is a convention in network analysis that two separate activities should not start and end at the same events. If the real activities could start and end at the same event, this is shown on the network by inserting a dummy activity, represented by an extra event node with a dotted line joining it to the next event. See Figure 11.4.

Incorrect

Correct

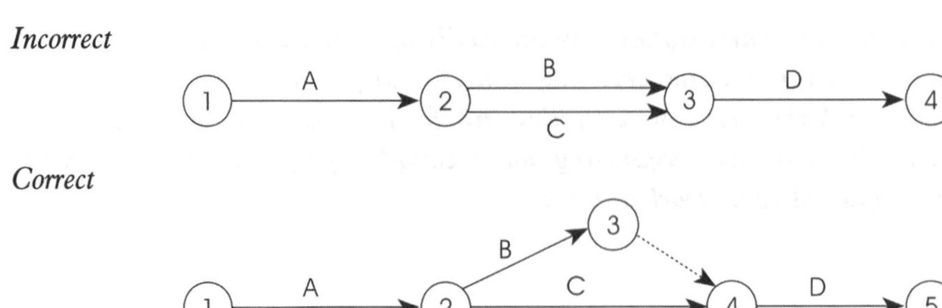

Figure 11.4: Network diagram with dummy activity

The correct version shows that Activities B and C both have to be completed before D can begin, and the dotted line indicates that no extra activity is actually done and no extra time is taken between Event 3 (completion of B) and Event 4 (completion of C). The two activities therefore do start and end at the same points in the sequence, but not at the same nodes on the diagram.

Activity 6 **(10 minutes)**

Here is the network activity required in the previous activity.

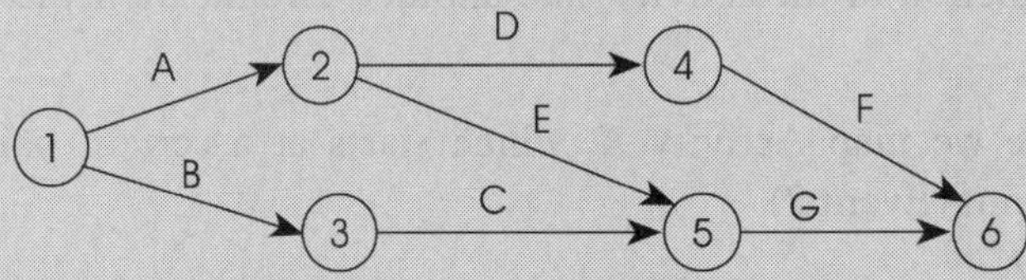

Now suppose that Activity G depended on the completion of activity D, as well as Activities C and E. Activity F still depends on Activity D alone. There is no extra time or activity involved; all you need to do is to indicate the link between Activities D and G. Draw the 'dummy activity' dotted line on our network diagram, to represent this scenario.

Another use of the dummy activity is to ensure that all activities end up at a single completion event, joining in any loose events.

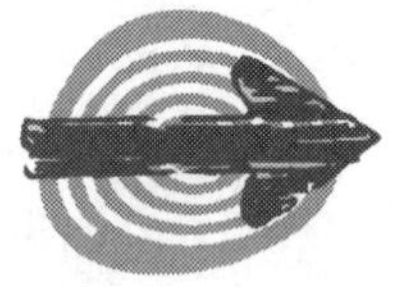

More information can be added to a network diagram, to describe not just what happens next, but when it should happen, and how long the whole project will take if each activity takes as long as it is supposed to. This technique is called CPA, or critical path analysis.

2.4 Critical path analysis (CPA)

If Activity A takes three days, it is shown like this.

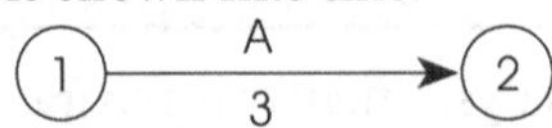

Let us say, building on our original A-G network, that:

Activity A takes 3 days
B takes 5 days
C takes 2 days

D takes 1 day
E takes 6 days
F takes 3 days
G takes 3 days.

Our network would be as in Figure 11.5.

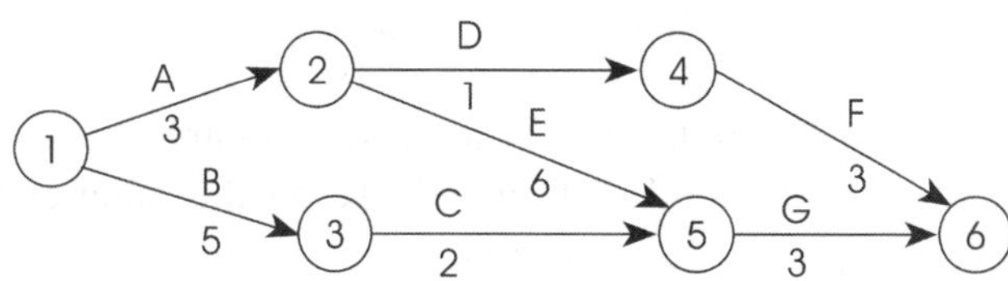

Figure 11.5: Network diagram with timings

Let us assume that you have all the resources you need to carry out the above project as drawn: in other words, you have enough workers to do Activities A and B at the same time, and so on. The shortest possible time in which you can complete the project is twelve days. See if you can work out why, before reading on.

Each of the 'routes' of arrows from the first event to the last event is called a pathway, or path.

Activity 7 **(20 minutes)**

List all the pathways in Figure 11.5, and add up how many days each path will take to reach Event 6.

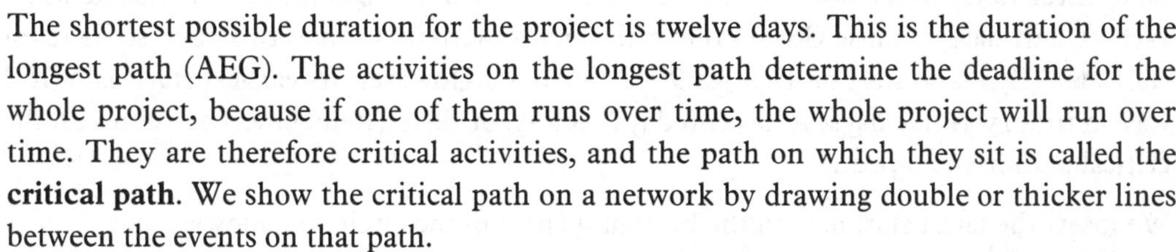

The shortest possible duration for the project is twelve days. This is the duration of the longest path (AEG). The activities on the longest path determine the deadline for the whole project, because if one of them runs over time, the whole project will run over time. They are therefore critical activities, and the path on which they sit is called the **critical path**. We show the critical path on a network by drawing double or thicker lines between the events on that path.

Activity 8 **(30 minutes)**

Draw a network for the following project, and identify the critical path.

Activity	Depends on activity	Duration (weeks)
A	–	5
B	–	4
C	A	2
D	B	1
E	B	5
F	B	5
G	C, D	4
H	F	3
J	F	2

Hint: all your activities should 'tie up' at Event 7.

Scheduling using the critical path

Once you have estimated activity durations and worked out the total project time, you can start scheduling. First of all, you work forwards from Event 1, working out the earliest start date of each activity. We show the earliest start date of an activity as follows.

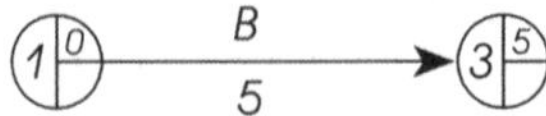

Obviously, Event 1 starts at 0 (on day one): the earliest possible time for C to start, given that B takes five days, is at the end of Day 5. If we do the same exercise with all the activities in our A-G example, we get Figure 11.6.

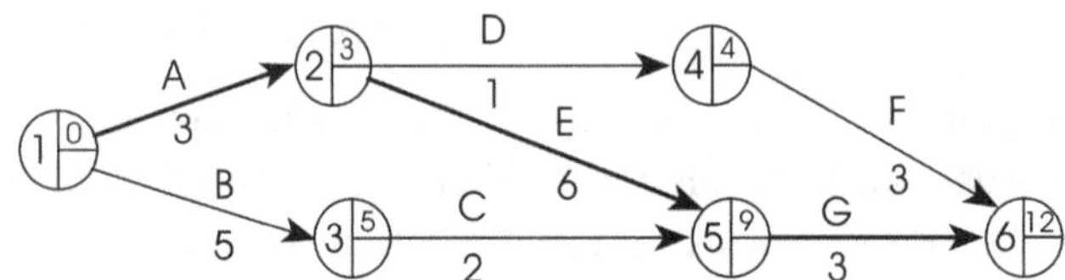

Figure 11.6: Network diagram showing start times

Note that the earliest start date for G (which has to follow A and E) is nine days. But B and C only take seven days: they can take two extra days, if necessary, without affecting the start of G.

We make this clear by next working backwards from Event 6 to Event 1, identifying the latest start dates when activities can start and still keep up with the timing set by the critical path. The earliest deadline of Event 6 is twelve days: this is also its latest deadline, because it is the end of the critical path, which must not run late. Activity G takes three days, so its latest start date is 12 – 3 = 9 days: again, this is the same as its earliest start date, because G is on the critical path. Activity C takes two days, so its latest start date (if G is to start on time) is 9 – 2 = 7 days. However, its earliest start date (if B was on time) was five days: it has two days' leeway, or float. (Remember: activities on the critical path have no float.)

We insert the latest start date in the bottom quarter of the circle, as follows.

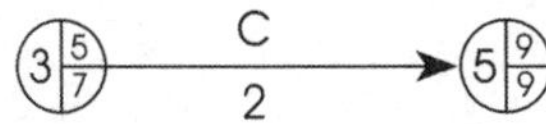

You can see just from this that Activity C can be started any time between days five and seven, giving the project manager a degree of flexibility, but that Event 5 is on the critical path and must not run late!

Activity 9 **(20 minutes)**

Starting from Event 6 and working backwards, fill in the latest start dates in Figure 11.6. Which activities can afford to start late, and by how much?

Attach actual dates to your days currently numbered 1 to 12, and you have a detailed and effective schedule.

3 RESOURCE ALLOCATION

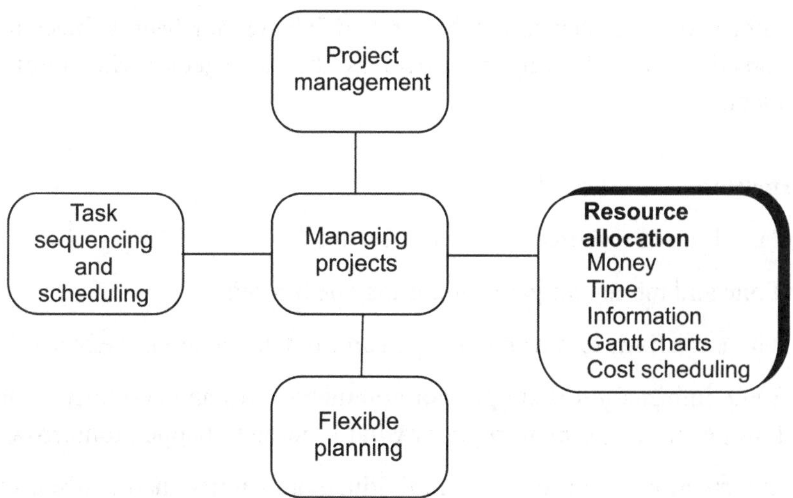

3.1 Money

Money, and the infinite variety of things it represents, is always **limited** and tightly **controlled** in organisations. Money allocated to different units represents cost to the organisation, whose **financial objectives** are likely to be profitability, return on investment and so on: in other words, to **maximise earnings and minimise costs.**

Individual unit budgets for expenditure are components of the overall organisational budget – like slices of a cake. A great deal of the politics and conflict within organisations is concerned with competing for bigger slices of the cake!

Limited financial resources therefore **constrain managerial decision-making** because:

(a) A limited budget can only be stretched so far, and the manager may not be able to obtain or retain all the other resources – quality materials, extra labour, new equipment and so on – that (s)he would want

(b) A manager may be tempted to spend up to the allocated budget, even though it is not required, so as not to have the allocation reduced next time round.

3.2 Time

You may not have thought about it, but **time** is a limited resource.

(a) There are only so many working hours available. If these are not sufficient to accomplish everything a manager wishes, (s)he will be constrained to:

   (i) Find extra labour or machine capacity, to cover the excess workload in the time available

   (ii) Eliminate, or simplify, tasks or 'cut corners' in order to get high-priority work done with the existing workforce

   (iii) Allow work to run late, and adjust the work plan for the knock-on effects

(b) **Deadlines** may be imposed by customer requirements or internal co-ordination. Compromises of cost or quality may have to be made to meet deadlines.

(c) Time for information-gathering and decision-making is also limited. This may constrain managers to make decisions which seem riskier or less informed than they might be, or which have not been subject to as much consultation with team members as the manager's style might otherwise dictate.

3.3 Information

Information is a limited resource for several reasons.

(a) Time and money for gathering it may be limited.

(b) There is a limit to how much a person can take in and use effectively.

(c) Some information is simply not obtainable with any certainty – for example, how people are going to react, or what is going to happen tomorrow!

(d) 'Information is power', and individuals and units in organisations tend to hoard it if they think it will give them extra influence or a competitive edge over others.

Limited information constrains the management of activities because:

(a) Decisions have to be taken on the basis of what is known: the full range of possible options can never be known, and a certain degree of uncertainty and inaccuracy remains

(b) It is not possible to predict the outcome of all decisions and actions, nor the contingencies that might affect them. Changes in the PESTEL, competitive or physical environment of an organisation cannot always be foreseen and planned for.

If management information is not made available to a manager – for example, the objectives and results of the organisation, or the attitudes of employees – then the ability of the manager to make effective decisions will clearly be impaired.

Activity 10 **(20 minutes)**

How does scarcity of:

(a) money
(b) time
(c) information

affect your management of your own activities? How are you constrained or limited by such considerations?

3.4 Gantt charts

As well as plotting **time to be taken** (and actually taken), Gantt charts can be used to estimate the amounts of **resources required** for a project.

Let us take the example we have been using so far in this section. We will be starting with our final network showing earliest and latest start times for A–G, so you may like to make a clean copy of the solution to Activity 9 and keep it by you for reference.

Suppose that, in addition to the information contained on our network, we know the number of workers required to do each job, as follows.

Activity				
Activity	A	requires	6	workers
	B	"	3	"
	C	"	4	"
	D	"	4	"
	E	"	5	"
	F	"	6	"
	G	"	3	"

Suppose that we have a team of nine workers, each of whom is paid a fixed wage, regardless of hours worked in a week (so we want to avoid idle time if possible). Each worker is capable of working on any of the seven activities involved in the project (so we can swap them round freely if required).

Figure 11.7 shows a Gantt chart, simply plotting the various paths against the 12-day timescale. We have assumed that activities will be started at the earliest start times, adding floats (where available) as a dotted line.

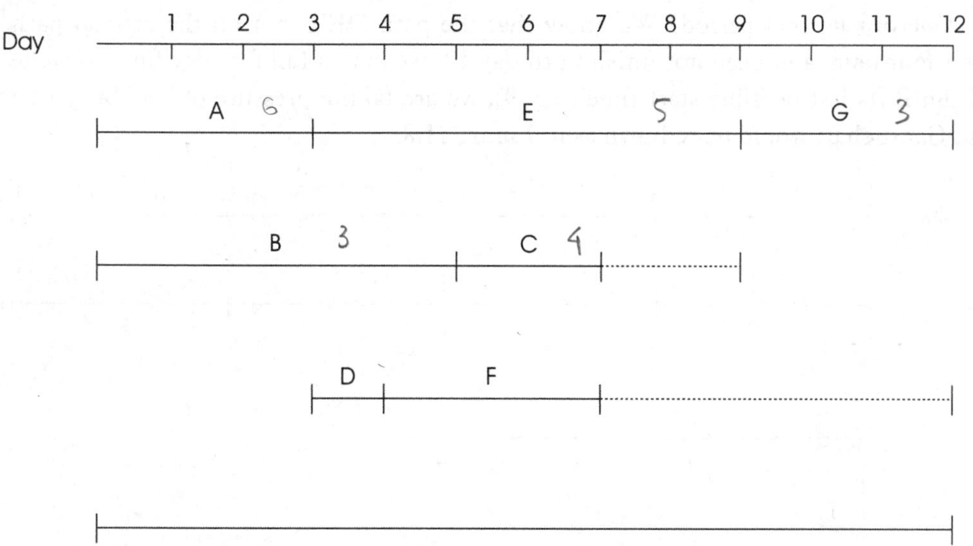

Figure 11.7: A Gantt chart showing floats

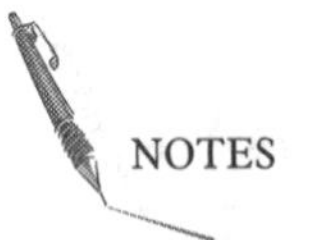

NOTES

Activity 11 **(30 minutes)**

1 On Figure 11.7 add the number of workers required, below the line under the relevant activity letter: A/6 and so on.

2 Now, label the line at the bottom of the chart 'Workers required'.

3 Draw a line vertically through the start and end of each activity, from the 'Time' line (days) to the 'Workers required' line. With each activity beginning or ending, the number of workers required will change.

4 In your first section of the 'Workers required' line, which extends from day 0 to 3, A and B are going on simultaneously. Mark 'AB' above this section of the line.

5 Activities A and B require six and three workers respectively: that is, nine workers. Mark '9' below the 'AB' on the 'Workers required' line.

6 Keep going until you have completed all segments of the 'Workers required' line.

From the answer to the above activity, you may note that on days 6 and 7 you need as many as fifteen workers though you only have nine. On days 8–12, you would have most of your team sitting about twiddling their thumbs. What are you going to do?

Let's look at the really busy period of days 4–7. Can you see any activities that need not be done during that period? We know that the path DF is not on the critical path. It takes four days, and need not finish until day 12: we have a full five-day float. If we leave DF until its last possible start time (day 9), we are taking pressure off the busy period. Our Gantt chart would be redrawn as in Figure 11.8.

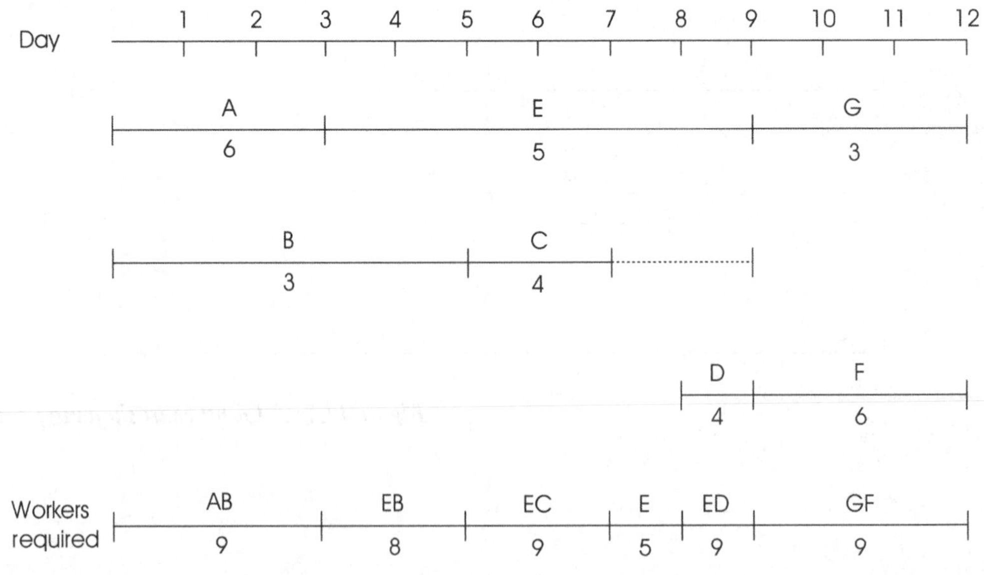

Figure 11.8: The final Gantt chart

The project can be completed without hiring any additional labour, and without running late. Good job! You can keep shuffling non-critical activities and re-calculating worker requirements like this until you are satisfied you have found the best solution. If there is too little float time at convenient stages to allow you do this, you may have to:

(a) Reschedule the project to find the minimum excess demand for labour, and hire in extra labour for those times

(b) Move critical activities as well as non-critical ones (thereby lengthening the project) to avoid excess demand for labour. The same method should be used to find the minimum extension of the project's duration required.

3.5 Cost scheduling

Cost estimating

It is usually not possible to say with certainty what the costs of a project will be, but some idea will be required in advance so that costs can be monitored and controlled. Estimates of costs can be based on rough guesswork (a 'ballpark' estimate), comparison with similar projects in the past, or the initial plans for the project (a 'feasibility' estimate).

The work breakdown structure will clearly be useful in devising estimates because it enables the project manager to compile a complete list of items that will attract expenditure. Estimation forms can be designed, based on the WBS, with columns for labour, materials, components and so on for each of the work units or tasks. This ensures that no items are forgotten, and speeds up the process of estimating, where jobs are routine or similar in type.

Cost scheduling

Costs can be scheduled, in exactly the same way as labour requirements.

(a) Draw a bar chart for the project.

(b) Estimate the cost of each activity.

(c) Divide by the duration of the activity to get the cost of the activity per week (or other appropriate time unit).

(d) Work out the cost of all activities going on in a given week: ie a total cost per week of the project.

For ease of cash-flow, the project manager may need to restrict cash outflows in any week. As with labour requirements, he may be able to do this by rescheduling tasks which have a float.

It may, however, be more important simply to keep within the planned amount for the total expense on the project. And even then, it may be preferable to spend extra finance on a project to stop it running over time.

FOR DISCUSSION

In what kinds of project would you consider the time deadlines more important than the expenditure budget? And vice versa? (What projects do you know of which have gone way over budget, or late? Look out for examples in the press.)

Activity 12 **(20 minutes)**

Find your answer to Activity 2 – your WBS for a dinner party menu.

(a) Make up a cost estimate, based on your WBS. Draw a column marked B for budget, down the right hand side of your list, and enter your estimated amounts for each task.

(b) Go out and find out what it would actually cost, and write down each amount in a column marked A for actual, next to your Budget column.

How was your estimating? If you gave your dinner party, you might have written down what you really paid for your ingredients in the Actual column. You could monitor how you were doing, compared to your budget. This is called budgetary control: another useful management technique!

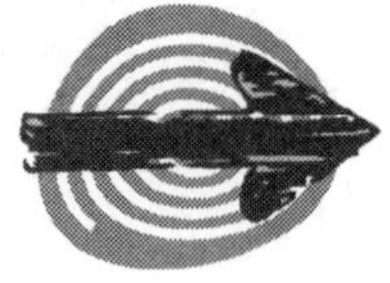

It should be clear from our discussion of 'estimates' that project planning is inexact and uncertain: the project manager does not have a crystal ball to tell him how long an activity will take, how much it will cost or how successful it will be. Finally, in this chapter, we look briefly at this problem of uncertainty, and how it can be planned for.

4 FLEXIBLE PLANNING

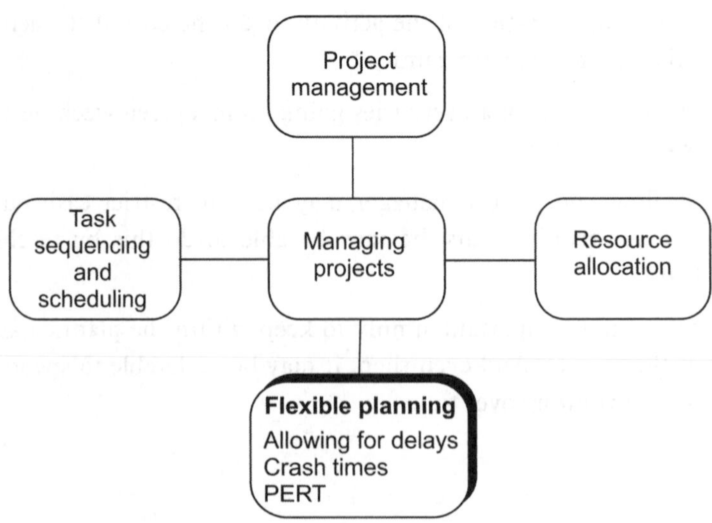

4.1 Allowing for delays

As we have already discussed, activities which are not on the critical path are non-critical, and can, within limits, start later and/or take longer, without holding up the completion time of the project as a whole. This slack time is called the activity's float. It allows unexpected delays to be absorbed and resources to be diverted, to avoid the late start of critical activities.

What happens if your critical activities are threatened with delays, though, and the final deadline simply cannot be extended?

4.2 Crash times

The crash time is the minimum time an activity can take to be completed. Crashing often involves the use of extra resources.

Job X takes one worker $1^1/_2$ days – say, twelve working hours. The worker gets paid £10 per hour, so the cost of the job is £120. If the project manager needs Job X completed at the end of a single day, (s)he might ask the worker to do four hours' overtime to complete the twelve hours work in a single working day. However, the overtime rate of pay is £15 per hour. So the crash cost is (8 hours @ £10) + (4 hours @ £15) = £140.

There would be no point crashing non-critical jobs, because you would not shorten the overall project duration or affect the critical path by doing so. However, crashing can be used to shorten the critical path itself, if necessary, to:

- Catch up with delays
- Shorten the project duration for any reason.

You may have noted that, in most cases, we are still only talking about estimated job times or durations. What happens if you get those wrong in the first place? One answer is to take account of uncertainty and contingencies at the estimating stage. A well-known technique for doing this is PERT.

4.3 PERT

Programme Evaluation and Review Technique (PERT) recognises that the activity durations in the network are in fact uncertain. Instead of one estimate of each activity time, three estimates are used.

- The most likely duration of the activity, given what is known about it (which we will call m)
- The most optimistic (shortest) estimate, assuming that all goes well (o)
- The most pessimistic (longest) estimate, assuming that things that are likely to go wrong will go wrong (p)

These can be converted into a 'mean' (or middle) estimate, which takes into account the small chance that things will go entirely well or entirely badly. The mean time is calculated using the formula:

$$\frac{o + 4m + p}{6}$$

As an example, here are some more data!

Activity	*Must be preceded by activity*	*Optimistic (o) days*	*Most likely (m) days*	*Pessimistic (p) days*
A	–	5	10	15
B	A	16	18	26
C	–	15	20	31
D	–	8	18	28

The mean times for each activity are as follows.

Activity	*(o + 4m + p)*	÷ 6 =	*Mean time*
A	5 + 40 + 15 = 60		10 days
B	16 + 72 + 26 = 114		19 days
C	15 + 80 + 31 = 126		21 days
D	8 + 72 + 28 = 108		18 days

Activity 13 **(20 minutes)**

Draw the network for A-D, using the mean times. Include earliest start and latest start times, and show where the critical path is.

Other calculations can be made using PERT, including the probability that a job will overrun by a given time. Because of their complexity, PERT systems are often run on computers, which generate the planning and control data required.

PERT is frequently used where there are a number of possible contingencies which would affect the project duration. Construction projects, for example, need to allow for delays due to unfavourable weather.

Chapter roundup

- Project management is directed at a particular end: achieving specific objectives within a limited time span.
- Project planning and organisation involves:
  - Breaking the project into units (work breakdown structure)
  - Determining the sequence and/or relationships between those units
  - Estimating the resources required for each unit
  - Scheduling time and allocating resources for each unit.
- Popular techniques for project planning include:
  - network analysis (including critical path analysis) and
  - Gantt charts.
- Network analysis aims to 'map' the relationships and dependencies of tasks in a project. The critical path is the longest path on the network, representing the shortest possible completion time of the project: if any activity on the critical path runs late, the project will run late. Non-critical activities may have some 'slack' time within which they can be extended without having a knock-on effect on the project duration: this is called a float.
- Estimating costs and job times is not an accurate science. One technique for taking uncertainty into account is Programme Evaluation and Review Technique (PERT) which calculates a mean time for each activity using most likely, optimistic and pessimistic estimates.

Quick quiz

1 What is a work breakdown structure, and what can it be used for?

2 What are (a) a critical activity and (b) a float?

3 What are the advantages and disadvantages of using bar charts for project planning and control?

4 What is depicted by (a) nodes, (b) arrowed lines and (c) thick arrowed lines, in a network diagram?

5 In what circumstances might you add a 'dummy activity' to a network diagram?

6 Is the critical path the shortest or longest line from start to end of the project network?

7 What do the numbers represent in the following segment of a network diagram?

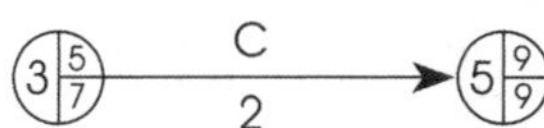

8 If you know how many workers are required for each job, and all team members can do all jobs, how might you go about scheduling your manpower in an efficient manner?

9 What is a 'crash time' and why might you not want to 'crash' a non-critical activity?

10 What is the mathematical formula for calculating a mean time for a job whose duration is uncertain?

Answers to quick quiz

1 It breaks a project down into its component phases or stages. It can be used to discover what work is needed and what resources are required and for sequencing and co-ordinating.

2 (a) One that must be completed on time.
(b) The amount of leeway there is for completion of the activity.

3 Advantages are that they are easily understood and do not require undue calculation. Disadvantages are that they give restricted information and links between activities are fairly crude.

4 (a) Events
(b) Activities
(c) Critical activities

5 When two activities could start and end at the same event

6 Longest

7 In the first node, 3 = event; 5 = earliest start; 7 = latest start; C2 means that activity C takes two days. In the second node 5 = event; 9/9 are the earliest and latest start day, so the activity must not run late.

8 Using a Gantt chart

9 It is the minimum time to complete an activity. Crashing a non-critical activity would not affect the critical path or shorten the overall project time.

10 $\frac{0+4m+p}{6}$

Answers to activities

1 You will have come up with your own ideas for different projects: here are some suggestions.

(a) Construction of a motorway extension, say, or the Channel Tunnel.

(b) Limited-edition production of a car, for example, or one-off tailor-made products.

(c) Implementation of a computer system, say, or mounting a trade exhibition or conference.

(d) Ironing out bugs in a system or product, completing a market research survey and so on.

Check that your own examples have a beginning, an end, and goals.

2 The answer will depend on your menu, but your WBS may include stages such as: the purchasing of the various ingredients; washing, peeling and chopping vegetables; mixing ingredients; cooking and/or preparing each dish; laying the table and preparing plates and utensils and so on. Your WBS should give you a fairly clear idea of what ingredients, in what quantities, you will need to buy: a more accurate cost estimate than trying to judge the cost of the meal as a whole. The same is true of the timetable, with the added advantage that it provides the basis for an action checklist and schedule for preparation.

3 To turn Figure 11.2 into a work schedule, you could put the days of the week across the top instead of the number of days given. So the excavations should take up Monday and Tuesday, the foundations start on Wednesday and so on.

4 The control line added to Figure 11.3 yields the result shown here.

DESCRIPTION OF WORK OR ACTIVITY	TIME (DAYS)													
	1	2	3	4	5	6	7	8	9	10	11	12	13	14
Excavate for foundations and services (drainage)														
Concrete foundations														
Build walls and soakaways for drainage														
Construct roof														
Fit garage doors														
Provide services (electric)														
Plaster														
Decorate														

You have made up your lost day of concreting because you had the float time on the door-fitting and were able to divert the door person to the roofing.

5

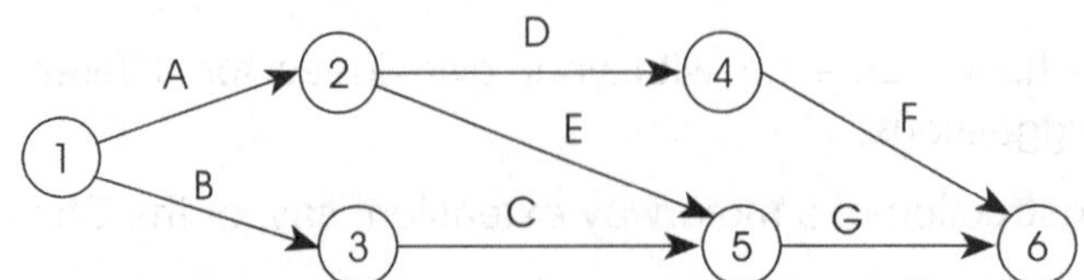

6 You should draw a dotted line from Event 4 to 5.

7 There are three paths, as follows.

ADF	= 3 + 1 + 3 days	= 7 days
AEG	= 3 + 6 + 3 days	= 12 days
BCG	= 5 + 2 + 3 days	= 10 days

8

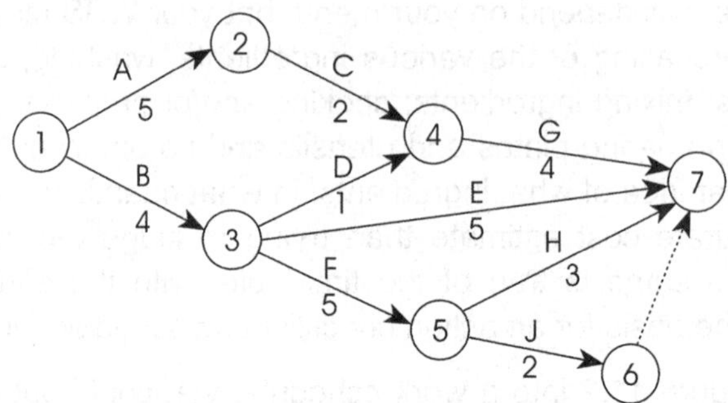

The paths are	ACG	= 5 + 2 + 4	= 11 weeks
	BDG	= 4 + 1 + 4	= 9 weeks
	BE	= 4 + 5	= 9 weeks
	BFH	= 4 + 5 + 3	= 12 weeks
	BFJ Dummy	= 4 + 5 + 2 + 0	= 11 weeks

BFH is the longest (and therefore the critical) path: the shortest time in which the project can be completed.

9

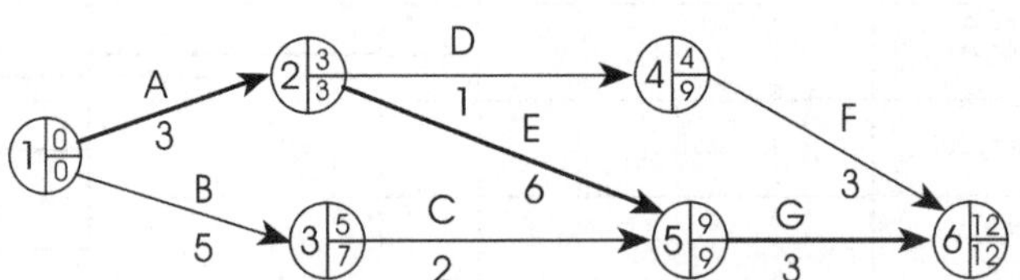

Activity C: anytime between days 5 and 7 (a 2-day float)

Activity F: anytime between days 4 and 9 (a 5-day float)

10 If you had difficulty answering this, review Sections 3.1-3.3, for some general ideas and then relate these to your circumstances.

11

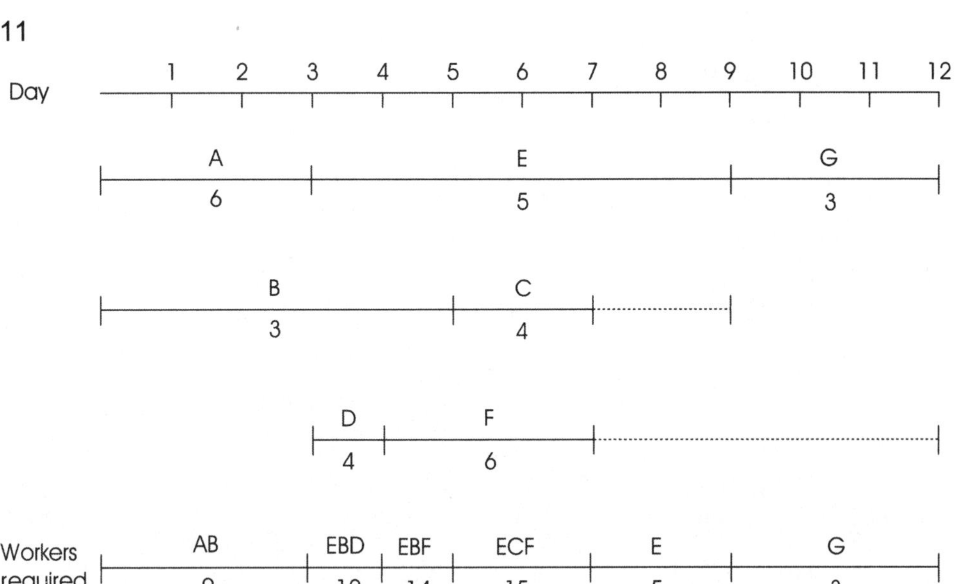

12 Did you totally underestimate your budget, and have to spend your food allowance for the next three weeks? If you did, it might be a good idea to go back to Section 3.5 and read up on cost estimating.

13

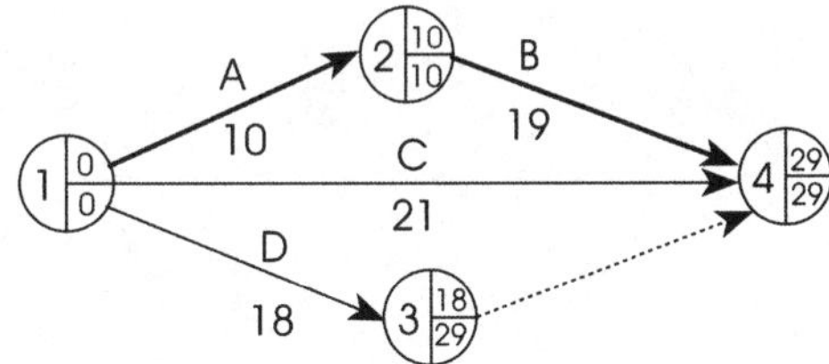

Chapter 12 :

TEAMS

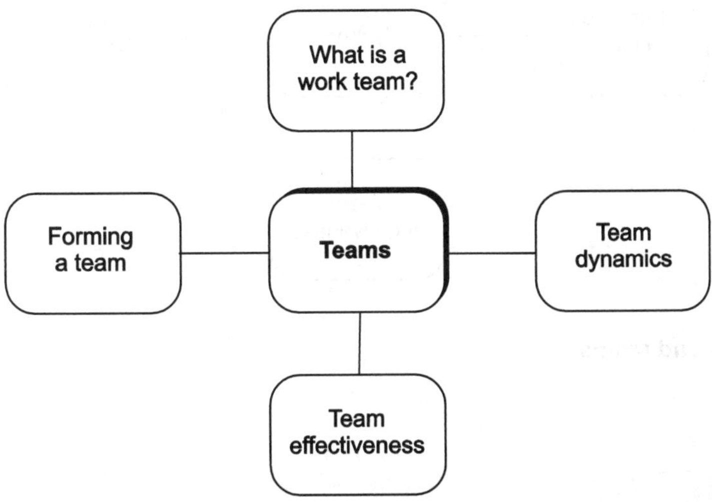

Introduction

You may have noticed that people behave differently in a group or crowd than they do on their own or when talking to one or two others: think about a gang of friends on an outing, or a crowd of people at a football match. The interplay and influences within groups that create this behaviour are called 'group dynamics'.

Groups in business organisations are, in effect, sub-organisations, and they require management for 'controlled performance of collective goals': not only their own collective goals, but those of the business organisation as a whole. This is especially important if the organisation wishes to empower work teams to realise its strategy. This chapter looks at what goes on, and why, when people work together in teams.

Your objectives

In this chapter you will learn about the following.

(a) Areas in which teamworking may be more or less effective

(b) Which stage of development a team has reached, and what comes next

(c) The types of people and behaviour required for an effective team

(d) Techniques for teambuilding and the dangers of too much 'team spirit'

(e) The dynamics of groups, with regard to behaviour, communication and decision-making

(f) The factors influencing the effectiveness of teams, and the contingency approach to team management

(g) The effectiveness (or otherwise) of a team

1 WHAT IS A WORK TEAM?

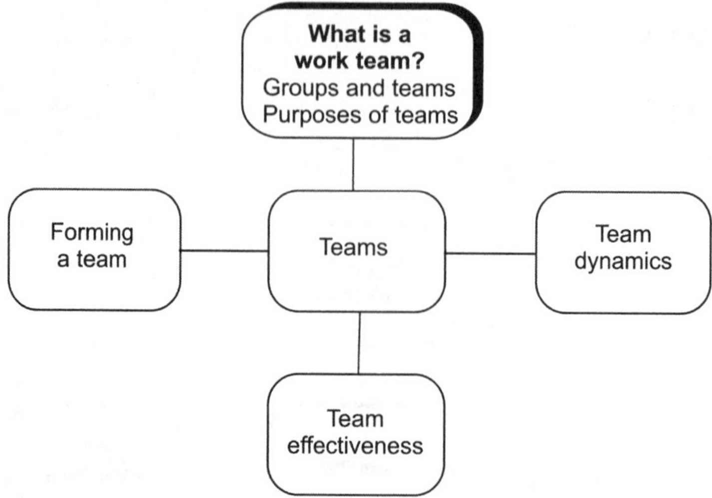

1.1 Groups and teams

Definition

A **group** is any collection of people who perceive themselves to be a group.

The point of this definition is that there is a difference between a random collection of individuals and a group of individuals who share a common sense of **identity** and **belonging**. Groups have certain attributes that a random crowd does not possess.

(a) **A sense of identity**. Whether the group is formal or informal, its existence is recognised by its members: there are acknowledged boundaries to the group which define who is 'in' and who is 'out', who is 'us' and who is 'them'.

(b) **Loyalty to the group**, and acceptance by the group. This generally expresses itself as **conformity,** or the acceptance of the norms of behaviour and attitudes that bind the group together and exclude others from it.

(c) **Purpose and leadership**. Most groups have an express purpose, whatever field they are in: most will, spontaneously or formally, choose individuals or sub-groups to lead them towards the fulfilment of those goals.

You should bear in mind that although an organisation as a whole may wish to project itself as a large group, with a single identity, loyalty and purpose, any organisation will in fact be composed of many **sub-groups**, with such attributes of their own. People will be drawn together into groups by a preference for smaller units, where closer relationships can develop and individual contributions are noticed; by the combined power of a group which individuals may not possess; and by the opportunity to share problems and responsibilities.

(a) **Informal groups** will invariably be present in any organisation. Informal groups include workplace cliques, and networks of people who regularly get together to exchange information, groups of 'mates' who socialise outside work and so on. The purposes of informal groups are usually related to group and individual member satisfaction, rather than to a task.

(b) **Formal groups,** put together by the organisation, will have a formal structure and a function for which they are held responsible: they are task oriented, and become teams. Leaders may be chosen within the group, but are typically given authority by the organisation.

A **primary working group** is the name given to the immediate social group of an individual worker: in other words, the people (s)he works with directly and most of the time. This group is the smallest unit of the organisation: the close relationships on which it depends cannot be formed among more than about a dozen people. People tend to be drawn into groups of this size, and if the organisation does not formally provide for them, informal primary groups – whose aims will not necessarily be in harmony with those of the organisation – will spring up.

It is only comparatively recently that organisations have realised the importance of primary working groups for harnessing the energy and team-spirit of employees. With the concept of **empowerment,** attention is being given to enhancing the purpose and leadership of such groups.

Activity 1 **(20 minutes)**

Anthony Jay has identified a primary workgroup of ten people as the descendant of the primeval hunting band, working together for mutual survival. He suggests that such a small band balances:

(a) The individuality which is necessary to generate new ideas

(b) The support and comradeship necessary to develop and put those ideas into action.

What primary groups are you a member of in your study or work environment(s)? How big are these groups? How does the size of your class, study group, work-team – or whatever – affect your ability to come up with questions or ideas and give you the help and support to do something you could not do alone?

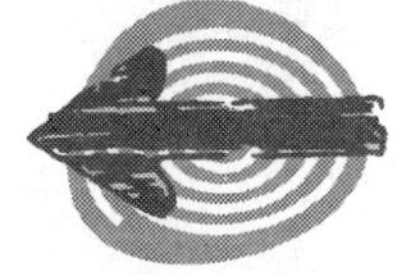

We have suggested that a small group can allow people to generate ideas, and encourage action. How might the organisation utilise these benefits? What might it use teams for?

Definition

While a group is informal, a **team** is formalised to achieve particular objectives.

NOTES

1.2 Purposes of teams

From the organisation's point of view, the advantages of teams may be as follows.

(a) Teams allow the performance of tasks that require the skills and time of more than one person, without involving co-ordination across structural boundaries.

(b) Teams encourage exchange of knowledge and ideas, and the creation of new ideas through 'hitchhiking': one person's idea or information sparks off an idea in someone else's head. They are thus particularly useful for:

- (i) Increasing communication
- (ii) Generating new ideas
- (iii) Evaluating ideas from more than one viewpoint
- (iv) Consultation, where a cross-section of views may help to produce better, or more acceptable, decisions
- (v) Job-related training, since they allow the testing of ideas in a realistic work-group context
- (vi) Resolving conflict, since argument can lead to agreement, compromise or consensus which will be reinforced by the group's sense of solidarity

(c) The power of the team over individual behaviour can be both:

- (i) A method of control – or, better still, self control
- (ii) A powerful motivator, if the aims of the group can be harmonised with the aims of the organisation.

All of these factors have encouraged the **empowerment of teams,** as opposed to individuals.

Examples of teamworking

Specific applications of teamworking may include the following.

(a) **Brainstorming groups**

Definition

Brainstorming is a process whereby people produce spontaneous, uncensored ideas, sparked off by a particular problem or task.

A brainstorming group would typically involve six to twelve people. The idea of brainstorming is to generate ideas, however irrelevant or impractical they may seem. The ideas are not, at this stage, criticised or examined, so people are free to think creatively and take risks, and to feed or 'hitchhike' on each other's ideas. The next stage would be for the ideas to be considered individually, and a decision made. Such an approach might be used to solve specific production problems, for example, or to come up with marketing or new product ideas.

FOR DISCUSSION

In a small group, imagine you are the advertising agency creative team given the task of recommending a new name for the charity Oxfam. This was a real task set by The Spastic Society, who felt that the word 'spastic' for sufferers of cerebral palsy had taken on negative connotations. Also, the name did not sound dynamic enough, and did not express the Society's purpose: to raise awareness of prejudice against sufferers, to emphasise their underutilised potential in the workplace, and to support their aspirations.

Oxfam may feel their title, although well known, is misunderstood (where's the famine in Oxford?). Brainstorm some ideas for a catchy and expressive new name. If you do this in class, you might like to have 'competing' groups of six to ten people, and get each to present what it considers its best idea. Remember to look for quantity, not quality, at the brainstorming stage, though: the real job candidates were observed spending too much time discussing single ideas, with not enough ideas on the table ...

The former Spastic Society is now SCOPE. Do you think that this is a good name?

(b) **Quality circles**

Definition

> **Quality circles** are groups of (typically 6 to 10) employees from different levels and/or disciplines, who meet regularly to discuss problems of quality and quality control in their area of work.

In these days of empowered teams, quality improvement is only one area in which responsibility is given to groups of employees – but it is still one of the most important. Quality circles are said to result not only in improved product quality, but also in higher morale among employees, higher productivity and a better level of awareness about organisational issues.

(c) **Project or product/service teams**, set up to handle:

(i) Strategic developments, such as new product development, or the introduction of computer systems

(ii) Tasks relating to particular 'cases' or customer accounts, products or markets

(iii) Tasks relating to a particular process within the production system (design, purchasing or assembly of components, say)

(iv) Special audits or investigations of current procedures or potential improvements and opportunities

(d) **Training or study groups**

Training groups (sometimes called 'T-groups') are often used to develop individuals' awareness of how they behave in relation to others, and particularly within a team: members are encouraged to observe and give

feedback on the group's behaviour and how they respond to it. T-groups develop skills in identifying and controlling group dynamics in a 'live' context and are sometimes used when new groups are formed due to reorganisation.

(e) **Employee representative committees**, such as the local branch of a trade union or staff association, or less formal groups which meet to discuss matters of interest or concern to staff. Such groups may meet jointly with representatives of management for the purposes of consultation and negotiation.

(f) **Other committees and 'panels'** – for example, employee selection panels; investigatory panels for disciplinary or grievance procedures; task forces set up to investigate and/or make decisions on a particular task or problem; advisory committees on specialist areas (a legal team, say) and so on.

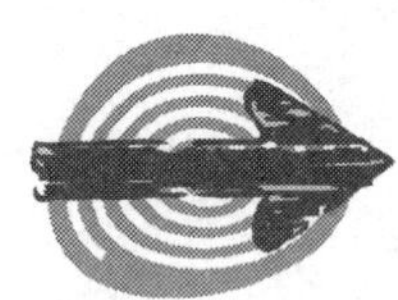

Small departments or sections might also be organised and managed as a team: we will look further at this area in Section 2 of this chapter, on teambuilding.

2 FORMING A TEAM

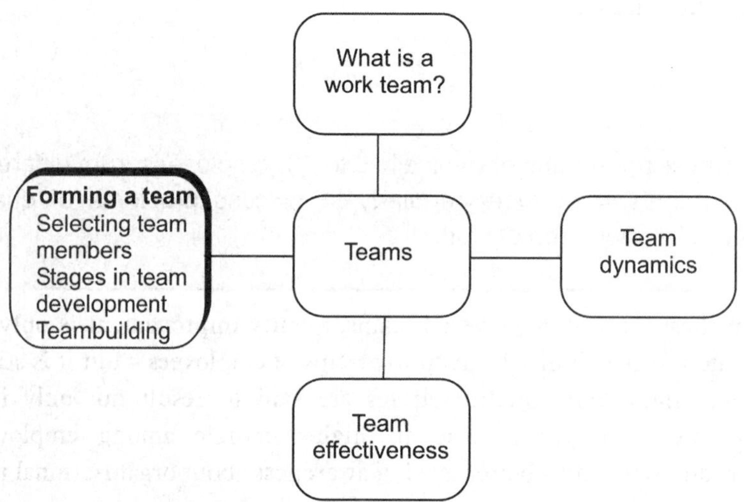

2.1 Selecting team members

Team membership may already be dictated by:

(a) Existing arrangements: a long-standing committee, section or department

(b) Organisation: a task force or project/product team may require a representative from each of the functions involved in the task, for the sake of co-ordination

(c) Politics: representatives of particular interest groups in the organisation might need to be included, so that they feel their interests are protected and so that decisions reached (if any) are likely to find broad acceptance

(d) Election: for example in the case of a staff association committee

Where a manager is able to select team members, however, (s)he should aim to match the **attributes or resources** prospective members are able to bring to the group with the **requirements** of the task.

(a) **Specialist skills and knowledge** may be required, from different areas in the organisation (or outside it).

(b) **Experience may be helpful**, especially if other team members are relatively inexperienced, and are therefore less likely to anticipate and know how to handle problems.

(c) **Political power** in the organisation may be a useful attribute in a member, particularly if the team is in competition for scarce resources, or its collective authority is unclear.

(d) **Access to resources**, such as use of equipment in other departments or information through specialist or personal contacts, may be helpful.

(e) **Competence** in the tasks likely to be required of the team member will be desirable, whatever other resources (s)he brings to the team.

In addition, both task performance and team maintenance (keeping the group together and satisfied) will require a mix of personalities and interpersonal skills.

Activity 2 **(15 minutes)**

Before reading on, list five 'types' of people that you would want to have on a project team, involved (say) in organising an end-of-term party.

Team roles

Belbin (1984) researched business-game teams at the Carnegie Institute of Technology. He developed a picture of the character-mix in a team, which many people find a useful guide to team selection and management. Belbin suggests that an effective team is made up of people who fill, between them, the following eight roles.

(a) The **co-ordinator** – presides and co-ordinates; balanced, disciplined, good at working through others.

(b) The **shaper** – highly strung, dominant, extrovert, passionate about the task itself, a spur to action.

(c) The **plant** – introverted, but intellectually dominant and imaginative; source of ideas and proposals but with disadvantages of introversion (unsociability, inhibition, need for control).

(d) The **monitor-evaluator** – analytically (rather than creatively) intelligent; dissects ideas, spots flaws; possibly aloof, tactless – but necessary.

(e) The **resource-investigator** – popular, sociable, extrovert, relaxed; source of new contacts, but not an originator; needs to be made use of.

(f) The **implementer** – practical organiser, turning ideas into tasks, scheduling, planning and so on; trustworthy and efficient, but not excited; not a leader, but an administrator.

(g) The **team worker** – most concerned with team maintenance; supportive, understanding, diplomatic; popular but uncompetitive; contribution noticed only in absence.

(h) The **finisher** – chivvies the team to meet deadlines, attend to details; urgency and follow-through important, though not always popular.

Belbin has also identified a ninth team-role, the **specialist**, who joins the group to offer expert advice when needed. Examples are legal advisers, PR consultants, finance specialists and the like.

FOR DISCUSSION

What role would you, and each of your study group or class-mates, fill in a working group, do you think?

Supposing that you are putting together a team from scratch, at what point do they stop being a collection of individuals and become a group or team? Of course, they will have to 'get to know one another', but there are more complex processes at work in team formation and development...

2.2 Stages in team development

Groups mature and develop. *Tuckman* identifies four stages in this development, which he names: forming, storming, norming and performing.

(a) **Forming**. The group is just coming together, and may still be seen as a collection of individuals. Each individual wishes to impress his or her personality on the group, while its purpose, composition, and organisation are being established. Members will be trying to find out about each other, and about the aims and norms of the group, without 'rocking the boat'.

(b) The second stage is called **storming** because it frequently involves more or less open conflict. Changes may be suggested in the group's original objectives, leadership, procedures and norms. Whilst forming involved toeing the line, storming brings out team members' own ideas and attitudes. This may encourage disagreement, as well as creativity.

(c) The third or **norming** stage is a period of settling down. There will be agreements about work sharing, output levels and group customs. The enthusiasm and creativity of the second stage may be less apparent, but norms and procedures may evolve which enable methodical working to be introduced and maintained. This need not mean that new ideas are discouraged, but that a reasonable hearing is given to everyone and 'consensus' or agreement (often involving compromise) is sought.

(d) Once the fourth or **performing** stage has been reached the group concentrates on its task. Even at earlier stages some performance will have been achieved, but the fourth stage marks the point where the difficulties of growth and development no longer get in the way of the group's task objectives.

It would be misleading to suggest that these four stages always follow in a clearly-defined progression, or that the development of a group must be a slow and complicated process. Particularly where the task to be performed is urgent, or where group members are highly motivated, the fourth stage will be reached very quickly while the earlier stages will be hard to distinguish. Some groups never progress beyond storming, however, because their differences are irreconcilable.

It is often the case that after a team has been performing effectively for a while it becomes complacent. In this phase, which has been called '**dorming**', the team goes into a semi-automatic mode of operation, with no fresh energy or attention focused on the task and with efforts devoted primarily to the maintenance of the team itself.

A manager might want to speed up the process of team development to the performing stage. Given the uncertainties and conflict of the storming stage, it might also seem apparent that team spirit and solidarity should be developed as soon as possible. So how do you build a team?

Activity 3 **(15 minutes)**

Read the following statements and decide to which category they belong (forming, storming, norming, performing, dorming).

(a) Two of the group arguing as to whose idea is best

(b) Progress becomes static

(c) Desired outputs being achieved

(d) Shy member of group not participating

(e) Activities being allocated

2.3 Teambuilding

Teambuilding involves:

(a) Giving a group of people a greater sense of their identity as a team; this is sometimes called '*esprit de corps*' or 'team spirit'

(b) Encouraging group loyalty or solidarity, so that members put in extra effort for the sake of the group

(c) Encouraging the group to commit themselves to shared work objectives, and to co-operate willingly to achieve them.

Activity 4 **(30 minutes)**

Why might the following be effective as team-building exercises?

(a) Sending a project team (involved in the design of electronic systems for racing cars) on a recreational day out 'karting'.

(b) Sending a project team on an 'Outward Bound' style course, walking in the mountains from A to B, through various obstacles (rivers to cross and so on).

(c) Sending two sales teams on a day out playing 'War Games', each being an opposing combat team trying to capture the other's flag, armed with paint guns.

(d) Sending a project team on a conference at a venue away from work, with a brief to review the past year and come up with a 'vision' for the next year.

These are actually commonly-used techniques. If you are interested, you might locate an activity centre or company near you which offers outdoor pursuits, war games or corporate entertainment and ask them about team-building exercises and the effect they have on people.

Team identity

A manager may be able to increase his work group's sense of itself as a team by any or all of the following means.

(a) **Giving the team a name**. A group name or nickname can express a lot about the team and encourage its members to identify with it: if the nickname naturally emerges from the group, as the way it refers to itself, even better. What sort of qualities of a group do names like 'The Monarchs', 'The Crazy Gang', 'The Gangstas' or 'The A Team' express?

(b) **Giving the team a badge or uniform**. 'Uniform' may sound offputting – but basically suggests any kind of shared dress norms. If a team has a distinctive identifying style or insignia, it will be expressing its boundaries: who is out and who is in. Think about how teams you know use baseball caps or T-shirts, badges or ties in this way.

(c) **Expressing the team's self-image**. One way of doing this is by identifying key phrases which tend to be repeated in the group, and turning them into group mottoes, or slogans. Think about the effect of slogans such as: 'You don't have to be crazy to work here, but it helps', or 'The impossible takes a bit longer'.

(d) **Building a team mythology.** Collecting and repeating stories about past successes and failures develops the group's self-image in the same way that experience shapes an individual's. Classic cock-ups make just as good team-building myths as hard-won successes or lucky breaks, as long as there is the sense that the team came through it together.

Activity 5 **(45 minutes)**

Consider the group of people you are studying with. Do you feel you are a team? Appoint a leader – someone you think is a 'co-ordinator' type, who will keep the discussion on track and under control – and try another brainstorming session. This time you are going to organise the end of term party.

Team solidarity

Another term for solidarity is 'cohesion' (literally, sticking together). Here, again, are some practical suggestions.

(a) **Expressing solidarity**. This is one of the more important uses of a team slogan. 'One for all and all for one' and 'United we stand' may be clichés now, but they caught on, to good effect, in their day. If you were a Polish trade union leader, why might you want to call a movement 'Solidarnosc' ('Solidarity')?

(b) **Encouraging interpersonal relationships**. Team members need to trust each other and be willing to work together – at the very least. Informal relationship-building activity should be encouraged and even provided (within reason, obviously: the main everyday focus of the group should be on its work objectives). Rallying round in times of need can be particularly powerful – but a team leader might want to pay attention to comparatively trivial things like members' birthdays, too.

(c) **Controlling conflict**. Personality clashes and disagreements should be dealt with immediately, and in the open – not left to fester and infect the whole team. The team leader needs to mediate between conflicting members, not to act as judge between them. In other words, (s)he needs to guide them in expressing and understanding their disagreement, and in finding ways of resolving the conflict that will be acceptable to both, if at all possible: a win-win situation.

(d) **Controlling intra-group competition**. Team members should all feel that they are being treated fairly and equally. The team leader should not show favouritism – which means that if there are inequalities of status, pay or 'say' in decisions, all members should be able to see that they are both reasonable and necessary to the success of the team as a whole. (You might give more of a say to someone who is an acknowledged expert.) Getting team members competing among themselves for bonuses and so on may spur them to better individual performance, but will not build the team.

(e) **Encouraging inter-group competition**. Competition with other teams, however, has been shown to increase cohesion within the competing groups, as they face what they perceive to be a threat from outside. The team closes ranks, and submerges its differences, demanding loyalty: it also focuses its collective energies more closely on the task. If a team lacks cohesion, or a task is particularly demanding of effort and loyalty, the team leader might pull the team together by finding an 'enemy', competitor or other perceived threat to face them with. (Warning: don't try this if it is important to the organisation as a whole to have teams working together!)

NOTES

Activity 6 **(30 minutes)**

Can you see any dangers in creating a very close-knit group? Think of the effect of strong team cohesion on:

(a) What the group spends its energies and attention on

(b) How the group regards outsiders, and any information or feedback they supply

(c) How the group makes decisions.

What could be done about these dangerous effects?

Commitment to shared objectives

The purpose of teambuilding is, ultimately, not to have a close-knit and satisfied team, but to have a close-knit and satisfied team that **fulfils its task objectives**. In fact, a cohesive and successful task-focused team may be more supportive and satisfying to its members than a cosy group absorbed only in its own processes and relationships.

Getting a team behind its objectives involves:

(a) Clearly setting out the team's objectives, and their place in the activity of the organisation as a whole

(b) Involving the team in setting specific targets and standards, and agreeing methods of organising work, in order to reach the objectives

(c) Providing the right information, resources, training and environment for the team to achieve its targets – involving the team in deciding what its requirements are

(d) Giving regular, clear feedback on progress and results – including constructive criticism – so the team can celebrate what they have achieved, and be spurred on by what they have not yet achieved

(e) Encouraging feedback, suggestions and ideas from the team, and doing something about them: helping team members believe that they can make an impact on their work and results, and that that impact is appreciated by the organisation

(f) Giving positive reinforcement (praise or reward) for creativity, initiative, problem-solving, helpfulness and other behaviour that shows commitment to the task

(g) Visibly 'championing' the team in the organisation, fighting (if necessary) for the resources it needs and the recognition it deserves

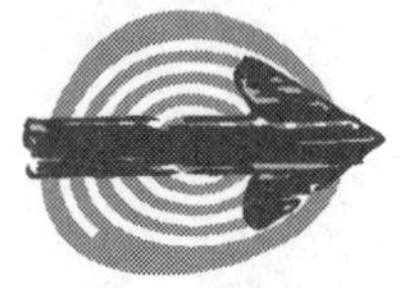

Assuming that we've now gathered and built a group of people into a close-knit, performing team, we can turn to the normal business of teamworking: the patterns and processes of team behaviour, or dynamics.

3 TEAM DYNAMICS

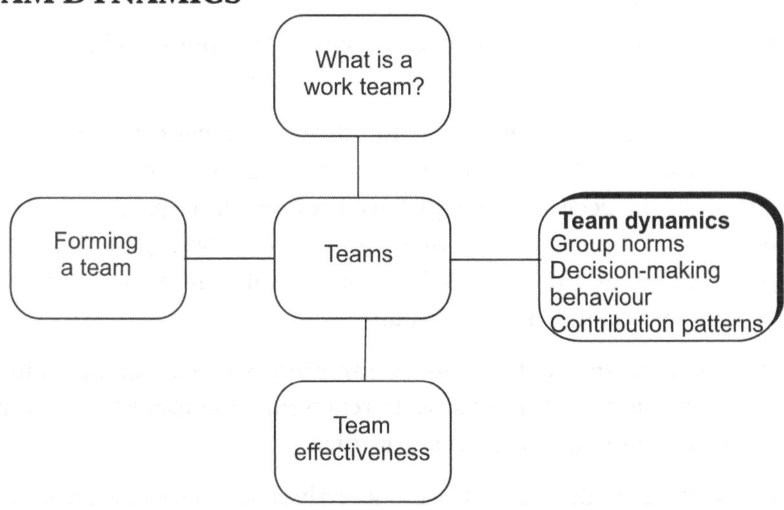

3.1 Group norms

Work groups establish **norms** or common patterns of behaviour, to which all members of the group are expected to conform. Norms develop as the group learns what sorts of behaviour work and don't work, in terms of maintaining the group and protecting its interests. There may be norms of interpersonal behaviour (the way the members speak to each other and so on), dress, timekeeping, attitudes (towards management, for example) and/or work practices and productivity. In other words, group norms are 'the way we do (or don't do) things round here'.

Norms may be reinforced in various ways by the group.

(a) **Identification with the group** may be offered as a reward for compliance, through marks of belonging, prestige and acceptance.

(b) **Sanctions or penalties** of various kinds may be imposed as a deterrent to non-conforming behaviour: ostracising or ignoring the member concerned ('sending him to Coventry'), ridicule or reprimand, even physical hostility. The threat of expulsion from the group is the final sanction.

In other words the group's power to influence an individual depends on the degree to which he values his membership of the group and the rewards it may offer, or wishes to avoid the negative sanctions at its disposal.

Activity 7 **(20 minutes)**

How might group norms:

(a) Cause problems for a new manager?
(b) Adversely affect performance?
(c) Help in the process of management control?
(d) Help in the process of change management?

3.2 Decision-making behaviour

As we have noted, empowerment involves groups in decision-making. This can be of benefit where:

(a) **Pooling skills, information and ideas** – perhaps representing different functions, specialisms and levels in the organisation – could increase the quality of the decision. Groups have been shown to produce better evaluated (although fewer) decisions than individuals working separately. Even the performance of the group's best individual can be improved by having 'missing pieces' added by the group.

(b) **Participation** in the decision-making process makes the decision acceptable to the group, whether because it represents a consensus of their views, or simply because they have been consulted.

However, it is worth considering how a group arrives at a decision. Depending on the personalities of its members and of its leader, and the nature of the task (for example whether it needs to be completed within a short or long time-frame), a team may arrive at decisions in a number of ways.

(a) Does it allow itself to be persuaded by its leader, or another dominant member?

(b) Does it defer to the member most qualified to make a particular decision?

(c) Does it collect information and views from all its members – but allow the leader/dominant member/qualified member to make the decision?

(d) Does it collect information and views from all its members and try to reach general consensus or agreement, however much discussion that takes?

(e) Does it collect information and views from all its members and take a democratic vote on the decision?

(f) Does it keep any dissenting views or contradictory information quiet, to allow consensus to prevail?

(g) Does it insist on dealing with dissenting views and contradictory information, even if it takes longer to reach a decision?

Depending which behaviour is adopted, there is clearly a trade-off between:

- The speed of the decision
- The acceptability of the decision to all group members
- The quality of the decision from the point of view of results

Activity 8 **(20 minutes)**

If you were team leader in the following situations, what kind of decision-making behaviour would you encourage?

(a) The computer expert in your team has suggested that the team should change over to a different, more efficient software package. Some of the team have only just mastered the current software, after quite a struggle. The new software will, however, iron out some very frustrating problems in the work.

Activity 8 cont'd

(b) The office manager has offered you a choice of yellow or blue, when the offices are redecorated next month, but she needs to do the purchasing almost immediately. What would your team prefer?

There are problems in group decision-making.

(a) **Group decisions take longer to reach than individual decisions** – especially if the group seeks consensus by trying to resolve all its disagreements.

(b) **Group decisions tend to be riskier than individual decisions**. This may be because:

   (i) Shared responsibility blurs the individuals' sense of responsibility for the outcome of the decision
   (ii) Contradictory information may be ignored, to protect the group's consensus or pet theories
   (iii) Cohesive groups tend to feel infallible: they get over-confident
   (iv) Group cohesion and motivation may be founded on values such as innovation, boldness and flexibility – which support risk-taking

(c) **Group decisions may partly be based on group norms and interests** – the group's own 'agenda' – rather than organisational interests: group maintenance is itself a powerful *raison d'être.*

3.3 Contribution patterns

One way of analysing the functioning of a team is to assess who (if anybody) is performing each of *Belbin's* team roles (discussed earlier). Who is the team's plant? co-ordinator? monitor-evaluator? and so on.

Another method is to analyse the frequency and type of individual members' contributions to group discussions and interactions. This is a relatively simple framework, which can revolutionise the way you behave in groups – as well as your understanding of the dynamics of a given team.

Who contributes?

The team leader should identify which members of the team habitually make the most contributions, and which the least. You could do this by taking a count of contributions from each member, during a sample ten to fifteen minutes of group discussion. (Count any spoken remark addressed to the discussion, not asides to other members, or mutters to self.) For example:

Robbie |

Martha

Jason |||

Mary ||||/ ||||/ |

Gary ||||/ ||||/ ||||

Paul ||

Mark ||||/ ||

If the same general pattern of high contribution (Mary, Gary), medium contribution (Mark) and low contribution (Robbie, Martha, Jason, Paul) tends to be repeated, irrespective of the matter being discussed, you might suspect that Mary and Gary are 'swamping' the other members, or that the other members have a problem communicating, or are not interested, or have nothing to contribute, or feel they have nothing to contribute. This team has a problem that needs to be addressed. Confronting the team with its contribution count may spark off an honest discussion of the problem.

How do they contribute?

Consultants *Neil Rackham* and *Terry Morgan* have developed a helpful categorisation of the types of contribution people can make to team discussion and decision-making.

Category	Behaviour	Example
Proposing	Putting forward suggestions, new concepts or courses of action.	'Why don't we look at a flexi-time system?'
Building	Extending or developing someone else's proposal.	'Yes. We could have a daily or weekly hours allowance, apart from a core period in the middle of the day.'
Supporting	Supporting another person or his/her proposal.	'Yes, I agree, flexi-time would be worth looking at.'
Seeking information	Asking for more facts, opinions or clarification.	'What exactly do you mean by "flexi-time"?'
Giving information	Offering facts, opinions or clarification.	'There's a helpful outline of flexi-time in this BPP Study Text.'
Disagreeing	Offering criticism or alternative facts or opinions which contradict a person's proposals or opinions.	'I don't think we can take the risk of not having any staff here at certain periods of the day.'
Attacking	Attempting to undermine another person or their position: more emotive than disagreeing.	'In fact, I don't think you've thought this through at all.'
Defending	Arguing for one's own point of view.	'Actually, I've given this a lot of thought, and I think it makes sense.'
Blocking/difficulty stating	Putting obstacles in the way of a proposal, without offering any alternatives.	'What if the other teams get jealous? It would only cause conflict.'
Open behaviour	Risking ridicule and loss of status by being honest about feelings and opinions.	'I think some of us are afraid that flexi-time will show up how little work they really do in a day.'
Shutting-out behaviour	Interrupting or overriding others; taking over.	'Nonsense. Let's move onto something else – we've had enough of this discussion.'
Bringing-in behaviour	Involving another member; encouraging contribution.	'Actually, I'd like to hear what Fred has to say. Go on, Fred.'
Testing understanding	Checking whether points have been understood.	'So flexi-time could work over a day or a week; have I got that right?'
Summarising	Drawing together or summing up previous discussion.	'We've now heard two sides to the flexi-time issue: on the one hand, flexibility; on the other side, possible risk. Now ...'

Each type of behaviour may be appropriate in the right situation at the right time. A team may be low on some types of contribution – and it may be up to the team leader to encourage, or deliberately adopt, desirable behaviours (such as bringing-in, supporting or seeking information) in order to provide balance.

You might draw up a **contribution profile**, by following the same procedure as a contribution count, but adding behavioural categories (perhaps a few at a time, at first). If you were worried about interpersonal conflict in your team, for example, you might look specifically for attacking, defending, blocking/difficulty stating, shutting-out and disagreeing: are such behaviours common in the team? Are particular individuals mainly at fault? Are attacks aimed at a particular person, who is forced to defend: a purely interpersonal conflict? Or is disagreement constructive and based on real objections – not linked to attacking or shutting-out? (See if you can see a problem in the following example.)

Contribution profile	*Mary*	*Martha*	*Paul*	*Gary*	*Mark*	*Jason*	*Robbie*
Attacking					卌	|||	|
Defending	卌						
Blocking			||	卌	||		
Shutting-out	卌			卌			
Disagreeing	|			|			

Activity 9 **(20 minutes)**

'The problem with teamwork is "the other people".' Is teamworking just a management fashion that imposes an unnatural way of working on individuals who would be more effective on their own?

Discuss in groups of six to ten people, for ten minutes. Appoint two extra people as observers: one to make a contribution count, and another to make a contribution profile. When your discussion is finished take another ten minutes to write down the implications of their findings.

4 TEAM EFFECTIVENESS

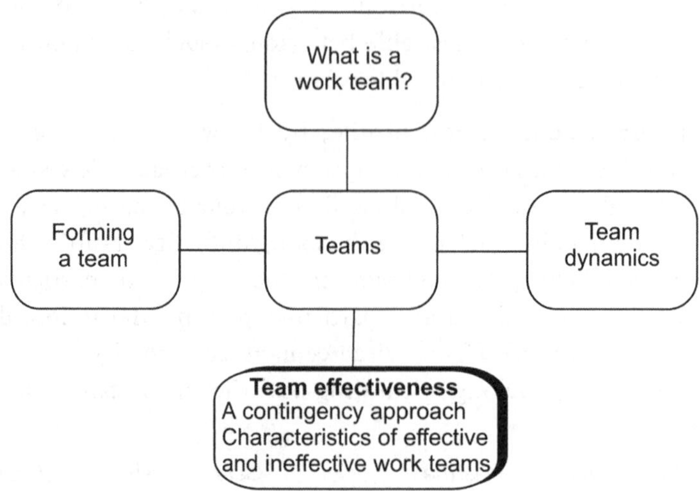

4.1 A contingency approach

An effective team is one which:

- Achieves its task objectives
- Maintains co-operative working through the satisfaction and interrelationships of its members

Unfortunately, no two groups of people are the same – and they may also be doing different work in different organisational set-ups. So the team leader will need to take a contingency approach. How much supervision does the team need? Should you let the team make the decisions? Do more team members need to contribute to group discussions? Should you discourage disagreement in the group? Answer: it all depends.

Charles Handy (1993) suggested the framework shown in Figure 12.1 as a guide to the factors that influence a group's effectiveness. The intervening factors are those that the team manager can manipulate in order to alter the outcomes, according to the situation (s)he has been given to start with.

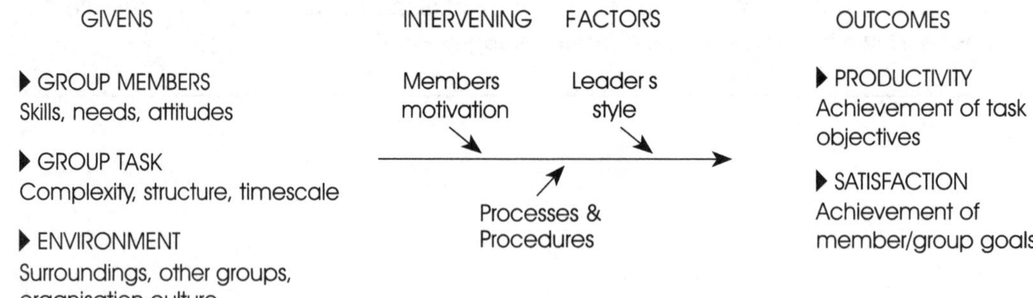

Figure 12.1: Group effectiveness

As an example, if the members have a high need for structure, but the task is very complex and ambiguous, and the organisation culture is intolerant of failure (all givens), the manager may need to adopt a relatively authoritarian management style, motivate team members by rewards for results, and establish 'safe' control procedures (intervening factors) if the team is to succeed without too much stress (outcomes).

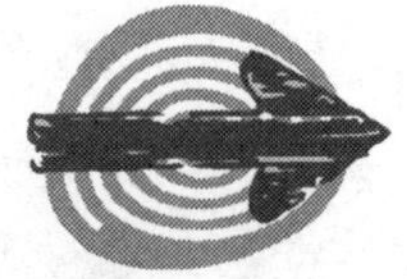

If a manager is to improve the effectiveness of the work team (s)he must have some idea of what an effective or ineffective group is like.

4.2 Characteristics of effective and ineffective work teams

Some pointers to group efficiency are **quantifiable** or numerically measurable factors; others are more **qualitative** factors, which can be observed, but are less easily measured. No one factor on its own is significant, but taken collectively they present a picture of how well or badly the group is operating.

Quantifiable factors

Effective work group	*Ineffective work group*
(1) Low rate of labour turnover	(1) High rate of labour turnover
(2) Low accident rate	(2) High accident rate
(3) Low absenteeism	(3) High absenteeism
(4) High output and productivity	(4) Low output and productivity
(5) Good quality of output	(5) Poor quality of output
(6) Individual targets are achieved	(6) Individual targets are not achieved
(7) Few stoppages and interruptions to work	(7) Time is wasted owing to disruption of work flow
	(8) Time is lost owing to disagreements between superior and subordinates

Qualitative factors

Effective work group	*Ineffective work group*
(1) High commitment to the achievement of targets and organisational goals	(1) Little understanding of organisational goals or the role of the group
(2) Clear understanding of the group's work	(2) Low commitment to targets
(3) Clear understanding of the role of each person within the group	(3) Confusion and uncertainty about the role of each person within the group
(4) Trust and open communication between members	(4) Mistrust between group members, and suspicion of leaders
(5) Idea sharing	(5) Little idea sharing
(6) New-idea generation	(6) Few new ideas generated
(7) Mutual help and encouragement, if necessary, through constructive criticism	(7) Competition, self-interest and hostile criticism within the group
(8) Group problem-solving, addressing root causes	(8) Superficial problem-solving, addressing symptoms, not causes
(9) Active interest in work decisions	(9) Passive acceptance of work decisions
(10) Consensus of opinion sought, through argument and mutual adjustment	(10) Interpersonal hostility, grudges and attempts to dominate
(11) Desire for self-development through work and career	(11) Boredom and uninterest in work
(12) Motivation and ability work in the leader's absence	(12) Need for leadership to direct and control work

Activity 10 **(20 minutes)**

Try to interview somebody who manages a work team, who would be willing to talk to you for just ten or fifteen minutes. Run through the checklist of factors given above, asking your interviewee to give a 'Yes' or 'No' to each of the statements. Put a question mark (?) where it was difficult for the respondent to answer, because the factor was not easy to define or measure. You might want to reconsider some of our factors, or the way they are phrased, in the light of the answers you get. What conclusions can you draw from your survey?

Chapter roundup

- A group is a collection of people who perceive themselves to be a group. A group with a strong sense of collaborating towards the fulfilment of their collective goals is a team.
- An effective team is one which achieves its tasks and satisfies its members.
- Collections of individuals develop into groups or teams through the stages of forming, storming, norming, performing (and possibly dorming). They can also be built into teams by enhancing their identity and solidarity as a group, and by focusing attention on their task objectives.
- Groups 'behave' differently from individuals. Some of the dynamics of groups of which a manager should be aware include:
  - The tendency of groups to develop norms of behaviour
  - The ways decision-making behaviour affects team performance and satisfaction
  - The way in which personal, interpersonal and task factors influence the contributions of team members.
- A contingency approach to team effectiveness includes attention to:
  - The givens: the group, the task and the environment
  - Intervening factors which the manager can manipulate: leadership style, motivation, processes and procedures
  - The outcomes: group productivity and member satisfaction.

Quick quiz

1 What is (a) brainstorming? and (b) a quality circle?

2 What should a manager look for when selecting team members?

3 What are *Belbin*'s eight roles for a well-rounded team?

4 Outline what happens in the 'storming' stage of team development.

5 What is 'cohesion', and what effect does inter-group competition have on it?

6 Suggest five ways in which a manager can get a team 'behind' task objectives.

7 Why do individuals comply with group norms?

8 Why are groups particularly (a) useful and (b) risky for decision-making?

9 List six of *Rackham and Morgan's* categories of contribution to group discussion.

10 Suggest five quantifiable characteristics of effective teams and five qualitative characteristics of ineffective teams.

Answers to quick quiz

1 (a) A process by which people produce spontaneous ideas, sparked off by a problem or task.

(b) Usually six to ten employees from different levels and disciplines meeting to discuss problems related to quality or quality control in their area of work.

2 Skills, knowledge, experience, political power in the organisation, access to resources, competence.

3 Co-ordinator, shaper, plant, monitor-evaluator, resource-investigator, implementer, team worker, finisher.

4 Storming brings out members' own ideas and attitudes. There may be conflict as well as creativity.

5 Solidarity. Faced with competition it causes a group to close ranks, focuses its energies and makes the group concentrate on objectives.

6 Set clear objectives, get the team to set targets/standards, provide information and resources, give feedback, praise and reward, and champion the team in the organisation.

7 To be accepted and to avoid sanctions or penalties.

8 (a) More ideas, suggestions, and participation usually make the decision more acceptable.

(b) Decisions take longer and may be based on group norms and interests.

9 Proposing, building, supporting, seeking information, giving information, disagreeing.

10 Refer to Section 4.2.

Answers to activities

1 The primary groups are probably your tutor group or class. If at work, it would be the section in which you work. If the groups are large, you may feel reluctant to put forward ideas or ask questions, but even within a large group you should feel there is support and that help is at hand if you need it.

2 For your ideal team, you might have listed: a person with originality and ideas; a 'get up and go' type, with energy and enthusiasm; a quiet logical thinker who can be sensible about the ideas put forward; a plodder who will be happy to do the routine leg-work; and a team player who can organise the others and help them reach agreement on ideas.

3 Categorising the behaviour of group members in the situations described results in the following: (a) storming, (b) dorming, (c) performing, (d) forming, (e) norming.

4 (a) Recreation helps the team to build informal relationships: in this case, the chosen activity also reminds them of their task, and may make them feel special, as part of the motor racing industry, by giving them a taste of what the end user of their product does.

(b) A team challenge pushes the group to consider its strengths and weaknesses, to find its natural leader, to co-operate and help each other in overcoming obstacles.

(c) This exercise creates an 'us' and 'them' challenge: perceiving the rival team as the enemy heightens the solidarity of the group.

(d) This exercise encourages the group to raise problems and conflicts freely, away from the normal environment of work, and also encourages brainstorming and the expression of team members' dreams for what the team can achieve in future.

5 You may have found it easier to work as a team this time. The group has probably generated a number of ideas as to what form the party should take. Activities may have been allocated (drinks, food, music) and decisions made on how to publicise the event. Hopefully, you have not yet reached the 'dorming' stage.

6 Problems may arise in an ultra close-knit group because:

(a) the group's energies may be focused on its own maintenance and relationships, instead of on the task;

(b) the group may be suspicious or dismissive of outsiders, and may reject any contradictory information or criticism they supply; the group will be blinkered and stick to its own views, no matter what; cohesive groups thus often get the impression that they are infallible: they can't be wrong – and therefore can't learn from their mistakes;

(c) the group may squash any dissent or opinions that might rock the boat. Close-knit groups tend to preserve a consensus – falsely if required – and to take risky decisions, because they have suppressed alternative facts and viewpoints.

This phenomenon is called 'groupthink'. In order to limit its effect, the team must be encouraged:

(a) to actively seek outside ideas and feedback;
(b) to welcome self-criticism within the group; and
(c) to consciously evaluate conflicting evidence and opinions.

7 Group norms might have the effect of:

(a) 'freezing out' a new manager who wants to change group behaviour;

(b) limiting output to what the group as a whole feels is fair for what they are paid: over-producing individuals are brought into line with the group output norm, so as not to make the group look bad;

(c) aiding management control by a process of self-regulation, if the group norms can be aligned with task objectives; under-producing individuals, for example, are brought into line by group pressure to pull their weight;

(d) aiding management in changing attitudes: if a manager can involve some individuals in accepting and communicating change, the rest of the group may be brought into line with the adjusted norm.

8 (a) The new software is clearly desirable for the task. You could make a decision yourself, supported by the expert advice of the relevant team member. However, there does not seem to be a time limit on the decision (it is only a suggestion) and there does seem to be a good reason for taking the time to consult the rest of the group. The change is something that will affect them all, and you can anticipate conflict (from the members who find technology a struggle); it should be brought into the open and worked through into consensus if possible. Agreement will make implementing the change much easier later on.

(b) This decision is more about acceptability than about quality: the colour is entirely a matter of taste, and the group will have to live with it, so they should be invited to share the decision. On the other hand time is short, and it is the sort of argument that could go to and fro for ever: you are unlikely to persuade people that one colour or the other is 'better', if they prefer the other one! A quick, democratic vote may show clear support one way or the other: if opinion is tied, the leader should make an authoritative casting vote, without wasting time over it.

9 In analysing the contributions, you may have found that strong characters were inclined to dominate the meeting. Attempts should have been made to draw quiet people into the discussion. There may have been arguments over certain points and perhaps peace restored by another member of the group. The observers may have noticed non-verbal communication taking place.

10 Hopefully, you found the checklist in Section 4.2 effective. If not, change the wording. From the answers you received you should be able to judge how effective the team/group is.

NOTES

Chapter 13 : STRATEGY IMPLEMENTATION

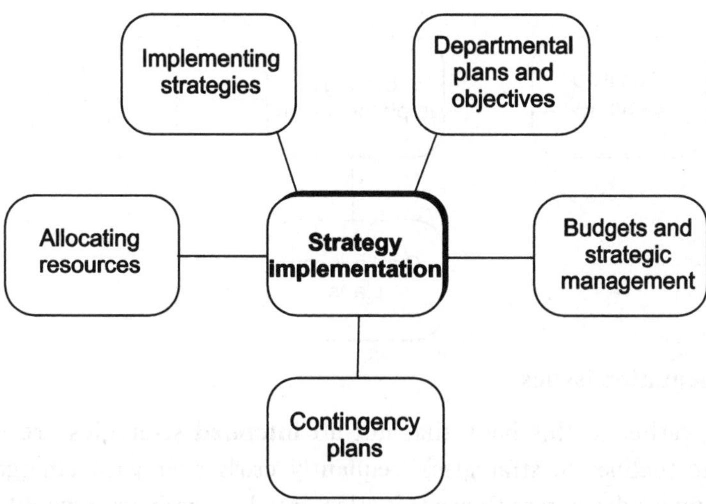

Introduction

Formulating strategic plans is one thing: implementing them is quite another as implementation requires converting plans into actual behaviour.

Following on from our discussions in the previous chapters on communication, projects and teambuilding, this chapter refines our focus and covers the process of putting the corporate strategy into practice. **Resources** have to be deployed – and the use of **critical success factors** indicates what needs to be done, by identifying key **tasks**. Management by objectives (MBO) is a technique which aims to integrate the business as a whole with the activities of individual managers at **operations level.**

The role of **budgets** in strategic management is covered in this chapter. Budgetary control assists with objectives ranging from resource allocation to setting targets and responsibilities.

Your objectives

In this chapter you will learn the following.

(a) Key issues in strategy implementation

(b) Different departmental plans and objectives, and how implementing strategies to achieve them may vary

(c) The concept of management by objectives

(d) Resource requirements and their allocation

(e) The importance of budgets in strategy implementation

1 IMPLEMENTING STRATEGIES

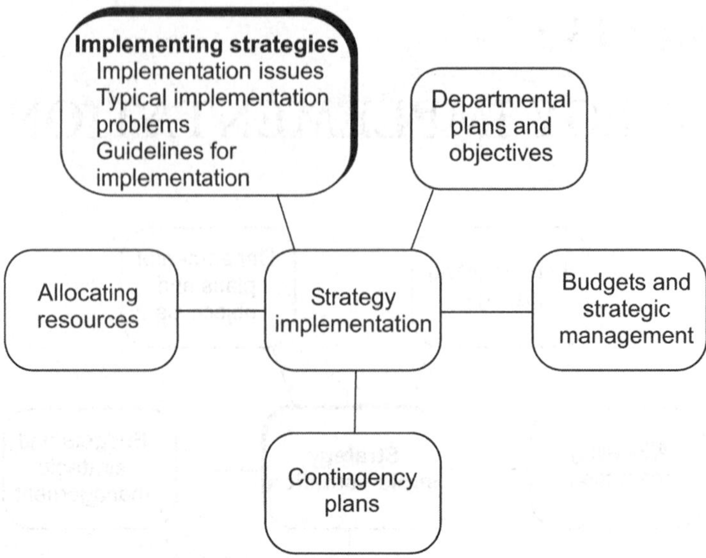

1.1 Implementation issues

We have seen earlier in this book that **not all intended strategies are implemented**. Those that are (deliberate strategies) frequently cross over with emergent strategies. Emergent strategies develop as they are implemented, so perhaps it would not be correct to talk about an implementation stage at all.

(a) It is impossible to plan for every eventuality. Some **decisions of strategic importance may not be anticipated** in the strategic plan.

(b) Implementation often involves **adjusting the plan** in the light of changed conditions.

(c) An organisation has to ensure that its resources are deployed at two levels.

- (i) Corporate; that is, between different businesses
- (ii) Unit or operations; that is, between functions and departments

(d) Decisions at operations level may be taken without any consideration of their overall strategic implications. A sudden cutback or delay in investment in a new technology for the sake of financial reporting, say, may have a damaging impact on the strategy. So, **resource allocation** is sometimes a strategic issue.

EXAMPLE

(a) A company wishes to expand into a new market. That is its strategic decision.

(b) In practice, this means that individual sales personnel have to persuade a host of new customers to buy the product. The strategy is made real by the work of many individuals, sometimes in isolation, sometimes in small teams, sometimes in large organisational formations.

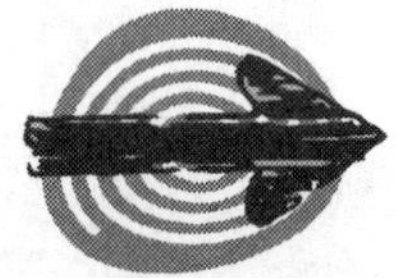

We looked at teamwork and communication in the previous chapters.

1.2 Typical implementation problems

- Implementation **takes longer** than expected
- Major unexpected **problems** arise
- Implementation activities are **inadequately co-ordinated**
- **Management's attention is distracted** from other activities
- Employees do **not have the necessary capability** or training to implement the strategy
- Managers **fail to give a sense of direction** at unit level
- The implementation **tasks are not defined properly**
- **Information systems** are not adequate
- The **overall goals** are not communicated

1.3 Guidelines for implementation

(a) **Envisioning**: Vision plays a role in strategy formation. This needs to be communicated at different levels and, if necessary, a separate 'vision' developed for each department supporting the corporate vision.

(b) **Activating**: ensure others **support** and share the vision.

(c) **Supporting**: leaders need to recognise the problems that subordinates actually face. This is particularly true in times of change.

(d) **Installing**: develop **detailed plans** to enact and control the strategy.

Step 1 Identify consequences of the change

Step 2 Identify the actions required to set up the change, in detail

Step 3 Allocate responsibility for the actions to be taken

Step 4 Establish priorities

Step 5 Provide budgets

Step 6 Set up teams and organisation structures, allocating human resources

(e) **Controlling**: there must be a control process to ensure that the work is done, deadlines achieved and so on.

(f) **Recognising** those who have contributed to the success of the organisation.

NOTES

2 DEPARTMENTAL PLANS AND OBJECTIVES

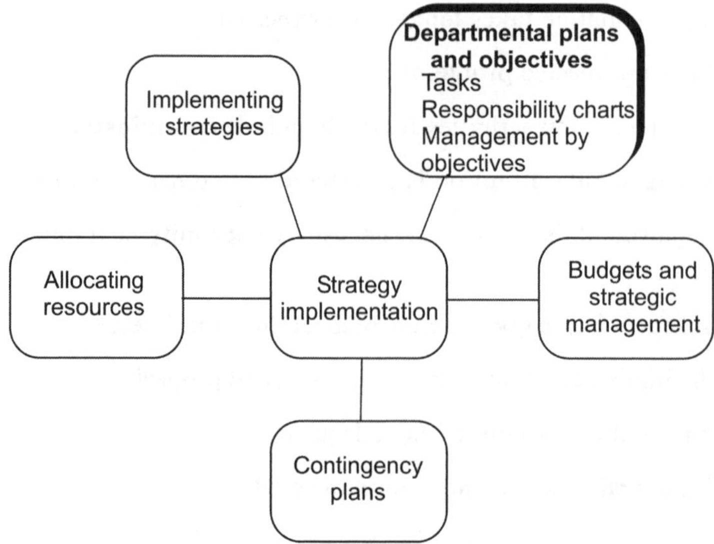

2.1 Tasks

Implementation of plans involves three tasks.

(a) **Document the responsibilities** of divisions, departments and individual managers.

(b) **Prepare responsibility charts** for managers at divisional, departmental and subordinate levels.

(c) **Prepare activity schedules** for managers at divisional, departmental and subordinate levels.

This process is sketched out in the diagram opposite.

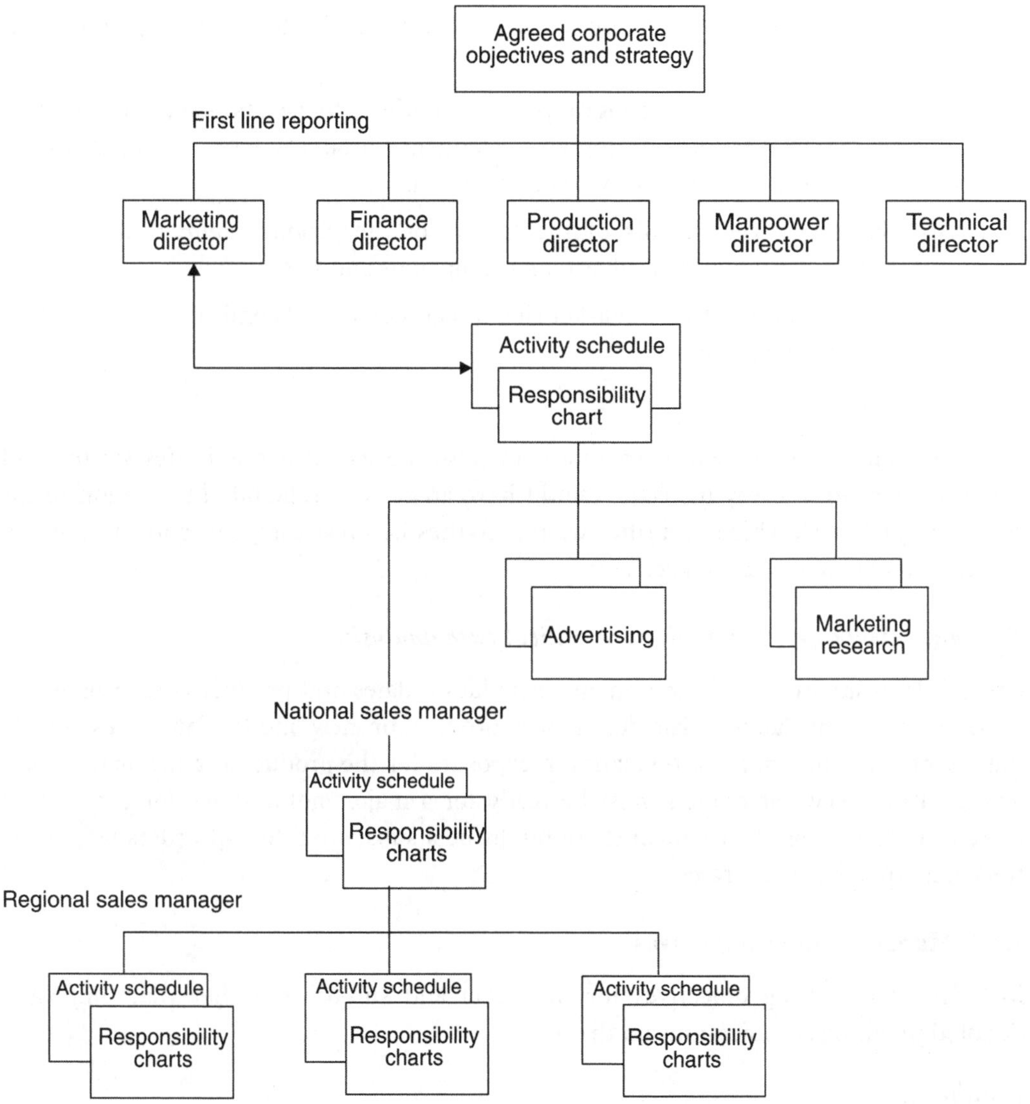

Agreed corporate objectives and strategy

First line reporting

Marketing director

Finance director

Production director

Manpower director

Technical director

Activity schedule

Responsibility chart

Advertising

Marketing research

National sales manager

Activity schedule

Responsibility charts

Regional sales manager

Activity schedule

Responsibility charts

Activity schedule

Responsibility charts

Activity schedule

Responsibility charts

Figure 13.1: Implementation of plans

2.2 Responsibility charts

These can be drawn up for management at all levels in the organisation, including the board of directors. They show the control points that indicate what needs to be achieved and how to recognise when things are going wrong. For each manager, a responsibility chart will have four main elements.

- The manager's major objective
- The manager's general programme for achieving that objective
- Sub-objectives
- Critical assumptions underlying the objectives and the programme

The responsibility chart for the marketing director might be drawn up along the following lines.

(a) **Major objective and general programme:** to achieve a targeted level of sales, by means of selling existing well-established products, by breaking into some new markets and by a new product launch.

(b) **Sub-objectives:** details of the timing of the product launch; details and timing of promotions, advertising campaigns and so on

(c) **Critical assumptions:** market share, market size and conditions, competitors' activity and so on.

Activity schedules

Successful implementation of corporate plans also means getting activities started and completed on time. Every manager should have an activity schedule in addition to his responsibility chart, which identifies what activities he must carry out and the start up and completion dates for each activity.

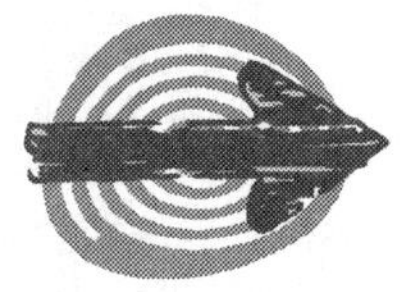

This may involve network analysis or critical path analysis.

Critical dates might include equipment installation dates and product launch dates. In some markets, the launch date for a new product or new model can be extremely important, with an aim to gain maximum exposure for the product at a major trade fair or exhibition. New car models must be ready for a major motor show, for example. If there is a delay in product launch there might be a substantial loss of orders which the trade fair could have generated.

2.3 Management by objectives

MBO involves setting objectives for managers and sub-units, rather than imposing **detailed** planning specifications on them.

Definition

Management by objectives (MBO) is a scheme, developed in the 1950s, of planning and control which co-ordinates short-term plans with longer-term plans and goals: the plans (and commitment) of junior with senior management and the efforts of different departments. It aims to harmonise individual managers' objectives with those of the organisation, seeking to achieve a sense of common purpose.

Achieving organisational goals

(a) **Direction**. Each job is directed towards the same organisational goals. Each managerial job must be focused on the success of the business as a whole, not just one part of it.

(b) **Target**. Each manager's targeted performance must be derived from targets of achievement for the organisation as a whole.

(c) **Performance measurement**. A manager's results must be measured in terms of his or her contribution to the business as a whole.

(d) **Each manager must know** what his or her targets of performance are.

Consequently, to ensure co-ordination, the various functional objectives must be interlinked:

(a) **Vertically** from top to bottom of the business.

(b) **Horizontally**, for example, the objectives of the production function must be linked with those of sales, warehousing, purchasing, R & D and so on

(c) **Over time**. Short-term objectives can be regarded as intermediate milestones on the road towards long-term objectives.

The hierarchy of objectives which emerges is this.

Figure 13.2: Hierarchy of objectives

Unit objectives are required for all departments.

Step 1 They must be set first of all in terms of primary targets. Here are some examples.

- Profitability
- Level of activity, or turnover
- Achievement of production schedules and delivery dates
- The quality of output or services
- Safety
- Efficiency in resources utilisation (labour, productivity, material usage)
- Plant utilisation

Step 2 For each of these primary targets, secondary targets (or sub-targets) will be set.

- Profitability: the contribution required from each individual product, and the method of fixed overhead allocation.
- Quality of output: the acceptable level of rejected units.

Step 3 **Identify which individual managers** within the unit are in a position to influence the achievement of each of them.

Step 4 Top management will then make a **unit improvement plan** for each unit of the business, setting out specifically the objectives for improvement, the performance standards and the time scale.

Key results are needed for managers.

Step 5 The unit improvement plan is then broken down into a series of **key results** and **performance standards** required from the various individual managers within the unit. For example, the key results of an information systems manager might be as given below.

ITEM	KEY RESULT
Service to users	To ensure that users get regular software upgrades, with appropriate helplines and training.
Use of resources and efficiency levels	The time when users cannot use the network must not exceed 5%.
Costs	The cost per operating hour must not exceed £60.
Quality	Queries from users must be responded to within ten minutes.

Step 6 A personal **job improvement plan** should be agreed with each manager, which will make a quantifiable and measurable contribution to achievement of the plans for the department, branch or company as a whole, within specified time periods.

Step 7 A systematic **performance review** of each manager's results is also necessary.

Activity 1 **(20 minutes)**

The Griswold Cutlery Company is an old established firm, selling high quality stainless steel cutlery to markets in the UK, France and Germany. It is based in Sheffield. The managing director, Mr Paul Griswold, great grandson of the firm's founder, has just taken over from his father, Matthew Griswold. Matthew Griswold was a manager of the old school. As the boss, he liked to exert power and employees were afraid to disagree with him. He encouraged strict conformance to company procedures: 'rules are rules, they are there to be followed, and I don't like changing them'. Paul Griswold wants to introduce MBO. Do you think this will be an easy task?

MBO implies an **organisation hierarchy.**

(a) It **empowers managers,** but still implies the existence of many management **layers,** between the strategic apex and the operating core.

(b) It **assumes that objectives** are not in conflict, or that they **can be reconciled easily**.

(c) It assumes that it is possible for senior and junior managers to co-operate as if they were equals.

FOR DISCUSSION

In a fast changing and increasingly competitive business world, more and more organisations are adopting strategic planning practices. Given this situation, what future do you see for the system of MBO?

3 ALLOCATING RESOURCES

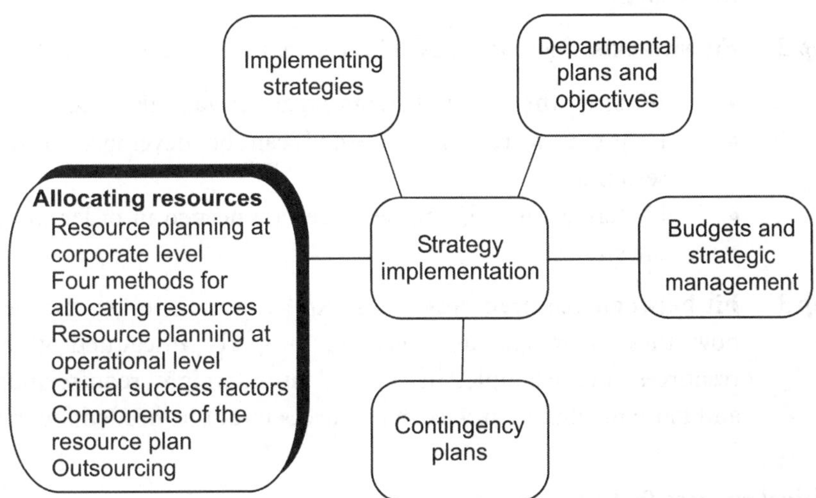

Corporations live in a world where some resources are more limited than others. A strategy requires decisions as to how resources should be deployed and this is an important issue in evaluation and implementation.

3.1 Resource planning at corporate level

The strategic plan, overall, might require a total change in the organisation's resources.

(a) **Degree of change**. Will the organisation need more or fewer resources of personnel, capital (for investment purposes) and so forth?

(b) **Extent of central direction.** How will these resources be allocated?

- By the corporate centre?
- According to the requests and decisions of the operating units themselves?

3.2 Four methods for allocating resources

		Change Low	*Change* High
Central direction	*Low*	**Bargaining** between departments or SBUs	**Competition** between units
	High	**Formula** (eg increase all depts by 5%)	Planners **impose** priorities

- Scarcity of key resources leads to higher central control.
- Resource allocation decisions, and hence the strategies that underlie them, are constrained by the **existing distribution** of resources and power.

3.3 Resource planning at operational level

Resource planning involves planning the resources (and identifying potential resources) of the undertaking in order that the defined and agreed corporate objectives may be achieved.

Step 1 **Resource identification**. What resources will be **needed** to implement the strategy?

Step 2 **Fit with existing resources.** Three assessments must be made.

- Whether the required resources are **already** in place
- If any **new** resources needed can be developed from existing resources
- If **changes** to existing resources are needed in order to implement the strategy

Step 3 **Fit between required resources**. An assessment must also be made of how these new resources can be properly integrated with current resources. For example, increasing output might require more people and more machines, and extra resources might be needed for training.

3.4 Critical success factors

CSFs can be used to **translate strategic objectives** into performance targets and tactical plans. Here is an example.

(a) Dogger Bank plc's **business objective** is increased profits.

(b) The strategy for increased profits is to **increase revenue per customer**.

(c) Increasing revenue per customer might not be possible unless **customers buy other services from the bank** (eg insurance).

  (i) The critical success factor will be the number of extra services sold to each customer.

  (ii) A key task might involve developing a customer database so that the firm can target customers with information about other services more effectively.

Some CSFs which cover both financial and non-financial criteria are outlined below.

Sphere of activity	Critical factors	
Marketing	Sales volume Market share	Gross margins
Production	Capacity utilisation	Quality standards
Logistics	Capacity utilisation	Level of service

Some criteria which are regularly used in choosing between alternative plans for specific aspects of marketing are outlined below.

Activity	CSF
New product development	Trial rate Repurchase rate
Sales programmes	Contribution by region, salesperson Controllable margin as percentage of sales Number of new accounts Travel costs

Activity	CSF
Advertising programmes	Awareness levels Attribute ratings Cost levels
Pricing programmes	Price relative to industry average Price elasticity of demand
Distribution programmes	Number of distributors carrying the product

3.5 Components of the resource plan

CSFs give some idea of the resources that are needed. For example, if the key task is the development of a customer database, then the resources needed might include the services of a systems analyst, hardware and so on.

The resource plan might use the following tools.

(a) Budgets

(b) Plans for obtaining and using human resources, such as recruitment and selection and training.

(c) Network analysis, indicating how resources will be deployed in a particular sequence.

3.6 Outsourcing

Definition

> **Outsourcing**: sub-contracting work to external suppliers, for example producing a subcomponent or providing a service.

Key issues in outsourcing

(a) **Resource usage**. When a company makes products in-house it is tying up resources which could be used for other more profitable purposes (ie there is an opportunity cost).

(b) **Supplier commitment**. If a company cannot produce all the output it needs in-house, it will be forced to use external suppliers to some extent. This might oblige the company to offer a supply contract to a supplier which guarantees a minimum supply quantity over a period of time.

(c) **Control**. In-house production might be easier to control in terms of product quality and the reliability of delivery. Certainly, the supplier has its own objectives.

(d) **Quality assurance**. External suppliers need to be reliable in terms of product quality and reliability of delivery times, and alternative sources of supply should be sought, in case one supplier becomes too unreliable or too expensive. One way of vetting suppliers is to check to see if they have BS EN ISO 9000 certification.

(e) **Compulsion**. Certain areas of the public sector are required to consider outsourcing.

(f) **Vulnerability**. If the outsourcing arrangement goes wrong a firm can suffer if it loses the expertise.

(g) **Contract compliance**. The outsourcing arrangement requires strict attention to contracts. This can be a source of operational inflexibility, if the contract has to be laboriously renegotiated when circumstances change.

(h) **Expertise.** Outsourcers can offer more expertise.

EXAMPLE

The pharmaceutical company AstraZeneca has made plans to outsource its entire drug manufacturing activities over the next ten years as it is not considered to be a 'core activity'. Executive Vice President of Operations David Smith outlined the major restructuring exercise as a way to cut costs given that over the next five years 38% of revenue will be lost as patents expire on key drugs. 11% of the global 66,000 strong workforce will be shed over the period of the transformation. In describing the ultimate corporate aim, David smith is quoted as saying:

"We will own the intellectual property, the research, the branding and the quality and safety issues but everything else would be outsourced. The idea is to take out as many stages as you can"

The company will shift emphasis and build its core competences namely the research and innovation and contract specialist pharmaceutical manufacturers at the production of medicines.

Adapted from Pagnamenta, D. (2007) 'AstraZeneca to outsource manufacturing' The Times 17.9.07

4 BUDGETS AND STRATEGIC MANAGEMENT

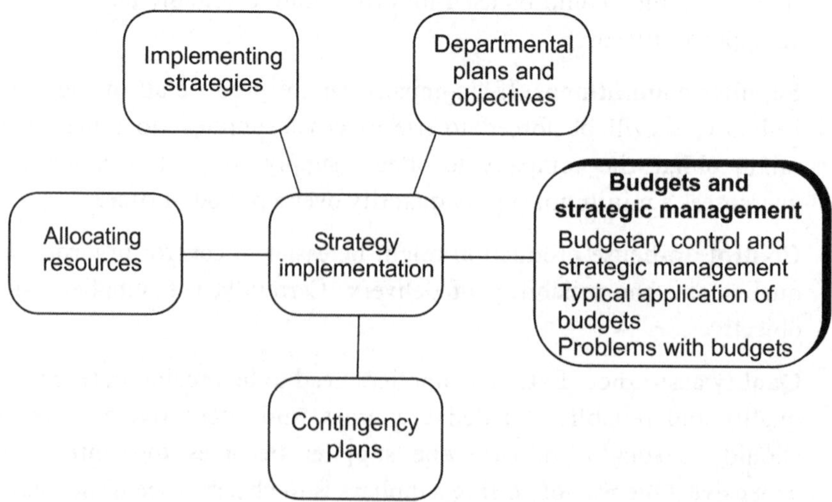

4.1 Budgetary control and strategic management

Objective	Comment
Strategic direction	Operations and resource plans, and hence budgets, should be derived from business strategies.
Resource allocation	Resources should be allocated according to the required outputs. Budgets should be directed towards achieving CSFs.
Continuous improvement	Firms should always seek to improve their performance in relation to customer needs, industry best practice and competitors. Budgets should support continuous improvement.
Goal congruence	Managers must understand the effect of their decisions on the work processes outside their department.
Add value	The time spent on budgetary activities should be worth more than its cost.
Cost reductions	When an organisation's targets include improved productivity, or restoring profitability, cost reductions are likely to be a crucial short-term target. The budget will be the planning mechanism.
Targets and responsibilities	Budgets will set targets for divisions, departments, and sub-sections of departments. Individual managers should be aware of what their personal targets are.

4.2 Typical application of budgets

Budget	Comment
Capital budgets	Reflect cash-flows for different projects, capital rationing decisions, funding methods
Working capital	Stock, debtor and creditor levels
Departmental budgets	This will clearly implement the allocation of financial resources between departments
Consolidated budgets	These enable planning of resource use as a whole across the company

The budget **should be properly related to the strategic plan**. Although many budgets are prepared for one year, the factors which should influence the **budget period** are as follows.

(a) Strategic plans have a **planning horizon** in excess of one year.

(b) **Implementation**. The long time required to purchase or erect new buildings, to move a company to a different location etc explain why the planning horizon for capital budgets is usually several years.

(c) **Resources**. A distinction can be made between long-term planning and short-term budgeting according to the 'fixed' or 'variable' nature of the resources of the business. In the long-term, all resources are variable in quantity, but in the short-term, although some resources are variable, others are fixed.

(d) **Error**. All budgets involve some element of forecasting and guesswork, since future events cannot be quantified with accuracy. The more distant the planning horizon, the greater the uncertainty and the wider the margin of error will be.

(e) The **greater the rate of change** that is likely in the future, the **nearer the planning horizon** should be.

4.3 Problems with budgets

(a) **Traditional budgets are based on the structure of the organisation**, with **responsibility centres** of different kinds representing where budgetary control is exercised. However, recent developments **require managers to think in terms of processes**, with the customer at the end of them, not of a **static organisation** structure.

(b) **Incremental.** At its worst, the traditional budgeting process commences with management setting a revenue forecast and financial targets. Departmental budgets are then prepared based on last year's costs and year-to-date actuals, 'plus or minus a bit'.

(c) Most budgets are prepared over a **one-year period** to enable managers to plan and control financial results for the purposes of the annual accounts. There is a need for management to satisfy shareholders that their company is achieving good results, and for this reason, the arbitrary one-year financial period is usually selected for budgeting. It is not necessarily relevant to the business strategy.

5 CONTINGENCY PLANS

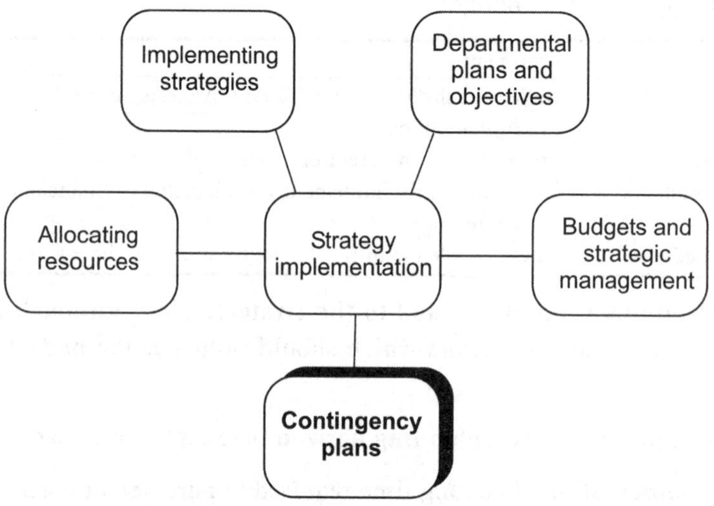

Definition

Contingencies are uncontrollable events which are not provided for in the main corporate plan.

Where contingencies are known about, **contingency plans** should be prepared in advance to deal with the situation if and when it arises. Such plans might be prepared in detail or in outline only, depending on the likelihood that the contingency will become a reality.

EXAMPLE

A company which exports or imports goods will be susceptible to fluctuations in foreign exchange rates. Although the risks of foreign exchange exposure can be reduced, by matching assets and liabilities in each currency the company deals in, and in the short term by means of forward exchange contracts, the company will almost certainly be unable to eliminate foreign exchange risks over its longer-term corporate planning period.

Contingency plans can be prepared to deal with adverse exchange rate movements, by speculating how far rates might alter and calculating the implications of various degrees of change. If the company's products are to remain competitive in their markets, 'trigger points' will need to be identified, and contingency plans drawn up containing outline instructions about what will need to be done if the exchange rate passes above or below a certain trigger point.

Other contingencies can be dealt with by insurance and providing backup facilities.

Chapter roundup

- Implementation consists of: envisioning, activating, supporting, installing, ensuring and recognising.
- Implementation has implications for projects, departmental plans, organisation structure, resources and so on.
- Plans are developed for individual units and programs. Management by objectives aims to co-ordinate unit and managerial objectives.
- The planning of resources requires consideration of three central issues: current resource needs, whether these needs are satisfied by existing resources, and future resources required. The various activities of the value chain can be examined to see if there is a fit between these elements. The mode of resource allocation depends on the degree of central direction of the organisation and the change to which it is subjected.
- Critical success factors can be used to determine where resources should be allocated.
- Budgets are statements in financial terms of the necessary resources for a plan.
- Contingency plans would be drawn up to mobilise resources in case of crises or matters not working out as anticipated.

Quick quiz

1. Identify the problems of implementation.
2. What are the guidelines for implementation?
3. Distinguish between responsibility charts and activity schedules.
4. Describe the system of management by objectives.
5. How might resources be allocated?
6. How do CSFs translate into resources?
7. What are the key issues in outsourcing?
8. What are the objectives of budgets if they are to support strategic management?
9. What types of budgets are there?
10. What are contingencies?

Answers to quick quiz

1. Time problems
   Inadequate co-ordination
   Distraction of management attention
   Lack of capability
   Lack of sense of direction
   Inadequate definition of tasks
   Inadequate information systems
   No communication of overall goals

2. Envisioning
   Activating
   Supporting
   Installing
   Controlling
   Recognising

3. A responsibility chart shows a manager's objectives and the main points to control. Activity schedules are more detailed, identifying those activities that need to be carried out, and the related timescales.

4. Management by Objectives is a principle of management which aims to harmonise individual manager objectives with those of the organisation. It is a means of integrating corporate objectives, such as profit and growth, with the needs of individual managers to contribute both to the organisation and to their own self development.

5. By bargaining between departments
   By competition between departments
   By applying a formula
   By having allocations imposed, due to priorities

6. Increase profits
   Increase revenue per customer
   Get customers to buy other services

7 Resource usage
Supplier commitment
Control
Quality assurance
Compulsion
Vulnerability
Contract compliance
Expertise

8 Strategic direction
Resource allocation
Continuous improvement
Goal congruence
Add value
Cost reductions
Targets and responsibilities

9 Capital budgets
Working capital budgets
Departmental budgets
Consolidated budgets

10 Uncontrollable events not provided for in the main corporate plan

Answer to activity

1 The company's existing culture does not appear to be one in which MBO could flourish. MBO requires that subordinates are relatively independent in negotiating with the boss and that the boss is willing to delegate. Neither of these conditions seems to be present in this company.

NOTES

Chapter 14 :
REVIEW AND MONITORING

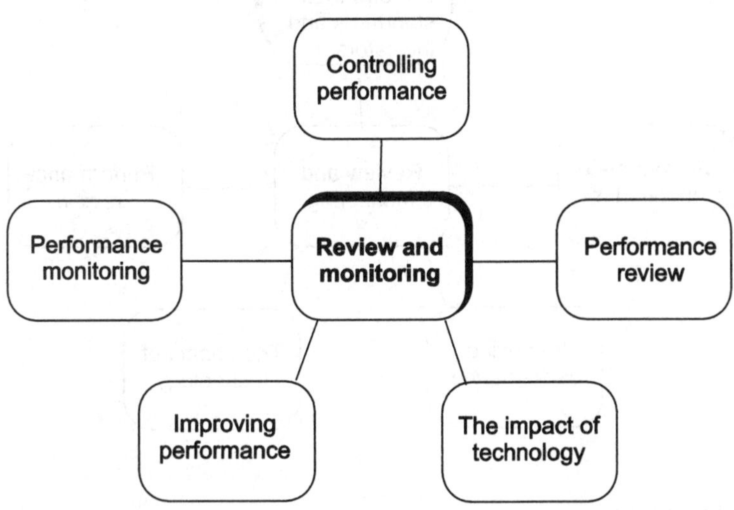

Introduction

Planning and organising are closely linked with control: the process whereby performance and results are monitored, compared with plans, schedules and budgets, and adjusted if necessary.

In this chapter, we discuss aspects of the organisation's control systems, and then, specifically, some of the techniques managers use to review the effectiveness of procedures, projects and tasks and to continuously monitor their progress and efficiency. This is obviously linked to employee appraisal and individual/team performance monitoring, but the emphasis here is on methods of working and managing tasks for the ultimate realisation of company strategy, rather than on the performance of the people involved.

Your objectives

In this chapter you will learn about the following.

(a) Defining a control system, and organisational examples

(b) Performance standards and indicators that might be used to evaluate your own effectiveness and that of others

(c) Techniques of performance review, including method study, systems analysis and value analysis

(d) How performance can be continuously monitored

(e) The impact of technology on the review and monitoring of performance

(f) How performance might be improved as a result of monitoring and review

1 CONTROLLING PERFORMANCE

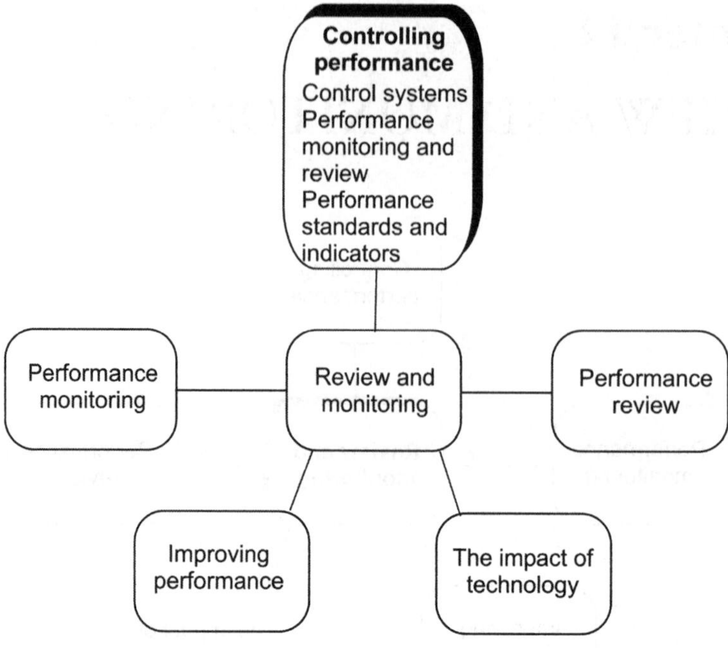

1.1 Control systems

Control is required to keep the performance of the organisation steady. Unpredictable disturbances continually affect the organisation system, so that its actual results deviate from its expected results or goals. A control system is used to ensure that the organisation is aware of these disturbances, and deals with them in an appropriate manner.

Activity 1 **(20 minutes)**

Give four examples of 'disturbances' to the smooth, planned operation of a business.

Control is achieved by setting standards and plans, monitoring actual performance, comparing actual performance with the standards or plans, and making any necessary adjustments to bring the two back into line.

A simple model of a control system may be drawn as in Figure 14.1.

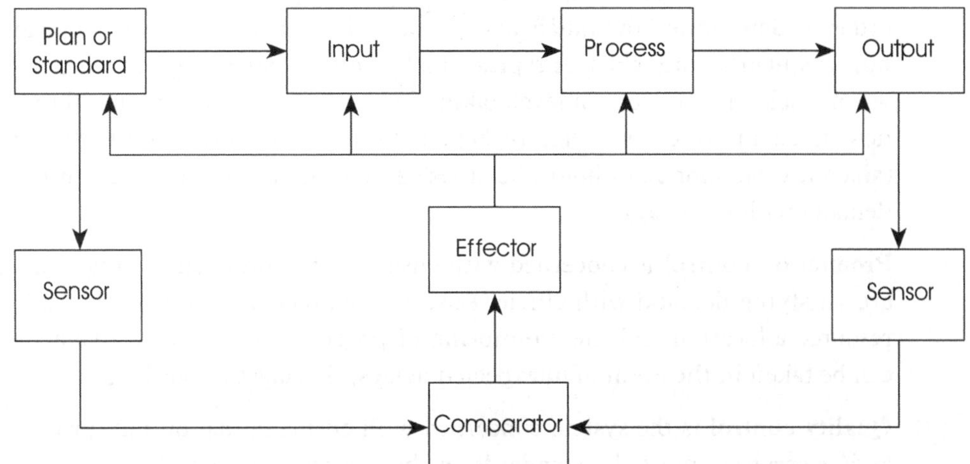

Figure 14.1 Control system

(a) The basis of any control system is the **standard** or **plan.** Control will be exercised to ensure that this is adhered to.

(b) A **sensor** is the device by which information about performance is collected and measured, or the person who does the collection and measuring.

(c) A **comparator** is the means by which the actual results of the system are measured against the pre-determined plans or standards. In a business organisation, comparative information might be provided by computers in the form of management reports. Managers, however, will also be comparators: they are expected to make decisions on the results of the comparison.

(d) An **effector** initiates control action. In a production department, an effector may be a component in some automatic equipment which regulates the functioning of the equipment (for example, a thermostat). An effector may also be a manager's instruction and a subordinate's action.

Types of control

Most organisations have formal control systems in place to control performance in the following areas.

(a) **Budgetary control**

Definition

A **budget** is a statement of desired performance, usually expressed in financial terms (expenditure, revenue, profit and so on).

An organisation will have budgets for each area of operation (production, sales, research and so on) as well as for each department: all these are drawn up into the master budget of the organisation. Budgetary control is the process whereby actual figures are entered against budgeted figures for each item and period, so that variances can be identified and dealt with.

We also looked at budgets in the previous chapter.

NOTES

(b) **Inventory (stock) control**. This system monitors the use of the organisation's stock of raw materials, components and other temporarily 'idle' resources, in order to determine how much new stock will need to be ordered or made, how frequently, and when. A typical stock control system triggers reordering when stock falls to a certain level, taking into account the time required to get new stock in: stock is therefore kept between a maximum desirable level (since it costs money to hold idle stock) and a safe minimum level (to meet demand without delay).

(c) **Production control** is concerned with ensuring that production programmes are satisfying demand with efficient use of resources. It involves scheduling, resource allocation and the monitoring of progress so that corrective action can be taken in the event of unexpected delays, shortages or bottlenecks.

(d) **Quality control** is the system concerned with ensuring that output (products and/or services) meet the standards set by the organisation. This is usually done by sampling output: if a certain proportion of sub-standard items is found, control action is triggered.

There may not be systems in place to offer feedback on performance in every situation. This is where performance monitoring and review come in.

1.2 Performance monitoring and review

As 'sensor' in a control system, a manager needs information about a unit's performance, to compare with the unit's plans and budgets. This may be done in two ways.

(a) **Performance monitoring**: 'keeping an eye' on progress, on an ongoing basis. Managers should constantly gather formal and informal control information. Progress may be monitored through observation, reports from team members or control systems, progress meetings, sampling of output quality and so on.

(b) **Performance review**: taking a look at results and/or methods used in a given period. This may be a major exercise, carried out only every few years: for example, a method study reviewing the systems and procedures of the organisation. It may be a regular procedure carried out at six monthly or annual intervals: for example employee appraisals, or the preparation of the annual report and accounts. Or it may be a kind of 'post mortem' examination of the success of a particular project or task, on its completion.

Activity 2 **(20 minutes)**

Think about your work for this course. Identify three methods by which it is monitored.

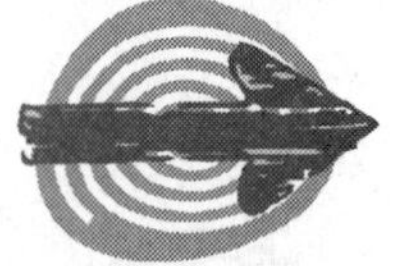

We will be discussing some techniques of performance monitoring and reviewing in the following sections of this chapter, but first, we will look briefly at performance standards and indicators. What is a manager actually looking for when (s)he monitors and reviews performance? How does (s)he know whether and how far the unit has in fact been successful?

1.3 Performance standards and indicators

What is a manager looking for that would indicate that successful performance has been achieved?

In general terms, there are certain attributes of successful performance which can be measured. (Rather neatly, they all begin with the letter 'e', as you will see below.) In specific terms, the manager should be measuring performance against clearly-defined goals and standards set out in the organisation's, and various units', plans and budgets.

The desirable 'E' factors of organisational performance are as follows.

(a) **Effectiveness.** Generally, objectives in this area relate to the firm's ability to serve the needs of its owners and its chosen market.

   (i) Market share of a specified market
   (ii) Quality of product or service
   (iii) Financial performance.

(b) **Efficiency**. Objectives in this area are to do with how resources should be used to achieve the goals of the firm.

   (i) Materials and energy usage and wastage rates
   (ii) Speed of response to customer enquiries and orders
   (iii) Completion of projects on time
   (iv) Productivity per person/hour, or per machine/hour.

(c) **Economy** concerns the financial aspects of the firm's operations and flows from the earlier objectives.

   (i) Cost per unit
   (ii) Contribution per unit.

(d) **Elegance**. Doing things the 'right way'.

   (i) Appearance of business premises and staff
   (ii) Punctuality and professionalism of service
   (iii) Appearance of corporate literature and communications.

(e) **Ethicality** concerns the firm's adherence to its social responsibilities and to business ethics.

   (i) Impact of operations on the natural environment
   (ii) Hiring and promotion of staff from minority groups
   (iii) Non-reliance on contracts with military or political connotations.

The organisation as a whole will have specific **financial performance indicators:**

(a) Profitability (and value added)
(b) Return on capital employed (ROCE) or return on investment (ROI)
(c) Survival, and/or growth
(d) Growth in earnings per share (EPS) or dividend payments to shareholders

In addition, there may be **non-financial performance indicators**, to do with:

(a) The maintenance of product or service quality

(b) The image and 'position' of the organisation and its products in the market-place

(c) Innovation – new ideas and products

(d) The organisation's ability to attract and retain highly-skilled labour

(e) The efficiency and effectiveness of the organisation's systems and management

(f) The social responsibility of the organisation

Activity 3 **(30 minutes)**

Give an example of a specific goal in (a) to (f) immediately above, which a manager might use as a yardstick for monitoring and review.

Clearly, goal-setting is essential to performance monitoring and review. If sub-units of the organisation have coherent and specific goals and targets, the extent to which those goals and targets are reached will be a helpful indicator of successful performance.

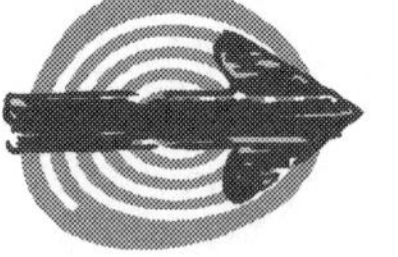

We will now look at some of the techniques organisations use for the monitoring and review of performance.

2 PERFORMANCE MONITORING

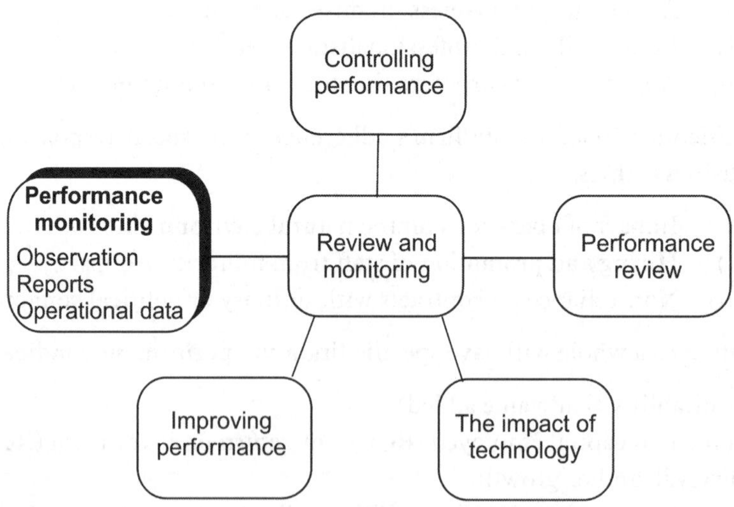

2.1 Observation

Managers may monitor performance by watching operations as they are carried out, or delegating such monitoring to a trained observer.

Task inspection

If the work is repetitive and directly observable, the observer may:

(a) Time particular tasks, logging when work is handed out and when it is returned completed

(b) Record levels of output

These figures can be compared with standard times or levels (determined by previous study or published standards).

This is obviously time-consuming for the manager or supervisor doing the monitoring. It may also be impractical in the following situations.

- There is a wide variety of work being done
- Large numbers of people are involved in the work
- A long time period is required to study a single 'cycle' of the work
- The work is infrequent
- The work is not readily observable – such as planning

Activity 4 **(20 minutes)**

Can you think of reasons why staff may not welcome task inspection as a method of performance monitoring?

Activity sampling

Activity sampling means taking a number of observations during the work cycle at random predetermined intervals. In this way, activity can be monitored with reasonable accuracy (since, statistically, the sample should reflect the whole) – without having to stand at the work-place for long hours taking observations. This technique (also known as 'work sampling'), has proved particularly useful for varied work such as that in offices, canteens, warehouses and supermarkets.

2.2 Reports

Instead of attempting direct observation, the manager may monitor performance via reports from operators, and others involved in the task.

As we have discussed elsewhere, **reporting by exception** should be the norm in any control system, so that the monitoring process only brings to the manager's attention variances from what (s)he expected and planned to happen. However, a manager may wish to monitor specific aspects of the work, such as time spent on particular tasks, or fluctuations in output.

Time sheets

Staff or supervisors may simply be asked to estimate how things are going, how long a task is taking and so on, from their experience.

Time and diary sheets are a more precise way of keeping track of the allocation and duration of tasks, provided that they are conscientiously maintained and truthful. Sheets are filled in on a daily or weekly basis and summarised for each individual or group to

NOTES

show amounts of time actually spent on various activities. This is particularly useful for activities which cannot be measured in output terms, only in time spent – eg answering phones, talking to supervisors, taking dictation, dealing with visitors, or running errands.

Similar monitoring can be carried out electronically, using computers. A clock-in, clock-out system may be used to log how long an individual spends at work, or on a particular task. Computers can also produce reports of who spent how long doing what.

Surveys

If performance criteria relate to service, such as staff attitude and friendliness, responsiveness, clarity of information, professionalism and so on, the monitoring mechanism may need to be a customer survey. Although management inspection may indicate some areas for approval or improvement, ultimately it is the impression given to the customer that matters.

Performance criteria related to being a responsible and desirable employer might likewise be monitored using staff attitude surveys, or staff feedback meetings.

2.3 Operational data

Operations will already have produced a number of records and documents, such as production and sales charts, accounts, order forms, customer complaint forms, stock requisitions and records and so on. These are not the same as management reports: they are designed primarily to provide and record data which are used in transactions and operations. However, a manager can also use them as management information about the level of output, materials usage, performance to schedule, quality problems and so on.

Activity 5 **(40 minutes)**

The British Airports Authority included the following service quality factors in its performance monitoring programme. For each, what mechanism of measurement do you think they use?

Service quality factor	*Measure*	*Mechanism*
(a) Access	Ease of finding way round	
(b) Aesthetics	Staff appearance Airport appearance Quality/appearance of food	
(c) Comfort	Crowdedness of airport	
(d) Communication	Information clarity Clarity of labelling and pricing	
(e) Friendliness	Staff attitude and helpfulness	
(f) Reliability	Number of equipment faults	
(g) Security	Efficiency of security checks Number of urgent safety reports	

3 PERFORMANCE REVIEW

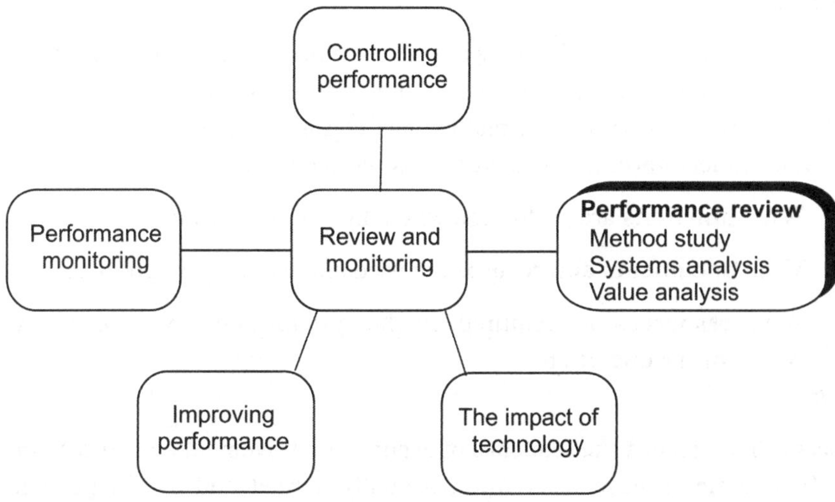

3.1 Method study

Definition

> **Method study** is the systematic recording and critical examination of existing and proposed ways of doing work, as a means of developing and applying easier and more effective methods and reducing costs.

Method study is concerned with how work could and should be done more efficiently. This may include concerns such as organisation structure, work environment, the co-ordination and economical use of resources, the streamlining of systems and procedures and so on.

The approach to a full-scale method study is as follows.

(a) Establish an area for investigation

(b) Establish terms of reference (say to improve productivity by 10%, or to find how the work force in a department can take on certain extra work without increasing staff numbers)

(c) Investigate the existing methods by:

   (i) Observation of procedures, forms and so on in action
   (ii) Discussion with people involved
   (iii) Studying existing records, such as procedure manuals, job specifications and so on

(d) Record the existing methods, by narrative, or using charts and diagrams (as discussed below)

(e) Analyse the existing methods, identify weaknesses and strengths, develop alternative methods and discuss these with the operations staff and management affected

(f) Develop an alternative method, and recommend it for implementation

(g) If accepted, install and later review and develop the new method as necessary

There are a number of ways of recording data on existing methods.

Narrative notes

Narrative notes (that is, an ordinary written description) have the advantage of being simple to record but are awkward to change. The purpose of the notes is to describe and explain the system, at the same time making any comments or criticisms which will help to deepen your understanding how it works. Notes need to cover:

(a) What **functions** are performed when, how and by whom

(b) What **documents and records** are used and where they 'go' at each stage

(c) What **resources** are required by the system, and where they travel in the course of the operation

Flow charts

Flow process charts record the sequence of events and movements using certain common symbols. Five symbols have been internationally agreed and are in general use, see Figure 14.2.

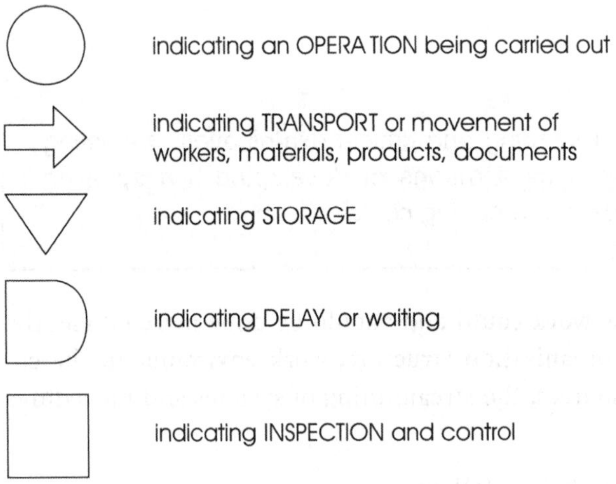

Figure 14.2: Flow chart symbols

Flow charts can be:

(a) Man type, recording what an operator does

(b) Machine type, recording how equipment is used

(c) Material type, recording what happens to materials

(d) Document type, showing how documents or other information are moved around within a system.

The symbols are linked, usually vertically, to show the chronological sequence of events (see Figure 14.3). You could also have columns: for each type of event, say, or each department of the organisation (to show physical movements between them), or destinations of various copies of documents (to show who gets them).

Each symbol is numbered, for ease of reference. This also helps the analyst to see at a glance if there are too many delays, too much moving about, too many different operations or insufficient inspection involved in a system.

Flow process chart for finishing and despatching booklets

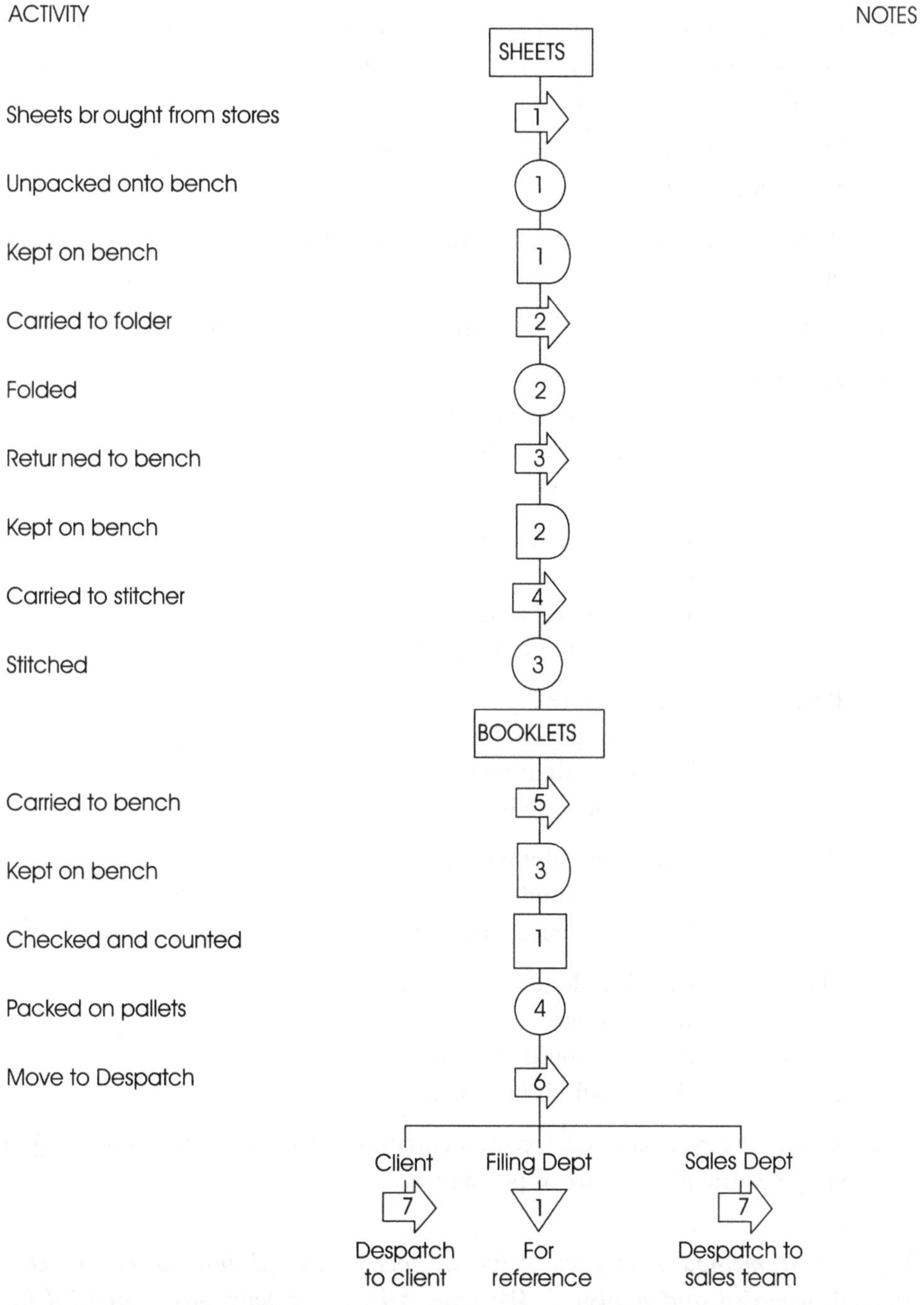

ACTIVITY		NOTES
	SHEETS	
Sheets brought from stores	1 (transport)	
Unpacked onto bench	1 (operation)	
Kept on bench	1 (delay)	
Carried to folder	2 (transport)	
Folded	2 (operation)	
Returned to bench	3 (transport)	
Kept on bench	2 (delay)	
Carried to stitcher	4 (transport)	
Stitched	3 (operation)	
	BOOKLETS	
Carried to bench	5 (transport)	
Kept on bench	3 (delay)	
Checked and counted	1 (inspection)	
Packed on pallets	4 (operation)	
Move to Despatch	6 (transport)	

Client	Filing Dept	Sales Dept
7 (transport)	1 (storage)	7 (transport)
Despatch to client	For reference	Despatch to sales team

Figure 14.3: Chronological flow chart

Activity 6 **(15 minutes)**

Can you suggest any areas where efficiency could be improved, judging by Figure 14.3?

Analysing the existing system

Data will be analysed to evaluate:

(a) How efficiently the system creates, moves and stores documents and utilises available personnel and resources of time, space, equipment, materials and services

(b) How effective the system is: for example, whether budgets, quality standards and deadlines are adhered to

(c) Whether the organisational structure as a whole is an effective framework for operations

The activities in a process can be tested by asking five sets of questions:

(a)	**Purpose**	What is being done? Why is it being done? What else can be done? What should be done?
(b)	**Place**	Where is it being done? Why there? Where else could it be done? Where should it be done?
(c)	**Person**	Who does it? Why that person? Who else might do it? Who should do it?
(d)	**Control**	When should it be done? Is it within budget? Is it of the correct quality?
(e)	**Means**	How is it done? Why that way? How else could it be done? How should it be done?

Once faults have been examined, recommendations can be drawn up, suggesting revisions to organisational structure or procedures.

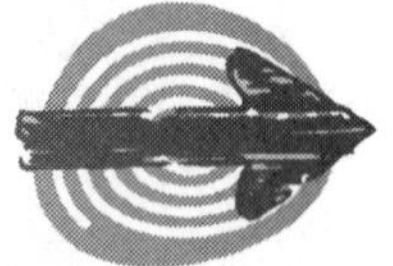

Having covered method study, we have in fact discussed how a system can be investigated, recorded and analysed. We now, briefly, see how this is applied in the process called systems analysis.

3.2 Systems analysis

Definition

> **Systems analysis** is the process of analysing methods, procedures, sequences of activities, paperwork flows and the inputs required and outputs expected in operational or informational processing systems which are based on computers.

The purpose of systems analysis is to improve existing systems or to design new systems for processing data. It is, in particular, the basis for:

(a) The selection or design of computer systems

(b) The selection or design of appropriate applications software, or computer programming

(c) Establishing the resources required to establish and operate a new system.

The sequence of activities in a systems analysis are similar to those involved in method study.

(a) Prepare a brief, defining the objectives of and constraints on the study itself.

(b) Investigate and record data on the current systems and procedures. This is done by flowcharting, as in method study, but with a greater emphasis on:

 (i) Inputs, processing operations (compilation, analysis, calculation, checks and so on) and outputs

 (ii) The way information is recorded and/or stored – as forms, files and so on

 (iii) Documents: what they are for, who uses them and how

 (iv) Document routes: where they originate, who sees them, how many are used, where they go and where they end up

 We give an example of a system flow chart in Figure 14.4.

(c) Prepare a specification for the new or modified system: what it will do and, broadly, how it will do it; whether existing computers could be used; what software would be required; what the costs might be.

(d) Design a new or modified system according to the specification.

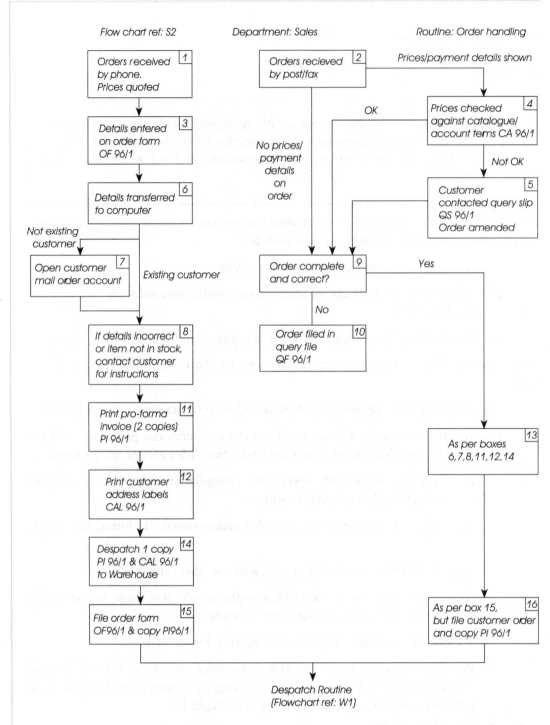

Figure 14.4: System flow chart

Activity 7 **(30 minutes)**

Think about applying for a job you have seen advertised in the local paper. Draw your own systems flow chart for the activities you will have to carry out.

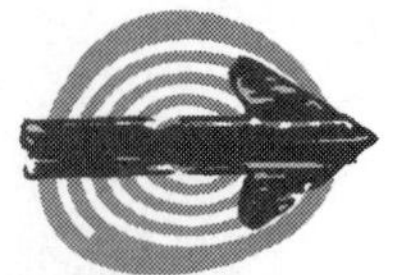
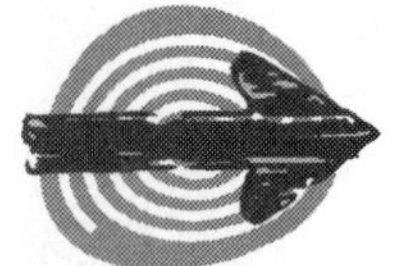

Method study and systems analysis are primarily concerned with the efficiency and effectiveness of systems and procedures. Resulting improvements should have the effect of reducing costs – or at least making the best use of them. We will now look at a review technique specifically aimed at cost reduction.

3.3 Value analysis

Value can be classified as either:

(a) **Use value** – the ability of a given item to achieve its purpose or function

(b) **Esteem value** – the perception that a given item is worth owning, because of its status or reputation, say

Definition

> **Value analysis** is a cost reduction technique aimed at identifying unnecessary cost elements in an item, by analysing its function and design in detail.

The objective of value analysis is to **maximise the value** of a product, while **minimising the cost** involved.

Value analysis involves six basic stages, as follows.

(a) Select the area(s) for analysis. Value analysis is likely to reap greater savings for products with a lot of parts or stages of production (some of which may be redundant), products which have 'been around' for a while without reappraisal, and products on which the margin between cost and value is currently low.

(b) Define the product's function. What do customers expect/want it to do? What does it do? What is it for?

(c) Record the components of the product.

(d) Calculate existing costs of making each component and the product as a whole.

(e) Consider alternatives which might eliminate some of these costs, without affecting the product's function or essential qualities.

  (i) Eliminating or simplifying components, design features or operations

  (ii) Using standard parts and/or bought-in (rather than made) parts, if cheaper

  (iii) Using lower-cost materials or manufacturing processes

  (iv) Relaxing quality standards (short of affecting value)

(f) Evaluate the alternatives and make recommendations. There is clearly a trade-off between:

  (i) Cost savings that can be made by a particular measure

  (ii) The extent to which the measure affects both use value and esteem value.

FOR DISCUSSION

What unnecessary 'frills' do you think there are on, for example:

(a) A Coca-Cola can?
(b) A Swatch watch?
(c) A top-range sports car?
(d) A food hamper from a store like Harrods or Fortnum and Mason?

What cost savings could the manufacturers make? How would such savings affect the use value and/or the esteem value of the product?

The following is a simple checklist of some of the programmes managers can implement to improve performance in three crucial areas.

4 IMPROVING PERFORMANCE

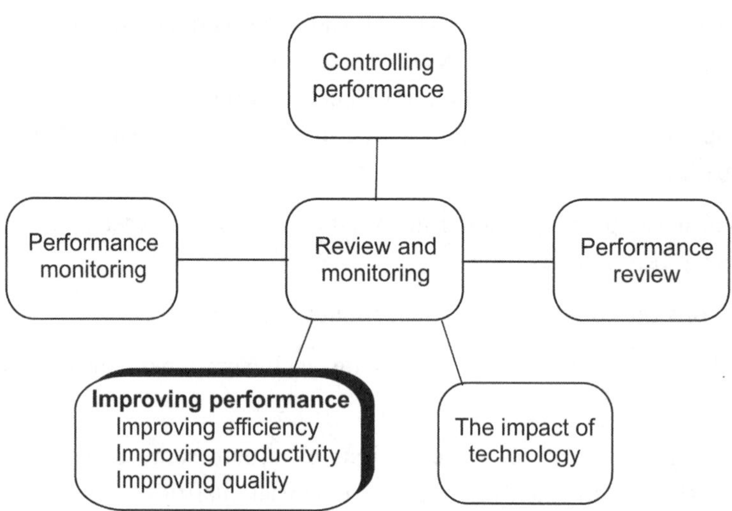

4.1 Improving efficiency

Efficiency (making best use of inputs to the organisation system) can be improved by:

(a) Using method study to identify bottlenecks, unnecessary activities and poor co-ordination

(b) Eliminating unnecessary paperwork routines and forms, duplicates, checks and so on

(c) Speeding up, streamlining or redirecting work flows

(d) Solving specific problems such as bottlenecks, duplications and gaps in workload, or waste of resources

(e) Investigating opportunities for cost savings by using machines (especially for labour intensive tasks), product simplification, value analysis and so on

(f) Training staff in methodical, economical working

4.2 Improving productivity

Productivity (the amount of output produced from organisational inputs) can be improved by:

(a) Work simplification – eliminating unnecessary operations

(b) Improving work environment, facilities, access and equipment – providing more efficient backup services, access to materials and tools, clear travel routes

(c) Improving labour usage: employing fewer but better-quality staff, improving the skills of existing staff, improving management

(d) Better planning, scheduling, organisation, co-ordination and communication

(e) Mechanisation (speeding up human work through the use of tools and equipment) and/or automation (replacing human labour with machines or equipment)

(f) Better motivation, incentives and productivity bargaining (negotiating with employee representatives to get agreement on work practices that will improve productivity in return for increased rewards)

4.3 Improving quality

Quality can be improved by:

(a) Operating quality control and quality assurance procedures to ensure that unacceptable levels of errors/defects are identified and investigated

(b) Solving identifiable problems of control, methods, equipment, worker training

(c) Training and involving workers in quality/service improvement issues

(d) Creating a culture in which quality and continuous improvement are key values

(e) Educating suppliers of materials and components, and retail outlets, in quality control and values

(f) Devoting resources to improving quality, if required

Quality control is not a new idea, but it has been elevated into a philosophy that guides every activity within a business: 'total quality management', or TQM.

The basic principles of TQM are:

(a) The cost of preventing mistakes is less than the cost of correcting them, so the aim should be to **get things right first time**

(b) It is always possible to improve, so the aim must be to get it more right next time.

5 THE IMPACT OF TECHNOLOGY

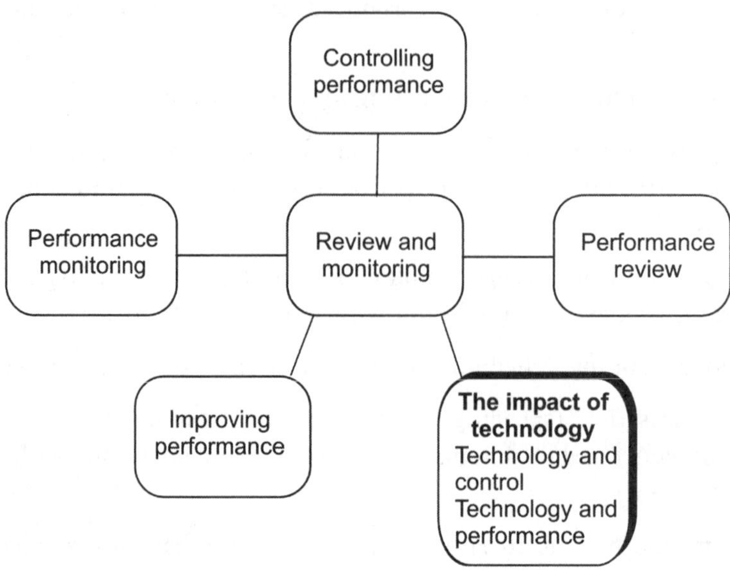

We will touch on some of the applications of technology to performance review and improvement.

5.1 Technology and control

Technology can be used in the processes of performance review, monitoring and adjustment, in the role of sensor, comparator and even effector (see Section 1.1 of this chapter). Computers, and related electronic systems, have had enormous impact on areas such as the following.

(a) **Automatic monitoring of processes**, and the production of control reports. Think of the 'black box' recorders used in aeroplanes and trucks to monitor speed and operation. Job reporting by computer may be effected via terminals at each work station, linked to a central processor, which visually display job status (set up, start, interrupted, completed etc) and/or progress:

   (i) For the manager or supervisor to allocate people or tasks to machines
   (ii) To notify the machine operator of his or her schedule

(b) Automatic monitoring and control of processes and machines. Many **manufacturing processes** are now fully automated, with output and quality monitored and regulated by computers or robots.

   (i) **Production monitoring** by computer keeps machines as smoothly and fully utilised as possible. Instruments in the machine tools are used to record the machine's on/off status, speed of operation, temperature, output rate and so on. The system can identify malfunctions or variances, produce exception reports, and adjust the operation.

   (ii) **Stock or inventory control** by computers allows usage rates and stock levels to be continuously monitored and updated; stock release to production teams, and re-ordering from suppliers, to be triggered automatically; and relevant documentation produced.

(c) High-speed, high-volume, complex **data processing** for management control information. Information technology allows data to be analysed, calculated, formatted and transmitted with far greater speed, accuracy and flexibility. Schedules, projections, simulations, models, flowcharting, networks, budgetary control reports and so on can be produced and disseminated with less and less human intervention.

5.2 Technology and performance

The same attributes and benefits apply to the use of technology in performance maintenance and improvement in general. Information technology (IT) and manufacturing technology can be used in several ways.

(a) In **planning and scheduling**, co-ordination and resource allocation, through the production of sophisticated management and decision-support information.

(b) In **computer-aided design** (CAD), producing designs, drawings and data for use in manufacture. This may involve graphic models, simulation, engineering calculations and drafting and so on. It increases the organisation's flexibility and ability to innovate, allowing experimentation with different designs.

(c) In **computer aided manufacture** (CAM), including the design of tools, the control of machines, process and materials planning, and robotics (the use of sophisticated machinery which can move parts or tools through specified – but quite complex – sequences of motions). An integrated CAD-CAM system can be used to control entire factory operations, with great savings on labour and space, and associated costs.

(d) In the gathering, processing, storage, retrieval and communication of **information.** This is the greatest impact of the so-called 'second Industrial Revolution'. **Electronic mail** allows computer users to communicate almost instantly, worldwide. The **Internet** allows access to a worldwide information database and communication channel. Meanwhile, even the smallest business has access to sophisticated technology in the 'electronic office'. For example:

   (i) Facsimile transfer (fax) of text or graphics

   (ii) 'Smart' telephones with memory and switchboard facilities

   (iii) Wordprocessing, spreadsheet and other business application packages available off-the-shelf for use on microcomputers, or PCs

   (iv) Networks of PCs allowing the sharing of data and tasks

   (v) The 'paperless' production and storage of data on disk; instant file retrieval and editing

   (vi) Documentation production with sophisticated text layout and graphics capabilities

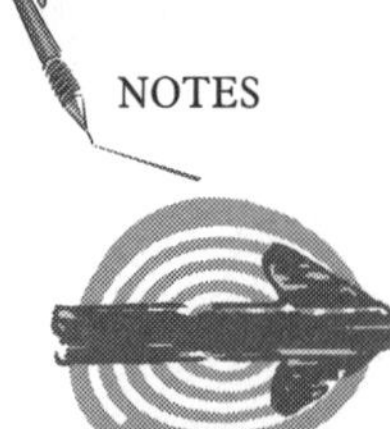

In all these areas, technology has the advantages of speed, capacity, versatility, reliability and accuracy. It can help the organisation to provide a faster, more accurate, more 'professional' service.

FOR DISCUSSION

Does technology offer the worker freedom from drudgery, a cleaner environment, an easier life, and new opportunities? Why is the introduction of technology so often resisted in the workplace?

Think about:

(a) Job security – and perceived job security: do machines replace people?

(b) Job interest: is the work more or less satisfying, and are the skills required more or less valuable and satisfying?

(c) Personal competence and humanity: do people feel threatened by machines, and is the environment and social system at work affected?

(d) Management and supervision: who has a say in the planning and control of work when it is automated?

(e) Where people work: is increased working from home, or on the move, a positive or negative experience for workers? Does it make life easier or harder for their managers?

There are two sides to each of these questions. Try to see both points of view.

Chapter roundup

- Control involves monitoring or reviewing performance, comparing actual results with expected/planned results and adjusting performance accordingly.
- A range of performance indicators and standards may be used as a yardstick for performance appraisal, including efficiency, effectiveness, economy, elegance and ethicality.
- Performance monitoring may be achieved by observation, reporting or the use of operational records.
- Performance review may be achieved using techniques such as: method study, systems analysis and value analysis.
- Technology offers benefits of speed, capacity, computational power, versatility, accuracy and predictability to the control process and also to operational and managerial processes.

Quick quiz

1 Outline two examples of control systems used in organisations.

2 Give six examples of non-financial performance indicators.

3 Give three examples of standards of ethicality.

4 Give three examples of financial performance indicators.

5 When might (a) activity sampling and (b) attitude surveys be used in performance monitoring?

6 What is 'activity sampling'?

7 What are the purposes of method study?

8 What questions are asked about an activity during a method study?

9 Name the four types of flow charts.

10 What are the four basic stages of systems analysis?

11 Distinguish between use value and esteem value.

12 What are the six basic stages of value analysis?

13 Suggest three ways of improving efficiency.

14 Give three ways in which quality can be improved.

15 Explain the terms 'production monitoring' and 'the electronic office'.

Answers to quick quiz

1 Budgetary control, stock control, production and quality controls.

2 Market share, quality, speed of response to customer, completion of projects on time, productivity per person/hour or per machine/hour, punctuality and professionalism.

3 Impact of operations on natural environment, hiring and promotion of staff from minority groups, non-reliance on contracts with military or political connotations.

4 Financial performance indicators include cost, profitability, return on investments, growth in earnings per share and many others..

5 (a) In varied work such as that in offices, canteens, warehouses, supermarkets.

(b) If performance criteria relate to staff attitude, friendliness, responsiveness, clarity of information and professionalism.

6 Activity sampling means taking a representative number of observations of a work activity at random predetermined intervals.

7 It is concerned with how work could and should be done more efficiently.

8 What functions are performed when, how and by whom; what documents and records are used and where they 'go' at each stage; what resources are required by the system and where they travel in the course of it.

9 Man, machine, material, document.

10 Define objectives and constraints; investigate; record data on the current system; prepare a specification for the new system; design the new or modified system according to the specification.

11 Use value is the ability of a given item to achieve its purpose or function. Esteem value is the perception that a given item is worth owning because of its reputation or status.

12 Select areas; define product function; record product components; calculate existing costs; consider alternatives; evaluate alternatives and make recommendations.

13 Use method study, eliminate unnecessary paperwork and solve specific problems.

14 Operate quality control and quality assurance, train workers and devote resources to quality improvement.

15 Production monitoring keeps machines smoothly and fully utilised. In computerised systems all details of the machine's operations are recorded. Computers can identify malfunctions or variances and can adjust operations. Examples of an electronic office include electronic technology such as email, smartphones, laptops and other hand-held computer devices and data storage systems.

Answers to activities

1 Obviously, there are many possible examples of disturbances to a planned business, but you may have come up with things like the entry of a powerful new competitor into the market, an unexpected rise in labour costs or scarcity of particular skills, the failure of a supplier to deliver promised materials or components, or even the tendency of employees to interrupt work for social chatter.

2 Ways in which your course is monitored include: your assignments and essays being marked; exam results; feedback from lecturers and tutors; end of year reports; and possibly peer assessment. You should, of course, be monitoring your own progress, for example by seeing whether your answers to questions in this book match up with ours (or are better than ours).

3 Goals where non-financial performance indicators might be used are, for example:

(a) Less than 5% errors in output; less than 100 customer complaints per month;

(b) Market leader (biggest share of the market); 80% awareness of the organisation in the general public;

(c) 50 new products per year;

(d) Lower rate of employee turnover than the industry average;

(e) A specific (low) ratio of inputs to outputs, ie efficiency in use of resources;

(f) Target hirings/promotions from minority groups; target giving to community causes; reduction in complaints of infringement of regulations, eg on the environment.

4 Staff may not welcome task inspection for several reasons. Allowances may not be made for necessary interruptions, the need for rest and refreshment and so on: the staff may feel that the assessment of performance is not fair or consistent. The conspicuous nature of the monitoring may cause resentment, if staff feel they are not trusted.

5 For the given service qualities, BAA use the following mechanisms.

(a) Customer survey
(b) Customer survey; management inspection
(c) Customer survey; management inspection
(d) Customer survey; management inspection
(e) Customer survey; management inspection
(f) Internal fault monitoring systems
(g) Customer survey; internal operational data

6 Figure 14.3 seems to suggest wasted labour to have the movement to and from the bench between operations, and there are delays in the process where the sheets/part-finished booklets lie idle on the bench. Scheduling could be improved so that the sheets move continuously through the process.

7 A systems flow chart for a job application might be as shown below.

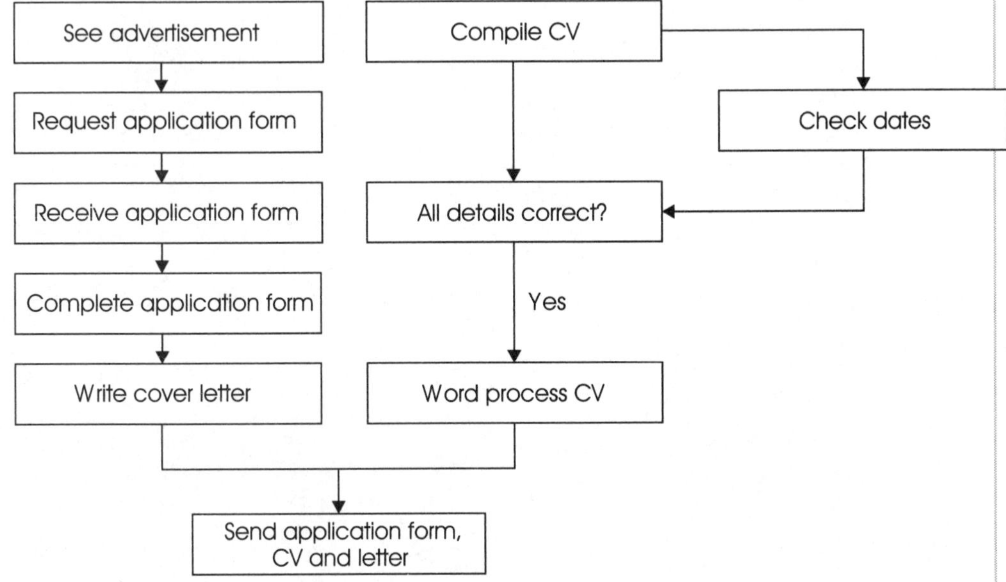

NOTES

Appendix

EDEXCEL GUIDELINES FOR OPTIONAL UNIT 7: BUSINESS STRATEGY

QCF Level 5

Aim

The aim of this unit is to give learners the knowledge and understanding of how a business unit can strategically organise and plan for likely future outcomes in order to be successful.

Unit abstract

One of the aims of this unit is to build on the learner's existing knowledge of the basic tools of business analysis such as PESTLE and draw it together so that the learner learns to think strategically.

Learners will be introduced to further tools of analysis needed for the process of strategic planning. Learners will be able to explain the significance of stakeholder analysis and conduct an environmental and organisational audit of a given organisation.

Learners will learn how to apply strategic positioning techniques to the analysis of a given organisation and prepare a strategic plan, based on previous analysis. Further, learners will learn how to evaluate possible alternative strategies (such as substantive growth, limited growth or retrenchment) and then be able to select an appropriate future strategy for a given organisation.

Finally, learners will learn how to compare the roles and responsibilities for strategy implementation and evaluate resource requirements for implementation of a new strategy for a given organisation. Learners will then be able to propose targets and timescales for implementation and monitoring of the strategy in a given organisation.

Learning outcomes

On successful completion of the unit a learner will:

1 Understand the process of strategic planning

2 Be able to formulate a new strategy

3 Understand approaches to strategy evaluation and selection

4 Understand how to implement a chosen strategy

Guidance

Links

This unit has links with the Management and Leadership NOS.

Essential requirements

For this unit it is essential that learners have good access to computers and to the Internet. Specialist packages for statistical analysis and network planning may be useful.

Employer engagement and vocational contexts

Centres should try to develop links with local businesses. Many businesses and chambers of commerce are keen to promote local business and are often willing to provide visit opportunities, visiting speakers, information about business and the local business context.

CONTENT		*Covered in chapter(s)*
1	**Strategic planning**	
	Strategic contexts and terminology: role of strategy, missions, visions, strategic intent, objectives, goals, core competencies, strategic architecture, strategic control.	1
	Strategic thinking: future direction of the competition, needs of customers, gaining and maintaining competitive advantage, Ansoff's growth-vector matrix, portfolio analysis.	6
	Planning systems: informal planning, top-down planning, bottom-up planning, behavioural approaches.	7
	Strategic planning issues: impact on managers, targets, when to plan, who should be involved, role of planning.	6
	Strategic planning techniques: BCG growth-share matrix, directional policy matrices, SPACE, PIMS.	6
2	**Strategy formulation**	
	Stakeholder analysis: stakeholder significance grid, stakeholder mapping.	1
	Environment auditing: political, economic, socio-cultural, technological, environmental and legal analysis (PESTEL), Porter's 5 force analysis, the threat of new entrants, the power of buyers, the power of suppliers, the threat of substitutes, competitive rivalry and collaboration.	2
	Strategic positioning: the Ansoff matrix, growth, stability, profitability, efficiency, market leadership, survival, mergers and acquisitions, expansion into the global market place.	4, 5
	The organisational audit: benchmarking, SWOT analysis, product positions, value-chain analysis, demographic influences, scenario planning, synergy culture and values.	3, 4, 5
3	**Strategy evaluation and selection**	
	Market entry strategies: organic growth, growth by merger or acquisition, strategic alliances, licensing, franchising.	9
	Substantive growth strategies: horizontal and vertical integration, related and unrelated diversification.	9
	Limited growth strategies: do nothing, market penetration, market development, product development, innovation.	9
	Disinvestment strategies: retrenchment, turnaround strategies, divestment, liquidation.	9
	Strategy selection: considering the alternatives, appropriateness, feasibility, desirability.	8, 9
4	**Strategy implementation**	
	The realisation of strategic plans to operational reality: communication – selling the concepts; project teams; identification of team and individual roles; responsibilities and targets; programme of activities; benchmark targets at differing levels of the organisation.	10, 11, 12
	Resource allocation: finance, human resources, materials, time.	13
	Review and evaluation: an evaluation of the benchmarked outcomes in a given time period of corporate, operational and individual targets.	14

Outcomes and assessment criteria

Learning outcomes On successful completion of this unit a learner will:	Assessment criteria for pass The learner can:
LO.1 Understand the process of strategic planning	1.1 Explain the strategy contents and terminology – missions, visions, objectives, goals, core competencies 1.2 Review the issues involved in strategic planning 1.3 Explain different planning techniques
LO.2 Be able to formulate a new strategy	2.1 Produce an organisational audit for a given organisation 2.2 Carry out an environmental audit for a given organisation 2.3 Explain the significance of stakeholder analysis
LO.3 Understand approaches to strategy evaluation and selection	3.1 Analyse possible alternative strategies relating to substantive growth, limited growth or retrenchment 3.2 Select an appropriate future strategy for a given organisation
LO.4 Understand how to implement a chosen strategy	4.1 Compare the roles and responsibilities for strategy implementation 4.2 Evaluate resource requirements to implement a new strategy for a given organisation 4.3 Discuss targets and timescales for achievement in a given organisation to monitor a given strategy

Glossary

Activities: The means by which a firm creates value in its products.

Activity scheduling: Provides a list of activities, in order in which they must be completed (called 'task sequencing' in part of the book).

Added value: An accounting term for the difference between the cost of raw materials and the sales price of the finished produict; ie the value that is perceived to have been added to inputs by processing within the organisational system.

Assumption: A statement of opinion about the occurance of an event which is outside the control of the planner.

Authority: The right to do something, or to get others to do it.

Benchmarking: Comparing the processes of one unit with those of another to improve performance.

Bottom-up decision-making: Subordinates are encouraged to think for themselves, and are involved in decision-making and planning.

Brainstorming: A process whereby people produce spontaneous, uncensored ideas, sparked off by a particular problem or task.

Budgets: Statements of expected results expressed in financial terms.

Business strategy: Concerned with how an organisation approaches a particular product market area.

Communication: The transmission or exchange of information.

Competitive advantage: A factor that enables an organisation to compete successfully with its main competitors on a sustained basis.

Competitive strategy: The taking of actions to create a defendable position and a return on investment

Contingency: Something which may or may not happen.

Contingency planning: The development of alternative plans to be used in the event that environmental conditions evolve differently to those anticipated, rendering original plans unwise or unfeasible.

Control: The overall process whereby goals and standards are defined, and performance is monitored, measured against goals and adjusted if necessary, to ensure that the goals are being accomplised.

Co-operation: Working or acting together.

Co-ordinate: To plan, or take action to improve, the interrelationships (especially of timing and methods of communication) between a number of various activities, which contribute to the achievement of a single objective, so that they do not conflict and the objective is achieved with a minimal expenditure of time and effort. *(Dictionary of Management).*

NOTES

Corporate: Relating to the whole organisation.

Corporate appraisal: A critical assessment of the strengths and weaknesses, opportunities and threats in relation to the international and environmental factors affecting the entity.

Corporate strategy: Denoted the most general level of strategy in an organisation. It is concerned with what types of business the organisation is in.

Cost/benefit analysis: Measuring the resources used in an activity and comparing them with the value of benefits.

Cost leadership: Being the lowest cost producer in the industry as a whole.

Critical success factors: Those factors on which the strategy is fundamentally dependent for its success.

Culture: The sum total of beliefs, knowledge, attitudes and customs which people are exposed to in an organisation.

Data: The raw material of information: facts and figures in an unprocessed state.

Database: A large file of data that is held on a computer and which can be analysed to provide useful information.

Decision-making: Making choices between alternative courses of action.

Decision support systems (DSS): An MIS (usually computerised), designed to produce information in such a way as to help managers make better decisions.

Demography: The study of population and population trends.

Differentiation: The exploitation of a product or service which is unique.

Distinctive competence: What an organisation does well, uniquely or better than its rivals.

Divestment: Selling off parts of a firm's operations or pulling out of certain product-market areas.

Economy: The reduction or containment of cost.

Effectiveness: The measure of how far an organisation, and its managers, achieve their output requirements, as defined by performance objectives and targets.

Efficiency: The relationship between inputs used and outputs achieved. The fewer the inputs used to obtain a given output, the greater the efficiency. Efficiency can be expressed as:

$$\frac{\text{output}}{\text{input}}$$

Emergent strategies: Those which arise from ad hoc choices and patterns of behaviour, in contrast to planned strategies.

Empowerment: Allowing workers to have the freedom to decide how to do their own work and making those workers personally responsible for achieving targets and controlling quality.

Evaluation: An attempt to obtain information on the effectiveness of a programme and to assess the results in the light of that information.

Feedback: Internally generated information about actual results achieved, the aim of the information being to help with control decisions.

Finance: Involves all aspects of the monetary dealings of an organisation, from attracting new investors to expenditure on office stationery.

Financial management: The control of all apsects of an organisation's monetary dealings.

Focus: Restricting activities to only a part of the market.

Forecasting: The identification of relevant factors and quanitification of their effect as a basis for planning.

Formal organisation: An organisation which is deliberately constructed to fulfil specific goals. It is characterised by planned division of responsibility and a well-defined structure of authority and communication. The organisation structure provides for consistent functions and roles, irrespective of changes in individual membership.

Gap analysis: The comparison of an entity's ultimate objective with the sum of projections and already planned projects.

Goals: The intentions behind decisions or actions that make organisations do what they do.

Group: Any collection of people who perceive themselves to be a group.

HR planning: The process of comparing an organisation's existing human resources with its forecast need for labour and in consequence specifying the measures necessary for acquiring, training, deploying, developing or discarding workers. It involves the estimation of the consequences of changes in working practices and the preparation of skills inventories.

Human resource management (HRM): Managing people in ways that integrate individual needs and objectives with those of the organisation in an effective and flexible manner.

Incrementalism: Small scale extension of past practices.

Informal organisation: One which is loosely structured, flexible and spontaneous, fluctuating with its individual memebership. Examples are colleagues who tend to lunch together and 'cliques'. Informal organisations always exist within formal organisations.

Information: Data which have been processed (selected, sorted, analysed, formatted) so as to have meaning for the person who receives it, and are suitable for a particular purpose.

Information technology: A combination of computer technology and communications technology.

Key tasks: What must be done to ensure each critical success factor is satisfied.

Limiting factor: A factor which at any time may limit the activity of an entity, often where there is shortage or difficulty of supply.

Logical incrementalism: Managers test new strategies in small steps as the organisation goes along.

Management Information Systems (MIS): A system designed to collect data from all available sources and convert it into information relevant to managers at all levels, for the purpose of planning and control of the activities for which they are responsible.

Marketing audit: A review of an organisation's products and markets, the marketing environment and its marketing system and operations.

Management by objectives (MBO): A system of control which aims to co-ordinate the goals of the organisation with the goals of individual managers.

Marketing research: The objective gathering, recording and analysing of all facts about problems relating to the transfer and sale of goods and services from producer to consumer or user.

Marketing: The management process which identifies, anticipates and supplies customer requirements efficiently and profitably.

Market share: One entity's sales of a product/service in a market expressed as a percentage of total sales in that market.

Method study: The systematic recording and critical examination of existing and proposed ways of doing work, as a means of developing and applying easier and more effective methods and reducing costs.

Mission: The organisation's basic function in society, in terms of the products and services it produces for its clients.

Monitoring: The process of obtaining and recording information on developments within a programme as they are happening.

Motivation: The process by which the behaviour of an individual is influenced by others, through their power to offer or withhold satisfaction of the individual's needs and goals.

Objectives: The anticipated end result of activity. They are the things that you hope to achieve.

Operations: The routine activities that convert the resource inputs into relevant activities.

Organic growth: Internal development and growth through the development of internal resources.

Organisation: A social arrangement for the controlled performance of collective goals.

Outsourcing: Subcontracting processes to external suppliers.

Performance criteria: The individual standards of performance that help to judge that work is being done satisfactorily.

Performance indicators: The criteria which indicate the standard of performance required for the successful achievement of the stated objective.

Performance measurement: Aims to establish how well something or somebody is doing in relation to planned activity and desired results.

Planning: (1) The process of deciding what, how and when things should be done.

(2) The process of deciding which objectives need to be achieved and of preparing how to meet them.

Planning period: The length of time between making a planning decision and implementing that decision.

Policies: General statements that guide thinking and action.

Position audit: A comprehensive study of an organisation and its current capabilities.

Priorities: Indicate the order in which tasks are completed.

Procedures: Customary methods of action.

Production: The function that plans, organises, directs and controls activities to provide products and services.

Product-market mix: The products/services a firm sells and the market it sells them to.

Products: Items produced by a manufacturing process.

Profit gap: The difference between the target profits (according to the corporate objectives of the organisation) and the profits calculated by the forecast.

Profitability: The prospect of a particular course of action generating profits for the organisation.

Programmes: Collections of activities that need to be carried out to achieve a desired outcome.

Project: An undertaking, often cutting across organisational and functional boundaries, and carried out to meet established goals within cost, schedule and quality objectives.

Protectionism: The imposition of tariffs, quotas or other barriers to trade to restrict the inflow of imports, in order to protect domestic producers from overseas competition.

Purchasing: The buying of goods and materials which the organisation needs.

Quality circles: Groups of (typically 6 to 10) employees from different levels and/or disciplines, who meet regularly to discuss problems of quality and quality control in their area of work.

Quotas: Limits that are imposed on the quantity of a particular good that can be imported.

Related diversification: Development beyond the present product/market but still within the broad confines of the industry. Takes the form of vertical or horizontal integration.

Research and development (R and D): The application of original research to develop new products and systems.

Resource audit: A review of an organisation's physical and financial resources as well as its systems.

Responsibility: The liability of a person to be called to account for his/her actions and results. It is an obligation to do something, or to get others to do it.

Review: The process of re-examining the information obtained by monitoring.

Reward: A token (monetary or otherwise) given to an individual or team in recognition of some contribution or success.

Risk: A general uncertainty which cannot be quantified, although its probability can be estimated.

Role: A part played by someone in any event of process.

Rules: Specific statements of what may or may not be done.

Sales: The disposal of products by different means for commercial purposes.

Scalar chain: The organisation hierarchy, from the most junior to the most senior. Also known as the chain of command.

Scenario: An internally consistent view of what the future might turn out to be.

Scenario building: The process of constructing a number of distinct possible futures so that deductions can be made about future developments of market, products and technology.

Services: Activities provided for customers.

Span of control: Refers to the number of subordinates working for a manager in the level immediately below the manager.

Stakeholder: A person or group with an interest in the organisation's activities.

Standards: The agreed quality measures that are used to judge whether a task has been satisfactorily completed.

Strategic analysis: An assessment of an organisation and its current and projected circumstances.

Strategic options: The suitable strategies for developing the organisation, from which choices have to be made.

Strategic planning: The managerial process of developing and maintaining a strategic fit between the organisation's objectives and resources and its changing market opportunities.

Strategies: Courses of action, including those that specify resources required, to achieve an overall objective.

Substitute product: A good or service produced by another industry which satisfies the same customer needs.

SWOT analysis: A method of analysing information which attempts to identify an organisation's strengths, weaknesses, opportunities and threats.

Synergy: When combined results produce a better rate of return than would be achieved by the same resources used independently.

Systems analysis: The process of analysing methods, procedures, sequences of activities, paperwork flows and the inputs required and outputs expected in operational or informational processing systems which are based on computers.

Tactics: Determine the most efficient deployment of resources in an agreed strategy.

Tariffs: Taxes imposed on an imported good.

Task sequencing: See Activity scheduling.

Team: A formalised group to achieve particular objectives.

Time scheduling: Adds to activity scheduling the timescale, or start and end times/dates, for each activity in sequence.

Top-down decision-making: Decisions are taken by managers and handed down to subordinates.

NOTES

Training: (1) The systematic development of the attitude/knowledge/skill/behaviour pattern required by an individual in order to perform adequately a given task or job *(Department of Employment).*

(2) Formal learning activity which may not lead to qualifications, and which may be received at any time in a working career.

Uncertainty: When the outcome cannot be predicted or assigned probabilities.

Unrelated (or **conglomerate**) **diversification:** Development beyond the present industry into products/markets which may bear no close relation to the present product/market.

Validation: Observing the results of a process (for example a training scheme), and measuring whether its objectives have been achieved.

Value analysis: A cost reduction technique aimed at identifying unnecessary cost elements in an item, by analysing its function and design in detail.

Values: basic (often unstated) principles and assumptions about what is right and/or important.

Bibliography

Books

Ansoff, I. (1987) *Corporate Strategy* (2nd edition), London: Penguin

Belbin, R. M. (1984) *Management Teams,* Oxford: Butterworth-Heinneman

Handy, C. (1993) *Understanding Organisations,* London: Penguin

Johnson, G. and Scholes, K (2000) *Exploring Corporate Strategy* (6th edition), London: Prentice Hall

Mintzberg, H. (1997) *The Structuring of Organisations,* Harlow: Prentice Hall

Mintzberg, H. (1999) *The Strategy Process,* Harlow: Prentice Hall

Mintzberg, H. Quinn, B. and Ghoshal, S. (1999) *The Strategy Process,* Harlow: Prentice Hall

Mintzberg, H. (2000) *The Rise and Fall of Strategic Planning.* Hemel Hempstead: FT Prentice Hall

Ohmae, K. (1982), *The Mind of the Strategist: The Art of Japanese Business,* New York: McGraw Hill

Porter, M. (1980) *Competitive Strategy,* New York: Simon and Schuster

Porter, M. (1996) *Competitive Advantage,* New York: Simon and Schuster

Porter, M. (1998) *The Competitive Advantage of Nations,* New York: Palgrave Macmillan

Articles

Blin (2001) 'Challenges are a piece of cake' *Sunday Times Fast Track 100,* Dec 9

Mortished, C. (2001) 'Ben and Jerry's keep the old hippy flavour', *The Times* Dec 10

Index

NOTES

BPP
LEARNING MEDIA

NOTES

NOTES

NOTES

BPP
LEARNING MEDIA

NOTES

NOTES

Review Form – Business Essentials – Business Strategy (12/07)

BPP Learning Media always appreciates feedback from the students who use our books. We would be very grateful if you would take the time to complete this feedback form, and return it to the address below.

Name: ______________________ **Address:** ______________________

____

____

How have you used this Course Book?
(Tick one box only)

☐ Home study (book only)

☐ On a course: college ______________________

☐ Other ______________________

Why did you decide to purchase this Course book? *(Tick one box only)*

☐ Have used BPP Learning Media Texts in the past

☐ Recommendation by friend/colleague

☐ Recommendation by a lecturer at college

☐ Saw advertising

☐ Other ______________________

During the past six months do you recall seeing/receiving any of the following?
(Tick as many boxes as are relevant)

☐ Our advertisement

☐ Our brochure with a letter through the post

Your ratings, comments and suggestions would be appreciated on the following areas

	Very useful	*Useful*	*Not useful*
Introductory pages	☐	☐	☐
Topic coverage	☐	☐	☐
Summary diagrams	☐	☐	☐
Chapter roundups	☐	☐	☐
Quick quizzes	☐	☐	☐
Activities	☐	☐	☐
Discussion points	☐	☐	☐

	Excellent	*Good*	*Adequate*	*Poor*
Overall opinion of this Course book	☐	☐	☐	☐

Do you intend to continue using BPP Learning Media Business Essentials Course Books? ☐ Yes ☐ No

Please note any further comments and suggestions/errors on the reverse of this page.

The BPP author of this edition can be e-mailed at: pippariley@bpp.com

Please return this form to: Pippa Riley, BPP Learning Media Ltd, FREEPOST, London, W12 8BR

Review Form (continued)

Please note any further comments and suggestions/errors below.